Our Daily Bread

German Village Life, 1500-1850

ALSO BY TEVA J. SCHEER

Governor Lady

Our Daily Bread

Village Life in Early Modern Germany

TEVA J. SCHEER

ADVENTIS PRESS

Published by
Adventis Press, 627 Downey Road, North Saanich, BC V8L 5M6, Canada

U.S. distribution by www.amazon.com

The photographs on the book cover and on pages 2, 19, 49, 71, 77, 99, 121, 130, 137, 145, 146, and 151 were taken by Hermann Bizer (1904-1964), a teacher and regional historian, with the kind permission of his descendants.

The photographs on pages 8, 10, 34, and 139 are reprinted from the book *Fürfeld* with the permission of the author and the publisher, Druckerei Odenwälder Buchen-Walldürn.

The map on page 5 is created using an image from Centennia Historical Atlas with the permission of Centennia Software.

The remaining illustrations are either in the public domain, or permission has been obtained from the web site sources.

Library of Congress Cataloging-in-Publication Guidance

Scheer, Teva J.
Our Daily Bread: German Village Life, 1500-1850
Teva J. Scheer.
Includes bibliographical references.
ISBN 978-1-453-72169-8.
1.   Germany — History, 1500-1850.
2.   Germany — Social Life and Customs.
3.   Villages — Germany.
DD901 2010
943

Contents

List of Illustrations

Acknowledgements

My purpose in writing this book was to create an easy-to-read narrative for members of the general reading public who have an interest in German history and genealogy. I relied heavily on the primary research completed by dozens of scholars from the disciplines of history, sociology, anthropology, religion, and cultural folkways, whose academic work is not always easy for the layman to absorb nor even to find in local public libraries. These scholars' names and books or articles are listed in the bibliography, and their work immeasurably enriched *Our Daily Bread*.

Early in my research, I was lucky to have the support of Eileen Moessle, whom I met through an on-line network, the Baden-Württemberg Rootsweb listserv. Eileen, who lives in southern Baden-Württemberg, acted as guide on my first research trip to Germany and as a gracious host on my second trip. Three other colleagues from the listserv—Tanya Nielsen, Wolf Haederle, and Kathy Bonnnell—read some or all of the draft chapters and provided me with valuable insights and suggestions. I wrote this book with the members of the listserv in mind, since they represent my intended audience.

As he did for my first book, my dear friend Carl Cipra read and commented on the entire manuscript, offering a valuable historical perspective and his enthusiastic support for this project. And as always, my husband Jon Scheer has been by my side, on each of three German trips and months of otherwise solitary writing. I am blessed in my friends and family.

I was fortunate to receive permission to use a number of photographs, also published in a book entitled *1950: Ein schwäbisches Dorf*. The book features a series of photographs taken by Hermann Bizer after the end of the Second World War in a small village called Isingen, Baden-Würtemberg, about 9 kilometers from the Neckar River and 145 kilometers south of the area where I located the fictitious village, Hochfeld, featured in *Our Daily Bread*. Although the photographs in this book are from the mid-twentieth century, I was struck by how little had changed for villagers in southwest Germany between 1950 and the early nineteenth century, when most of this book's chapters are set. Other than the villagers' clothing and their use of some modern machinery, village life remained essentially the same during the 100 years between 1850 and 1950. The photographs are a remarkable documentation of these villagers' communal life and of their constant toil to earn their daily bread.

1

Our Daily Bread

The church bell rang just once that cold, rainy morning. The villagers knew why it rang. They had been expecting it; there was no need to summon them with a second pealing. Silently, they congregated at the church for the procession to the graveyard. Johann Adam Mann was burying his youngest daughter. In the space of a month, he had already buried his wife and three other children. As he fell into step behind the pastor, beside him walked his last surviving child, ten-year-old Johann Jacob. Four men led the procession carrying the body, which lay on a bier covered with a white cloth. There was no coffin, just as there was no funeral sermon, because Johann Adam lacked the money to pay for them. Nevertheless, despite his poverty, the community considered Johann Adam an honorable man, and his daughter would receive a respectful Christian burial with all the citizens in town in sympathetic attendance.[1]

While the villagers walked, the schoolmaster led his students in a slow and mournful hymn: "*Mitten wir im Leben sind, Mit dem Tod umpfangen*": "Though in midst of life we be, Snares of death surround us."[2] Johann Adam Mann focused on the distant fields, jaw clenched, as he clasped the shoulder of Johann Jacob. Arriving at the graveyard, the bearers gently lowered the body into a tiny grave next to her mother and the pastor began to pray. Jacob flinched as the first clumps of clay struck his sister's shroud-covered body.

The pastor asked the villagers to recite with him the Lord's Prayer, *Vater Unser*: "*Unser tägliches Brot gib uns heute*," they prayed. "Give us this day our daily bread." But for Johann Adam's family the prayer went unanswered. It was late December 1816, remembered in history books as the Year Without a Summer, when cold and damp destroyed crops and people rioted for food across Europe. In Hochfeld, the church bells rang for many other villagers that season. Following a string of bad or failed harvest years, the poor yield of 1816 drove the people to slaughter their cattle because there was no fodder to feed them. Swarms of mice, driven by hunger and flooded fields, overran the village. Compounding the series of poor harvests, troops from the recently ended Napoleonic wars had, over the last several years, been confiscating what little food the villagers had been able to grow. To pay for the wars, the villagers were forced to give more than half of their harvests in taxes, in addition to their usual burden of rents, tithes, and fees. The meager supply and increased demand for food had resulted in a doubling of prices

since 1810. By the end of the winter, Johann Adam's neighbors from
Hochfeld and nearby villages streamed out of the area, bound for what they
hoped would be better lives in America. Officials in Württemberg issued
3,000 passes that winter to emigrants, while the Grand Duchy of Baden —
Johann Adam's country since 1806 — issued passes for 18,000, or 2 percent of
the duchy's population.[3]

Figure 1. Villagers return from a funeral.

Although his land holdings were small, Johann Adam had thus far been
able to support his family, supplementing his income by growing vegetables
in the family plot and hiring himself out as a day laborer. That year,
however, his crops failed, and he could not earn enough to feed his family
and warm his hearth. When influenza struck the village, his vulnerable
family was among the many to be struck down.[4]

A grim dichotomy existed in the villages of early modern Germany. For
those who owned, rented, or controlled enough land to feed their families, or
who were prosperous merchants, innkeepers, or millers, life could be
pleasant. But for those who had no land, or not enough, life was an
uncertain, even desperate struggle for survival.[5] "Give us this day our daily
bread" signified far more than simple words in a prayer; they were a fearful
entreaty, a harsh reminder that the majority of villagers were just one bad

harvest or one major illness away from potential malnutrition, homelessness, or even death.

Johann Adam Mann is an imagined character. Although he did not actually exist, the circumstances of his fictional life and of his family's deaths played out in villages throughout the kingdoms, duchies, and independent principalities that comprised the territory now known as Germany. In many cases in this book, the experiences of Johann Adam and his fellow villagers were drawn directly from historical individuals, as noted in the book's endnotes. In all cases, the history and sociology of their lives are as historically accurate as existing sources permit. Johann Adam's given name and surname, for example, were typical of his location and time period; Mann is among the 300 most common surnames in Germany today, and it appears more frequently in his geographic locale of present-day Baden-Württemberg than in any other part of the country.[6]

This book presents the lives of Johann Adam's family, his neighbors, and their ancestors in a hypothetical village called Hochfeld am Neckar. The purpose for the invention of the fictitious villagers is to bring to life the historical and cultural elements of German village life, as opposed to the often dry and lifeless factual presentations that characterize many academic works. What was family life like? What about courtship? How important was religion to the villagers? How did their village function? What were their occupations? What about their schooling, their social life, their customs and superstitions? The villagers of Hochfeld illustrate these most important aspects of life in the German lands in a period that began with the Reformation in the early sixteenth century and extended until the great waves of German migration to North America in the mid-nineteenth century. The book's time frame is roughly equivalent to the European early modern period, which is defined by some historians as running from the late fifteenth century to the mid-nineteenth century.[7]

The book's first chapters cover three topics that form the essential scaffolding for the lives of the villagers: peasant status, religion, and war. It is impossible to understand why these people thought, acted, and reacted in the ways they did, and why their culture and worldview acquired such unique features, if one does not have a general understanding of the impact of the important issues of the times. Some of these issues were the relationship of the people with their lords; the repercussions of the Reformation on Germany; and the scars left by war, particularly the Thirty Years' War. Once these foundations are established, the book moves on to the daily aspects of villagers' lives: their families, livelihoods, inheritance customs, self-governance practices, and village institutions such as the school. Finally, the book closes with an examination of the reasons that millions of Germans left their homeland for North America; what they experienced on their journeys; and how they created new lives for themselves in a German diaspora.

A query on the word "Genealogy" on the Google search engine in 2010 resulted in almost 51 million hits; while accurate statistics about the popularity of genealogy are impossible to find, the topic is generally rated among the top five most popular subjects on the World Wide Web. In the U.S. census of 2000, almost 43 million Americans, or 1 in 6 individuals, identified themselves as descendants of German immigrants—the largest ethnic affiliation in the nation. The total dwarfed all other ethnic groups, including African-American (24.9 million), English (24.5 million), Mexican (18.4 million), and even the Irish (30.5 million). In Canada, over 3.5 million persons—more than 10 percent of the total Canadian population as of 2005—claim German descent.[8] This book was written primarily for the tens of thousands of North American genealogists and the millions of German descendants in the United States and Canada who are curious about the lives of their German ancestors.

I am one of those descendants, as is my husband. After I identified several of the home villages for our German ancestors, which were scattered over the breadth of the German territories, and after I had traced our family trees as far back as the records permitted, I said . . . "So what? Now I know where they came from, and what their names were. But how did they live?" I headed to the library to check out books on everyday German life, but I found not one. I found dozens of books on German history, religion, economy, anthropology, and law, most of which were written for the academic audience, but I found nothing that told me how my ancestors lived their daily lives. So I decided to write this book.

This is not an academic work; however, it *is* densely footnoted to allow interested readers to seek out additional information on many topics relating to the lives of these people: war, religion, agriculture, economics, anthropology, sociology as related to the book's time period. Whenever possible, I chose to cite English-language sources so that those of you who are not fluent in German could nevertheless learn more about the topics that most interest you. I also made liberal use of German terms, since as a genealogist, I found I often ran into these terms when I was researching my own family (you'll find a glossary at the back of the book). I would have liked to have known what they meant, so I thought you might, as well.

For the most part, the Germans in the time period covered by this book, both the villagers and their noble lords, lived out their lives in small, rural, and isolated worlds. By the time that Johann Adam's wife and children died in 1816, his imagined village of Hochfeld am Neckar had been incorporated into the Grand Duchy of Baden in Southwest Germany. However, when our fictitious protagonist was born in 1784, Hochfeld was part of a tiny independent entity owned by the family of an imperial knight, a member of the minor nobility of the German Holy Roman Empire, or in German, das Heilige Römische Reich Deutscher Nation. During the sixteenth and seventeenth centuries, in southwest Germany alone, there existed about 350 separate territories, which were not subject to any overrule except the nominal control of the emperor himself. These territories included about 250 fiefdoms, properties held by imperial knights and various other noblemen. There were also about 75 ecclesiastical lands—bishoprics and abbeys—which together covered about 15 percent of the land mass of Germany; the bishops and abbots who ruled these territories were temporal nobles as well as spiritual rulers. Finally, there were about 25 imperial cities such as Wimpfen, which were not part of any territorial entity such as Württemberg, Hessen, or Saxony. Each of the imperial cities and independent territories had its own laws and its own customs (see Figure 2).[9]

Clearly it would be impossible to write a comprehensive book that covers the customs and history of *all* German villages, so this book will concentrate on a small area of Evangelisch-Lutheran villages at the northern end of today's Baden-Württemberg. However, the book's coverage of major historical subjects such as the Reformation and the Thirty Years' War is

Figure 2. Map of the German territories, ca. 1800. The approximate area in which this book's fictitious events take place is shown with a circle and arrow. The tiny fiefdoms discussed in this book are too small to show with their individual names and boundaries on this map. (Map courtesy of Centennia Software, ©2009)

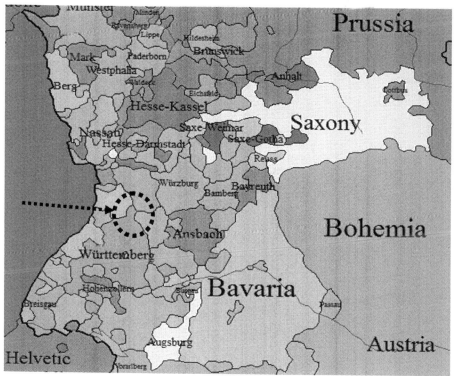

relevant to almost all of Germany. In addition, the book explains several significant differences between southwestern Germany and the other German lands—for example inheritance customs and peasant status—so that even if your ancestors came from another part of Germany, you will gain a greater understanding of their lives.

I am confident that *Our Daily Bread* is true to the general experience of early modern villages from southwest Germany, and that it will help German genealogists to better understand the lives of their ancestors. Nevertheless, I know that readers who have already studied aspects of village daily life may well question some of the facts cited in this book because they are not consistent with the readers' own research. It is critical that you keep in mind how much the specifics of life in early modern Germany varied from region to region and even from village to village. Terminology, customs, and institutions were unique to each small area. Therefore, all I could do was to document the sources for each fact, custom, and scene pictured in this book. I encourage readers with questions to study the relevant endnotes and to use the citations listed there as a starting point for additional research.

I hope you find this book useful and informative.

2

Hochfeld am Neckar
and its Universe

Johann Adam Mann lived in a half-house that he inherited from his mother, Maria Magdalena Mann geb. Lymbach (geb. is short for *geboren*, and its use signifies a maiden name). When his mother and her siblings made a final division of their parents' assets following the death of both parents, the house was partitioned into two separate dwellings. The front half opened up onto the principal street that ran through Hochfeld. On the first level, there was a single room, the living room or *Wohnstube*, in which the family lived and ate. At one end, a kitchen had been fashioned around the Wohnstube fireplace, since the original kitchen was partitioned into the other half-house. The sole table, used for both eating and food preparation, sat in front of a bench attached to the wall. The family also owned three movable stools.

Upstairs, there was a single sleeping room, which contained a bed for the married couple, sleeping pallets for the children, and one chest for the single change of clothes and other small articles belonging to the family members.[10] It was there, at bedtime, that Johann Adam felt most acutely the loss of his wife and children. The room seemed melancholy, cold, and empty. Most of all, he missed the sweet, lisping voice of his youngest daughter as she recited her evening prayer.

The other half-house opened to the back alley, and it also contained one room above, one below, the lower level being the former kitchen before the house was divided. In many houses in this part of Germany, a small barn or stabling area for farm animals was attached to the house, with the barn area having storage space for hay and fodder on the second floor. However, Johann Adam's house did not have an attached barn. Instead, it had an outbuilding that was reached through the alley; in it he kept his few farm tools and his sole milk cow. The house had been built by his maternal grandparents in the typical half-timber style called *Fachwerk*. Fachwerk houses have frames of heavy lumber, in which the spaces between the logs are filled in with brick, rocks, or discarded building materials and then usually covered with plaster or clay.[11]

During the eighteenth and nineteenth centuries, houses were frequently divided into two or more dwellings as a result of inheritance divisions in this part of Germany. In Johann Adam's case, the other half of his house was owned by his mother's elderly sister, Praxedis Keller geb. Lymbach. The relationship between the two families, unfortunately, was hostile. Praxedis was the kind of woman who held a grudge, and she had been angry about the house division ever since Johann Adam's mother drew the straw for the front half-house. Praxedis was a sour, spiteful woman, and the neighbors joked that her husband had been happy to die since at last he would have some peace. Johann Adam's wife used to say that the reason Praxedis was so unhappy about the house division was that it was much harder to spy on the other villagers because her windows did not overlook the street.

Figure 3. Fachwerk houses with their associated outbuildings

Praxedis was well-known by the village's local court officials, the *Gericht*, because of her constant complaints about her neighbors' every infraction of village ordinances. But her one saving grace, in Johann Adam's eyes, was her tenderness for her retarded adult daughter, Anna Sabina. When the inheritances of her four other living children had been settled following her husband's death, Praxedis insisted on keeping the half-house as Anna Sabina's share, fearful that her other children would fail to take proper care of their sister. Sometimes as he lay in his bed late at night, Johann Adam could hear Praxedis crooning a lullaby to Anna Sabina through their common bedroom wall.

In 1816, Hochfeld's population was 627 inhabitants, which was about the same size as most of the neighboring villages. In such a small place, everyone knew everyone else's business. Houses were built closely together, and most shared a wall with at least one other dwelling. At the center of the village and at its highest point stood the only church, and on the other side of the street stood the city hall or *Rathaus*. The church was of the Lutheran or Evangelisch denomination. The town had been Evangelisch since the earliest days of the Reformation, and about 88 percent of the villagers were members. There were only 4 Catholic families in Hochfeld, and they attended mass in another village. Hochfeld also had 5 Jewish and 5 Mennonite families.[12]

The village's streets and alleys stretched out in each direction from the church like a spider web. In good weather, people sat outside and chatted with neighbors, or leaned out half doors and watched the village comings and goings. Even in winter, the low windows and the common walls meant that there were few secrets in the town. Everyone knew who drank too much, which couples were quarrelsome, and who was courting whom. Most people's ancestors, or at least the majority of their ancestors, had lived in Hochfeld since the end of the Thirty Year's War in 1648 or earlier, so almost everyone was related. Johann Adam's parents had been third cousins. Old stories, relationships, and grudges survived a very long time, sometimes for generations.[13]

In this part of southwestern Germany, the villagers' houses and outbuildings were clustered together in a compact area in a pattern known as a *Haufendorf*. Surrounding the Haufendorf were the fields, meadows, and woodlands that belonged to each village. The boundaries (*Gemarkung*) of each village were carefully marked by a series of boundary stones or *Grenzsteine*. Each year, a deputation of village officials and citizens walked the boundaries of their village, clearing brush and insuring that their boundary stones were still in place.

The villages around Hochfeld were compact, but they could be much larger in the area called Swabia, which lay to the south. Near Hochfeld, villagers followed the custom of partible inheritance or *Realteilung*, in which all children shared equally in their parents' estates. Most Hochfeld farmers held strips in two or more of the village's three fields rather than a continuous plot of land. Since these strips were subject to division among all the children, it was not possible to build homes on the fields because the strips were subject to redistribution with each new generation. Even the richest five farmers in Hochfeld, called *Hofbauern*, had their land divided among the villages' three cultivated fields. Therefore, most villagers lived in the center village and walked out each day to farm their various segments of land.

Conversely, the pattern was quite different in areas of impartible inheritance, where one child inherited the bulk of his parents' assets. In general, northern Germany practiced impartible inheritance and southern Germany partible inheritance, although there were exceptions—notably parts of the Rhineland and part of Württemberg followed impartible inheritance practices. In the areas practicing impartible inheritance, villagers were much more likely to live in houses located on the holdings instead of a

Figure 4. A village near fictitious Hochfeld, laid out in the Haufendorf pattern, from 1835. The village's fields and meadows are labeled with their names. Note the individual field strips.

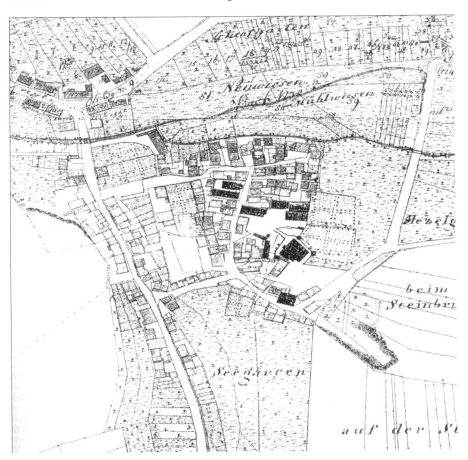

central village. Therefore, the villages in those areas looked very different than Hochfeld.[14]

The main street that ran in front of Johann Adam's house was called the Wimpfener Straße[15] (or Strasse) because it led to the free imperial city of Wimpfen, about 9 kilometers to the south.[16] The road to Wimpfen was a deeply rutted dirt pathway that turned to mud in rainy weather. In many locations, it was only wide enough for a single cart to travel in one direction. The road ran along the high crest that marked the west bank of the Neckar River. The bank of that crest formed the eastern boundaries of both Hochfeld and Wimpfen. To the west of Hochfeld was a gentle, largely flat plain. There were some small patches of woods and meadow, but for the most part, the fertile land was divided into long, intensively cultivated and carefully tended fields.

From almost any location across the plain, two or more church spires could be seen, marking the sites of the villages just a few kilometers apart. Because of its vantage point over the river, Hochfeld's skyline featured not just the church spire but also an ancient guardtower, dating to the thirteenth century, which stood next to the home of the local lord. The guardtower was erected when Holy Roman Emperor Frederick I of the House of Hohenstaufen, nicknamed Barbarossa because of his red beard, established an imperial palace in Wimpfen, and subsequently built a series of castles along the river as protection for his palace and city. He ceded each castle to a noble administrator. Hochfeld Castle he gave to the barons, or *Freiherren*, of the von Oberdorf family.

In 1449, the Freiherr von Oberdorf sold the castle and the village of Hochfeld to a neighbor, the Freiherr von Steinweg. The Steinweg family still lived in the castle in Hochfeld in Johann Adam's day, and continued as the major landlords for Hochfeld and five other villages nearby.[17]

*   *   *

The plain on which Hochfeld sits is in a region called the Kraichgau, an area of about 1,600 square kilometers. Today, it is merely a geographic designation for an area that stretches roughly from the Rhine on the west to the Neckar on the east, and from the Oden Forest (Odenwald) on the north to the Black Forest (Schwarzwald) on the south. During the time of the Frankish emperors from the fifth to the tenth centuries, the Kraichgau was a political division or Gau of the empire. By the time that Steinweg purchased Hochfeld, the term Kraichgau was used merely to designate a loose confederation of imperial knights. These imperial knights or Reichsritter joined together in the voluntary federation called the Kraichgauer Ritterschaftskanton. In 1599, about 75 knights, who ranged from prosperous to poverty-stricken, belonged to the confederation.

The average size of the knights' individual territories was less than 14 square miles. Their lands were not part of any larger duchy or mark, but were independent "countries," and the knights answered to no overlord except the Emperor himself. The knights looked back nostalgically at their heyday in the medieval period, when they held real power and prestige. By the sixteenth century, however, with the rise of the cities, increased trade, and the earliest signs of proto-industry, their military skills were no longer needed. They were territorial anachronisms.[18]

The Kraichgau federation found itself squeezed between the powerful territories of France and Austria, and their nearest neighbors were the much larger German territories of Württemberg, the Palatinate, and Baden-Durlach. Although it was not military, the federation gave its member knights some measure of protection in the larger, threatening world of German geopolitics. The federation endured until the Napoleonic invasion and the reorganization of German territories between 1803 and 1806. In 1806, the last Holy Roman Emperor abdicated, and the Holy Roman Empire ceased to exist. The Napoleonic reorganization abolished Germany's tiny states, dividing them among their larger neighbors. It was at that point that Hochfeld and three other Steinweg villages became part of Baden; the other two Steinweg villages were incorporated into Württemberg, whose border was less than seven kilometers away.

The Holy Roman Empire, parts of which would eventually become modern Germany, was founded on Christmas Day in the year 800. When Pope Leo III crowned Charlemagne as the Holy Roman Emperor that day, the participants hoped that their act would inaugurate the rebirth of the Roman Empire, which had ended when the last emperor in the western Roman Empire was deposed in 476.

In its earliest period, the Holy Roman Empire stretched from the Atlantic Ocean in the west to present-day eastern Austria, Slovenia, and the Balkans on the east and south. However, this ungovernable amalgamation of peoples, cultures, and languages lasted only until 843, when the Empire was split into three entities. The western third evolved into France; the middle third eventually became Burgundy; and the eastern third became known as Germany in recognition of its primary language. By the late fifteenth century, this last portion would be known as the Holy Roman Empire of the German Nation.

By the time that Holy Roman Emperor Frederick I Barbarossa established his capital in Wimpfen sometime around 1182, Germany was a major power in Europe. Under the Hohenstaufen dynasty, Germany was a strong, well-populated empire with a growing urban population. Located in the center of the continent, the German third of the Holy Roman Empire contained most of the continent's major trade routes, by land and by river. However, during the early modern period, while England, France, and Spain evolved into great nation states, unified under their strong monarchies, Germany remained divided into hundreds of independent "countries."

There were several reasons for Germany's failure to consolidate. First was the Thirty Years War, lasting from 1618 to 1648, which devastated the German countryside and impeded the Empire's economic and political development. Second, the Empire stretched across the central plain of Europe, and it lacked mountain ranges or other geographic boundaries that could help to consolidate the country territorially and defensively. In order to hold the empire together, the emperors were forced to cede large tracts and power to their subordinates, who over time turned the grants into semi-independent hereditary fiefs. These lords resisted the development of a strong central monarch, which would have limited their own autonomy.

Third, even after it lost the western two-thirds of the Carolingian empire, the Holy Roman Empire still remained a disparate assortment of peoples and languages. At one point it encompassed most (but not all) of present-day Germany, Austria, Switzerland, Liechtenstein, Luxembourg, the Czech Republic, Slovakia, Slovenia, Belgium, and parts of present-day Poland, France, and Italy. Many German-speaking people lived outside the Empire's boundaries, while at the same time many of the Empire's German princes also ruled lands that lay outside the Empire. As one commentator notes, "The entire course of Germanic history has been an argument about poorly defined borders."[19]

Finally, the position of emperor was elective rather than hereditary, and the nobles tended to elect those monarchs who could not threaten their own positions. A vicious cycle developed in which weak emperors were forced to grant ever more powers of government to the dukes, barons, and princes, which further diminished the central administration. One scholar has aptly summarized the authority of the Holy Roman emperors as an alchemy of the shadows.[20]

As strong central monarchies arose in England, Spain, and France, their kings stood at the apex of a unified pyramid of feudal allegiance; at the bottom was a base of the peasant workers, who worked the lands of small local lords who owed fealty to barons, who in turn were the kings' men. This tidy arrangement never developed in the Holy Roman Empire because of the power relationship between the emperor and the nobility, which were known collectively as the imperial estates or *Reichsstände*. Instead, emperor and nobles became mutually dependent. The dukes, princes, and territorial bishops or archbishops needed the alliance of the empire to protect themselves from foreign encroachment; but in order to provide this measure of protection, they had to contribute men and money to common imperial undertakings.

Meanwhile, most imperial knights such as the Steinwegs simply opted out of the Reichsstände. These knights had no money or interest in contributing financially to imperial projects, so they also forfeited their rights to vote and to participate as members in the imperial assemblies.[21]

By the thirteenth century, one noble house had begun to dominate the imperial throne. The Habsburgs were originally from southwestern Germany and the area that is now Switzerland. In 1273, Rudolph I of Habsburg was elected Holy Roman Emperor. Through battles and diplomacy, he eventually acquired present-day Austria and made it a heritable part of the family holdings. The Habsburgs continued to be elected, at first intermittently but later continuously, to the position of Holy Roman Emperor.

The problem with Habsburg rule for the Holy Roman Empire was that the Habsburgs were a powerful dynasty whose boundaries were not consistent with those of the Empire. The Habsburgs held some hereditary territories, such as Hungary, which were outside the empire's boundaries; but they had no hereditary right to many parts of the empire itself, including Württemberg, Baden, Saxony, and Hanover. These widespread holdings caused a conflict between the Habsburg's dynastic interests and their imperial responsibilities.

By the seventeenth century, Habsburg Austria-Hungary was rivaling France as the superpower of Europe. This meant that the Habsburg rulers were far more interested in the fortunes of their own dynasty than the fortunes of the Holy Roman Empire. Even if he could have dominated the independent princes and barons of the Empire, no Habsburg emperor would be likely to take such an action, because it would threaten the position of his own family's patrimony.[22]

Below the rank of Austria, there were five other states in the empire that by 1700 comprised the middle rank of size and power: the electorates of Brandenburg-Prussia, Hanover, Saxony, Bavaria, and the Rhineland Palatinate. (Elector was the title given the powerful dukes, princes, and archbishops who together had the right to elect the Holy Roman Emperors. The number and composition of the electors changed over the centuries.)

Below these five were the three ecclesiastical electorates of Mainz, Cologne, and Trier, as well as the duchy of Württemberg and the landgraviate of Hessen-Kassel. Baden fell into the next tier, along with other minor states such as Hessen-Darmstadt and Braunschweig-Wolfenbüttel. At the very bottom were the tiny independent holdings of the imperial knights.[23]

By the time Johann Adam Mann was born in 1784, the Holy Roman Empire was in its last days. There was nothing left of the political dominance the Empire had commanded in its early centuries; in its place, Austria and an ascendant Prussia were locked in a battle for German leadership. On the economic front, Germany had failed to join England, Spain, France, and the Dutch in voyages of exploration and colonization beginning in the late fifteenth century. Germany's mines, once the primary European source of silver for coinage, were playing out just as gold and silver began to pour into Europe from South America. Germany's importance as the center of European trade was eclipsed as trade routes moved from the inland waterways to the sea, so that the new trade powers became coastal cities such as Antwerp and London. In the south, commercial centers such as Augsburg and Ulm were unsuccessful in maintaining their former lucrative trading routes through Italy. In the north, the German Hanseatic League lost its monopoly when Denmark and Sweden forced open the Baltic to other nations' ships.[24]

In England during the second half of the 1700s, steam power and mechanization ushered in the period known as the Industrial Revolution. Manufacturers and financiers took advantage of the new power source and England's raw materials, cheap labor sources, and modernized transportation systems to create the world's first factories. Consequently, capital and manufacture began to replace land ownership as the basis for wealth. Germany, however, would not embark on its own Industrial Revolution until the latter half of the nineteenth century. As late as 1850, it was still a net exporter of foodstuffs and raw materials and an importer of manufactured goods.

During Johann Adam's lifetime, Germany remained overwhelmingly a rural nation, and the local nobles such as the Steinwegs retained significant power over the lives of villagers. Even trade between territories in Germany was fairly limited until the end of the eighteenth century. The poor quality of roadways severely restricted the movement of goods and raw materials, but as late as the eighteenth century, officials remained ambivalent about improving roads and bridges. Experience had taught the Germans that good roads were an open invitation to invading armies.[25]

The poor harvests, which remained an intermittent factor until the 1830s, would finally bring about change, although too late to save Johann Adam's family. One historian has noted,

Immediately after 1830, the economic situation of agriculture improved. A series of poor harvests raised grain prices, and land values climbed. The beneficial effects of the *Zollverein*, or German Customs Union, which had become a virtually national institution in 1834, began to be felt in agriculture as trade movement to the cities increased. Until 1840, then, no important sudden changes in the agricultural economy occurred. The total effect of the many profound changes which touched agriculture on the German economy as a whole was one of freeing it from virtually feudal restrictions of many kinds; in a land which was soon to embark on a phenomenal commercial and industrial boom, freedom in the essential sector of agriculture was a fundamental precondition of the rapid development of manufacturing and commercial pursuits.[26]

In the meantime, villages remained profoundly conservative — suspicious of strangers and hostile to any innovation, such as new crops or agricultural innovations. The inhabitants lived too close to the prospect of starvation and ruin to be open to experimentation. Each village tried to be as self-contained as possible.

Male citizens who were born in a village were entitled, when they married and assumed adult status, to the protection of *Bürgerrecht*, or local Bürger law and the privileges that Bürger status conferred. Women born in a city or village into a Bürger family also had Bürger status, but could not pass it to their husbands or children.

Outsiders who wished to live in a city or village were required to apply and to show financial solvency. Some would be granted Bürger status. Some would be denied permission. Others might only be granted temporary permission to stay as inhabitants or *Beisitzer* or *Einwohner*, subject always to possible expulsion for economic or other reasons. The Jewish families in Hochfeld, for example, were Beisitzer, but would never be granted Bürger status. They lived in Hochfeld under the protection or *Schutz* of the Freiherr, so they were also known as *Schutzverwandte*, or persons who lived in Hochfeld under sufferance of the local lord, subject to payment of a yearly fee called the *Schutzgeld*.

The English word "Burgher" is roughly equivalent to the German Bürger, but the English term is most often reserved for inhabitants of the early modern cities. Actually, both terms simply refer to a citizen of any city, town, or village. Most books and articles on early modern Germany use the term "peasant" when they discuss residents of the small agricultural villages, because this is generally the translation of the German word "*Bauer.*"

"Bauer," however, can be problematic as a term. In addition to being translated as "peasant," it also refers to the occupation of farmer, and it can carry a connotation of churlishness and backwardness, dating to the time when peasants were objects of scorn and ridicule. "He was either an animal to be laughed at or a person of such low caste as to be completely ignored," wrote one historian. Conversely, Bürger is a term of respect and dignity, and as such, will be used in this book rather than "peasant" when discussing individuals who possess Bürgerrecht in Hochfeld. In writing about the inhabitants of Hochfeld in a more general sense, the term "villager" will be used, since this term also includes inhabitants such as the Jewish families, who lacked Bürgerrecht.[27]

Fees for obtaining Bürger status could be steep. Bürger citizenship could not be transferred from one place to another, so it had the effect of locking most individuals into their places of birth. One historian has observed that there was little escape for the German villager from his predestined place. "People knew too much about him. A bad craftsman found neither friends nor influence; the morally deviant found neither customers nor office; political contrariness tainted a man's workshop and the tavern he frequented. Community citizenship was what he had, and he had it all the time, his pride and his prison."[28]

The pressures of too many people and not enough land caused most villages and their lords to enact ordinances that ensured that they would not be overwhelmed by beggars, the homeless, and "foreigners," whom they defined as anyone not from the home village. Cities and villages had an obligation to support their own legal residents if they became destitute, but they were determined not to assume responsibility for those from any other towns.

In order to protect themselves, villages and cities either wrote detailed regulations pertaining to outsiders or, as in Hochfeld, they simply amended existing local ordinances to exclude the poor and control the admittance of others. The Hochfeld ordinance set a fairly low entry fee of 4 florin for a man and 2 florin for a woman, at a time when the cost of a sheep was about 8 Florin. [For an explanation of German monies, see this endnote.[29]]

The Hochfeld provisions as of 1763 were:

➢ Any person who desires to move into Hochfeld must have the approval of the village council (Gericht). He must attest that he is free of Leibegenschaft (i.e., not the serf of another lord) and of good reputation and standing in his own community. The new subject must at a minimum possess 1,000 florin, pay an entry fee of 4 florin, and must attest to the Bürger oath. Applicants who wish to practice a trade in Hochfeld will be denied if the village administration determines he would injure the livelihood of any Hochfeld Bürger. No one other than Evangelisch (i.e., Lutheran) persons will be accepted as inhabitants without express permission of the town council and the Freiherr.

➢ Foreign women who wish to marry a legal resident of Hochfeld also require permission of the Gericht and the Freiherr. If approved, their entry fee is 2 florin.

➢ Any person who owns or inherits property in Hochfeld, and who intends to sell it, must first offer it to a legal Hochfeld resident. The Gericht has the right to approve any foreign purchaser if no local purchaser can be found. If someone outside Hochfeld inherits part of a house, he must first offer it for sale to the local inhabitants of the house. If buyer and seller cannot agree on a price, the local court (Gericht) will determine the amount.

➢ No Bürger or other inhabitant may sell or renovate his property without advance permission from the Gericht and from the Freiherr, if he is the landlord. Any foreigner (i.e., anyone from outside Hochfeld) who buys or lives in a house or piece of land and who does not intend to become a Bürger here must offer his property for sale to a Hochfeld Bürger within one year.

➢ Without the approval of the Freiherr, as appropriate, no one may mortgage his land or house, either to another resident or a foreigner. A resident who seeks a mortgage because he needs to raise cash may apply to the *Gericht*. The council will question the applicant concerning the nature and urgency of his need, and may decide to advance him the money. The *Bürgermeister* (i.e., the village's financial administrator) will maintain a record of the loan and repayment in the village account book.

➢ Neither residents nor the tavern keeper may lodge a foreigner, especially disreputable peddlers or tinkers, without the advance permission of the mayor (*Schultheiß* or *Schultheiss*)."[30]

This last ordinance highlighted the suspicions that villagers harbored about the strangers, not just beggars but also itinerant peddlers and craftsmen, who passed through their town. These people were different; they had traveled and seen many sights, so that they knew things and had thoughts that were foreign—even frightening—to the Hochfeld residents. Strangers also made the Gericht nervous because they were not subject to the rules and controls that circumscribed the behavior of all village residents.

Fortunately for the village inhabitants, there was little need for peddlers in Hochfeld. Although the village was too small to support a weekly market, most of the villagers' needs, including sale and purchase of animals, tools, foodstuffs, and services, were handled locally, through cash or barter, between village residents. One of the Jewish family men in Hochfeld, Josua Hirsch, was a peddler who traveled from village to village, buying and selling. He lived his life on the road; at best, he was able to visit his family once a week. Because he was known to the villagers, he was not subject to the same unease with which they viewed strangers, and he was able to meet their needs for most small items such as needles that could not be produced by a local craftsman.[31]

On rare occasions, the villagers might travel the 9 kilometers to the small weekly markets in Wimpfen. Johann Adam himself had never ventured farther from Hochfeld than Wimpfen, and he seldom had reason to make that trip. However, one of the earliest and most vivid memories of his life was when he was ten years old and his father took him to the Talmarkt, the market fair which had been held annually in Wimpfen since the year 962.

The experience assaulted his every sense. He was jostled in the street by more humans than he had ever seen in one place, pressed together in the narrow streets as they moved from one stall to another. He almost choked on the mingled odors of unwashed bodies, animals for sale, fish, soap, flowers, herbs, even perfumes. There were vendors and merchants hawking everything from food, wine, and cloth to tobacco, elixirs, musical instruments, books, toys, leather goods, and furniture. There were horse races and wrestling contests. There were fallen women, shysters, and common pickpockets. There were exotic foreigners from across Europe and the Levant, dressed in outlandish clothes and head coverings. There were the performers: actors, acrobats, singers, and puppets. But what Johann Adam most remembered was his sense of a larger world, of people and lands far distant from Hochfeld, and his mixed emotions of wistfulness and relief that he would never know these places and things.

Figure 5. Village cooper.

In February 1817, a miracle occurred—or at least so it seemed to Johann Adam. Johann Adam's eldest brother, Georg Stephan, suffered a heart attack and died. Johann Adam's father had been one of Hochfeld's two barrel makers or coopers (Küfer), and Johann Adam had worked alongside him, learning the trade. However, so had Georg Stephan; and as the eldest son, his father designated him to carry on the family business. No man could practice a trade in Hochfeld without the permission of the Gericht, and Johann Adam knew they would never allow him to work as a Küfer. The village could only support two barrel makers; with three none of them would earn enough. Now there was but one, and Georg Stephan had only daughters, no sons to take up his place; perhaps Johann Adam would be granted the second license.[32]

The council members were very aware of Johann Adam's sufferings. They considered him an honest, hard-working man; perhaps just as important, several of them were related to him by blood or marriage. His petition was granted. He would not earn a great deal of money as a part-time Küfer, but combined with his farming and his earnings as an intermittent day laborer, he that he would earn enough so that that he and his son would never again suffer through a hungry winter.

3

Peasant Status

In 1449, Caspar Freiherr von Steinweg purchased Hochfeld and two other nearby villages from the von Oberdorf family. The Steinwegs had owned land and villages in southwest Germany since the ninth century, but their property was scattered across the Kraichgau; they even owned two villages west of the Rhine River and two other villages to the south in Württemberg.

Ever since the outbreak of the Black Death in Germany in the mid-1300s, families like the Steinwegs, who lived off their rents and the sale of their agricultural produce, had watched their income drop. Accurate mortality rates for the Black Death are nonexistent, leaving historians to draw conclusions from isolated reports. One report stated that the plague killed two-thirds of the population in Hamburg, and another reported 2,000 deaths during a 72-day period in Frankfurt. Whatever the actual rate was in southwest Germany, the drop in population in Germany translated into lower demand for grain and competition for the reduced supply of peasant labor.

Many surviving villagers took advantage of the chaos to either migrate to the cities or to move to the lands of lords who offered their tenants better terms. Caspar was resolved to improve his family's financial situation; he decided the best way to do that was to consolidate his land holdings. If he eliminated the substantial distance between his villages, he would improve his ability to oversee and control his tenants and to squeeze the maximum income from their labor.[33]

There was another reason that Caspar wanted to consolidate his holdings near the Neckar. As lord of Hochfeld, he was an independent noble who answered to no one but the Emperor. Some of his other properties, however, he held as fiefs from other lords, specifically the bishops of Speyer and Worms and the Count of Württemberg. He wanted to free himself from the interference of these intermediate lords, who meddled in his affairs and took part of his income. Over the next few years following his purchase of Hochfeld, Caspar continued to sell off his most distant properties and to purchase more holdings near Hochfeld. By 1457, he still held one property in Württemberg but the bulk of his land, consisting of six villages and their associated fields and forests, was now consolidated on the west bank of the Neckar river. In 1451, Caspar moved his family and his administrative center to the old castle in Hochfeld.[34]

Caspar's Neckar Valley purchases made him the landlord or *Grundherr* for most, but not all, of his villages' inhabitants. It was not uncommon during this period, and in the following centuries, for a village to have multiple Grundherren. But for those villagers whose personal holdings were on "his" land, he could expect to receive rents, labor services called *Frondienst*, and certain other dues and payments.[35]

The twenty-first century concept of ownership, which is grounded in Roman law, would have been foreign to Caspar and the villagers in the mid-fifteenth century. Roman law had been forgotten after the fall of the Roman Empire, and its concepts did not begin to penetrate the Holy Roman Empire until the end of the fifteenth century. Under Roman law, ownership of a piece of land was exclusive and absolute. Had Roman law been in force in Germany when the Freiherr purchased Hochfeld, he would have been acknowledged as the sole owner of whatever land he had purchased. But he would *not* have become the Grundherr of any villager who held a title to his own plot. In other words, the real estate transaction would have functioned just as it does in twenty-first century America: one sole owner for each plot of land.

During Caspar's time, Germany was still operating under the "good old law" of Germanic custom, which had been

Figure 6. Woodcut of a lord and his peasant.

practiced there for centuries, and under this law the concept of ownership was more complex.[36] Under the "good old law," anyone who possessed a piece of property, and who received an economic benefit from it, held the *Seisin* for that property. This is a simple concept as long as only one person both possesses and is the sole beneficiary of any profit from a property. Indeed, the territorial lords in eastern Germany generally directly controlled their holdings, using the labor of servile peasants who were much less free than in the southwest. This system was called *Gutsherrschaft*. But in southwest Germany, tenants actually held their own lands, sharing the proceeds with the Grundherr through rents and fees, so that both parties held a Seisin over the property. No one perceived a contradiction in the concept that both the lord and the tenants "owned" segments of property at the same time.

The concept of ownership was further complicated by the fact that traditionally, villages held a substantial portion of the available land — meadows, pastures, and forests — in common, shared by all the villagers who enjoyed Bürgerrecht in that community. There was also an understanding that villagers could have different levels of use rights and "ownership." Some, for example, were not technically tenants of the Grundherr, but instead owned their land free and clear — an arrangement that today we call a freehold. Other villagers were tenants, but held the right to pass on their holdings to their children. Still others held only a time-limited right to a piece of property, a right that the Grundherr could terminate with the death of the villager or, in some cases, at any time. Nevertheless, all parties recognized the right of the Grundherr to collect rents and dues, regardless of who "owned" a piece of property.[37]

Grundherrschaft was only one aspect of lordly rights, or Herrschaft. There were at least two other types of Herrschaft: *Gerichtsherrschaft*, or the right to administer legal justice, which Caspar held by virtue of being the sole lord in Hochfeld; and *Leibherrschaft*, or the right to control the villagers themselves, as opposed to their land. When one wishes to use a general term to encompass *all* the rights that a local lord held, one can simply use the term *Ortsherr*, which means "local lord."

Just as the villagers owed rent and, in most cases, labor, to their lord, so he owed them protection, a concept called *Schutz und Schirm*. While the era of protecting villagers from marauding bands of thugs was, for the most part, past, the lord was expected to help villagers through years of bad harvest and other disasters. There was an implicit assumption in the concept that Herrschaft was legitimate only if the subjects accepted the rule of their lord. Herrschaft was

> . . . a very complex term because it may be construed as an abstraction, a bundle of interrelated claims that represented 'rule' . . . [It] connoted reciprocal relationships, and in order for rulers to achieve legitimation through the exercise of Herrschaft they, too, had to recognize some reciprocal obligations . . . But villagers had no illusions that the reciprocal obligations between lord and subject were evenly balanced.[38]

In addition to his rights as Grundherr to those villagers who were his tenants and/or who owed him fees based on land usage, Caspar was also the Leibherr for some Hochfeld residents, as well as for other serfs scattered across the Kraichgau, northern Württemberg, and the Rhineland Palatinate. A Grundherr had rights over a piece of property, but a Leibherr had rights over the people themselves; to use a common term, they were his serfs. Many of these individuals were in the villages Caspar owned, but many others were the tenants of other Grundherren. For a man whose goal was to increase his control over his people and his property, this state of affairs was a serious problem, one he shared with most other lords in southwest Germany.[39]

How did relationships between common man and lord become so confused? The roots of the problem dated back to the wandering Germanic tribes who began to move into northern Germany in the eighth century B.C. and whose continued spread southward led them into conflict with the Romans by the late second century B.C. The Germanic tribes were nomads whose economy was based on summer military campaigns, in which the men earned the tribes' living by plunder. As long as their agricultural endeavors were limited to nomadic grazing and sporadic farming, it was no hardship for all the men to leave their temporary homes each year for several months of warfare.

However, as the tribes began to establish permanent homes and to earn more of their livelihood through agriculture and livestock, it became impossible for most men to leave during the growing season. In return for a release from fighting in order to tend their land and to insure that they would be protected from other bands of fighters, some men took pledges of service and fealty to their warrior overlords. By the end of the middle ages, there remained little need for the military services of the overlords, so the overlords also settled down. Land and the income from agricultural products replaced plunder as their primary source of income, and the relationship of overlord and peasant farmer became firmly established.

By the seventh century A.D., peasant farmers had lost their freedom and were tied as serfs to their lords' lands; in other words, these farmers' lords now became their Leibherren. When Vikings, Saracens, and Hungarians began to invade the Germanic lands in the eighth and ninth centuries, many peasant farmers took advantage of the confusion to seek better lords. While they still had to agree to perform labor services and to pay their new lords rents and fees, at least they were again free men. There was another period of mobility in the fourteenth century as a result of the enormous death toll from the Black Death. At the beginning of the fifteenth century, therefore, men in southwest Germany were generally free to move, to select their own lord, and to marry as they chose, irrespective of the local Grundherr. In addition, because the villagers were not bound to the land in southwest Germany, their Leibherr did not change just because their Grundherr sold his interest in a village.[40]

This was the muddled situation that Caspar von Steinweg was determined to remedy. One of his first acts after purchasing Hochfeld in 1449 was to require all the villagers for whom he was already the Leibherr to swear that they would take no lord but him, or face expulsion from the village. Next, as tenancies came up for renewal or as any tenant died who could not prove that he held *Erblehenrecht* or inheritable rights to his property, Caspar made the new tenant swear to become his *Leibeigene* or serf; with this vow, they voluntarily gave up their personal freedom.

Those villagers whose families owned their land outright were still obligated to pay the Freiherr a death tax when the head of household died. Caspar set the death duty so high that many villagers were forced to give him their land to settle the debt, after which he would allow them to continue as his tenants—provided they agreed to become his *Leibeigene*. To speed up the consolidation process, Caspar worked a series of trades with other lords in the years between 1450 and 1461 in which they exchanged their Leibeigene, either in ones and twos or in large groups, with a goal of insuring, to the maximum extent possible, that each villager would owe rent, fees, labor, and fealty to just one lord. Since children of a Leibeigene inherited their parents' servile status, even if one of the parents was free, within 20 years of his purchase of Hochfeld, Caspar was both the Grundherr and the Leibherr for more than 85 percent of the village residents.[41]

The actual conditions of Leibeigen status changed from region to region in Germany, and even from village to village, depending on the conditions agreed to or forced upon each locale. Certainly, conditions were much harsher in regions where Gutsherrschaft was practiced, as it was in eastern and parts of northern Germany. Indeed, not all researchers agree that the term Leibeigenschaft should be used for southwest Germany, preferring instead the term *Untertan* or subject. But for convenience, this book will use the term "serf" to describe the unfree status of most villagers in Hochfeld.[42]

Despite a lack of clarity in the terms that researchers have used to describe the villagers' unfree status, as well as the great variety of conditions that relate to a villager's legal status in Early Modern Germany, there are certain overall statements that apply to the servitude of the German villager:

➤ Free and unfree are relative terms when one speaks of the status of German villagers between 1500 and 1850. An individual peasant's legal status depended on his geographic location, the rules and practices of his individual overlord, and the specific time period, since the peasant's status, rights, and responsibilities all evolved over time.

➤ Serfs were not slaves. They could not be killed, mutilated, sold off, or separated from their families. The overlord did not own their bodies, although he might own all or part of their labor. However, some peasants were tied to a specific parcel of land, particularly in northeastern Germany, so that they transferred with the land if the territorial lord sold or traded it.

➤ It was not necessarily undesirable to be a serf. Some villagers freely accepted sevile status in return for protection by an overlord or in order to receive a choice tenancy. In many cases, serfs were far better off than free peasants, who had no financial security and less or no land to work.

➤ Within their own villages, serfs could enjoy considerable freedom, relative wealth, and prestige despite their Leibeigene status. There was no relationship between an individual's social status and his personal freedom or lack thereof. Serfs regularly served in positions of village leadership, including as Schultheiß (Schultheiss).

As long as a village met all its tax, tithe, and work obligations owed to the overlord, state, and church, many lords allowed villagers to administer their own affairs—subject, of course, to lordly oversight. Over time, as the money economy grew and barter dwindled, it became economically advantageous for both the overlord to receive and the peasants to pay their rent in money rather than in bound labor.

The legal death knell for serfdom came with the establishment of the Napoleonic Code in the first decade of the nineteenth century, although it had already begun to be abolished in some territories. That did not mean, however, that mandatory unpaid labor or Frondienst was immediately abolished; in most villages, it took decades before the villagers freed themselves completely of this hated practice.

As serfdom ended and Roman law was applied to the fuzzy question of property ownership in the eighteenth and nineteenth centuries, villagers were often given the opportunity to buy out the interest of their Grundherr in their property. However, some villagers who were unable to come up with the funds continued to be required to sign onerous contracts, including labor requirements, in order to keep their tenancies. Vestiges of the ancient relationship between lord and villager continued to exist well into the twentieth century in many villages.[43]

*   *   *

Shortly after his purchase of Hochfeld, Caspar von Steinweg ordered the villagers to assemble in front of the church. Even though he was not yet the Grundherr or Leibherr for all the villagers, he was their *Gerichtsherr*. Given his status as the village's sole overlord, Caspar and his dictates represented the only form of "government" that existed for Hochfeld in the fifteenth through eighteenth centuries. As such, each village inhabitant was subject to his dictates, taxes, and fees, irrespective of whether Caspar was that individual's Grundherr or Leibherr.

In recognition of his position as Hochfeld overlord, Caspar required that all the Bürger and other inhabitants swear homage to him, both personally and on behalf of their families. Each man was directed to raise his right hand with three fingers extended: the thumb for God the Father, the index finger for God the Son, and the middle finger for the Holy Ghost. Then, as Caspar's *Amtmann* or bailiff read the words of the oath, they repeated after him:

> I swear to God to be true and faithful to my lord, Caspar von Steinweg, and to be obedient to his commandments and prohibitions. I will safeguard his property and dedicate myself to his well-being, and I will contribute my

labor to his profit and advantage. I pledge to help enforce his will, insuring that his mandates are obeyed by all persons, be they neighbor or stranger, rich or poor, and I will accept no inducements from others that might contravene my lord's best interests. I will inform the lord or his representative of any transgressions by others against his commandments. I will not agitate against the lord in any way, nor will I attempt to move from Hochfeld without informing the lord. I swear to account for the faithfulness of my service before God Almighty on the Day of Judgment.[44]

After all the villagers had sworn their fealty and obedience to Caspar, he announced that he had drawn up a set of village ordinances or *Dorfordnungen*. The purpose of the new ordinances, he informed them with an ironic smile, was to guide them so that they could live together in harmony, both with him and among themselves, in a godly and productive manner. Caspar then directed his Amtmann to read them aloud to the assembled crowd.

The Amtmann began to read, and he continued to drone on and on, to the villagers' shock, for almost an hour. As he read one prohibition after another, a murmur of protest swept through the crowd in the form of muttered comments and head shakings as the villagers began to comprehend the degree to which these Dorfordnungen would intrude into their personal lives and prerogatives. For example, the village strictures concerning the treatment of strangers, discussed in Chapter 1, grew out of the restrictions listed in Caspar's original Ordnungen. But there were dozens of other restrictions and requirements, many far more intrusive than those listed in Chapter 1, including:

> ➤ All villagers are directed to attend church each Sunday, festival day, and for weddings and funerals. Only on very important grounds may someone miss a service. Persons who fail to attend will be fined; continued absences will result in physical punishment. Likewise, any sacrilegious acts or blaspheming will be punished.

> ➤ No one may work on Sundays and holidays except during harvest, unless bad weather threatens the crop or the hay is in danger of blight from the rain.

> ➤ The Freiherr reserves the right to select and to dismiss at any time, any villager for any office or official duty, including the mayor (Schultheiss) and the village council (Gericht). If an individual for a lower office is selected by the community, the Freiherr reserves the right to affirm or to overturn the community's selection.

> ➤ In case of a riot, death, or inappropriate disturbance in the town or within its boundaries, the Schultheiss and other officials may require the help of everyone in the town. If someone is not involved in an impending

disturbance but he knows or hears about it, it is his duty to hasten to the scene and render whatever kind of aid is possible.

➢ If the Freiherr, the Amtmann, or the Schultheiss call together the entire community and someone fails to appear, he will be penalized 8 pfennigs.

➢ No Bürger should wantonly or willfully inflict any disgrace, dishonor, or damage on another. The subjects should live with one another in a Christian and friendly manner. If something results in a grievance, he should take it to the Gericht. The Schultheiss and Gericht will determine and implement an appropriate remedy. Under pain of punishment, it is forbidden for any citizen to pursue his grievance in a court outside the village. If there is a debt owed of 20 gulden or more, one should bring the case before the Herrschaft. Any inhabitant or stranger who is assessed a fine must pay it within 8 days. In case this deadline is missed, the fine will be doubled. If someone is too poor to pay a fine, he will be locked in the tower for a period to equal a fourth gulden for each day.

➢ Each inhabitant has pledged himself in accordance with his oath that he will inform the authorities concerning anything detrimental that relates to the rights, annuities, rents, mortgages, interest or anything similar that has or will take place. Also, each person has pledged that if the community, the church, the school, the sacristy, is affected, he will notify the authorities. Each person should alert the authorities if a stranger or neighbor has overused the pasture or sheep-run, if a boundary stone has fallen, or if the authorities have been defrauded concerning rents, tithes, or taxes. If anyone has seen or heard something concerning a death, murder, robbery, marital breakup, or other similar evil, his oath requires him to report it.

➢ Anyone who drinks to excess or is thriftless will be punished. Anyone found in the tavern after 9 p.m. in summer or 8 p.m. in winter will pay a fine of a half gulden, and the tavern keeper will be fined a gulden for serving him. No one should be out on the streets after these hours without a significant justification.

➢ Excessive gambling is prohibited. Anyone who engages in dice, cards, or any other game is not allowed to bet more than a pfennig. Anyone who exceeds a daily total of 15 kreuzer a day will be fined 5 schillings.

➢ No subject should deal with a Jew or take money from him at a usurious interest rate. Anyone who nevertheless does this will be subject to high punishment by the Herrschaft. Jews may receive nothing for their lent-out money, their attendant expenses, or their penalties.

➢ Anyone who hires a farm servant or laborer from outside the village must present the servant to the Schultheiss within 14 days. The servant must swear to the Schultheiss that he will abide by the same requirements and prohibitions as all the other residents of Hochfeld.

➤ Concerning marriages for Leibeigene villagers: No one should live with, have lewd dealings with, or pair off his children with a dishonorable person. Clandestine marriages, i.e., entered into without the blessing of the Freiherr or the pastor, will result in corporal punishments, fines, and time in the tower. One may marry only with the advanced knowledge of the Gericht, parents, guardian, or the next of kin. The Freiherr must consent to all marriages. Any villager who wishes to make a marriage outside the village must also have the assent of that place's ruling authority.

➤ No village festivities and weddings may take place without the knowledge and consent of the Herrschaft. No one is allowed to spend too much money on a wedding. Even when rich people marry, they may not invite more people than can be seated at four tables unless they have special circumstances and the approval of the lord.

➤ Bakers, innkeepers, and butchers are warned to measure their products accurately and to insure that they do not cheat anyone. They must maintain accurate scales to insure that their bread, meat, and drink products match the mandatory amounts. Bread, meat, and wine must meet a consistent quality standard. Any violations will be punished.

➤ From now on, no one is allowed to pick grapes before the general harvest, except for the pastor, wardens, cellar master, the Freiherr's cooper, or the herdsman.

➤ Likewise, no one may take in his harvest before the Freiherr's servant has removed his share (*Zehnt* or tithe) from the fields.

➤ The Herrschaft retains the right to invalidate any sales agreement entered into by one or more villagers, for the four-week period following the agreement.

➤ No villager may hunt, cut wood, or herd cattle in the Herrschaft forest or anyplace else within the boundaries of the village. No villager may take eggs out of the nests of the wild ducks and other fowls. Likewise, it is forbidden to fish or to trap crabs in the brooks of the Herrschaft. The fine for violating these prohibitions is 6 florin. If someone allows his dog to run in the forest, his fine is 1 florin. Anyone caught in the forest with a rifle or crossbow is subject to a fine of 3 florin.

➤ In the past, it has been customary for villagers in the autumn to graze their livestock in the Herrschaft woods on fallen acorns and beechnuts. This practice is now strictly forbidden, subject to a fine of 6 florin or more.

➤ All the villagers' garden plots along the Wimpfener Strasse must be fenced so that cows will stay out. Anyone whose cow does damage is liable for a penalty of 6 pfennigs, more if the damage is serious.

➢ After harvest, the village swine will be penned in the fields to forage, then the cattle, and finally the geese. If a village herder fails to wait until receiving permission for his turn, he will be fined 5 schillings.

➢ No one is allowed to harvest grass from the pastures. It is the duty of each inhabitant to inform on any violators of this rule. Anyone who holds a piece of ground with pastureland must insure that their grass does not spill over into a neighbor's holdings.

➢ No one may cross a common field, not even on foot, but must stay on the designated paths. An exception would be if the path is covered by water, so that to use it would cause damage. In this case the Schultheiss must be informed so that an alternative temporary path can be designated.

➢ Anyone who takes down a straight, well-growing tree from the Herrschaft woods or the community woods will be assessed a fine of 3 Pfunds. Anyone who trespasses in the Herrschaft woods will be fined 5 schillings. Effective immediately, residents may take lumber or firewood only after paying the Herrschaft the appropriate fee.

➢ No inhabitant may sell or give away firewood, kindling, stakes, or other wood outside of the community, although he may sell or give it away to another village resident.

➢ Residents whose holdings abut the Herrschaft estate or forest and whose property is not adequately maintained will be fined. If any villager whose field abuts the Herrschaft forest allows undergrowth to become established, his land may be confiscated. No subject is allowed to create new paths over the meadows of the Herrschaft through the act of driving, riding, or walking across them.

➢ Houses, barns, sheds, and stables must be maintained in good condition. Whenever a house is constructed, the foundation may not sit directly on the ground but must rest on at least two footings. These regulations should insure the durability of any building.

➢ It has been the practice that if a house's fire goes out, the residents send their child to a neighbor to borrow some embers from their hearth. Because of fire hazard, this practice must be stopped. Every subject should be aware of fire hazard at all times. Each house must keep a leather bucket and an axe handy and be ready to assist in putting out a burning house or other building.

➢ The village must employ two house and field inspectors whose job it is to insure fireplaces and buildings are fire-worthy. Anyone cited by these individuals will be subject to a 3-pfund fine. Anyone whose fields or vineyards are not maintained in an orderly fashion will be subject to the same fine.

➤ No one may break flax and hemp or dry fruit within the village proper because of the danger of fire. Flax and hemp are to be broken only outside of the residential area in the area called the Breakhole. Penalty for noncompliance is 1 gulden.[45]

By the time the Amtmann finished reading, the villagers had given up their muttering and were standing before him silently, in shock and disbelief at what they had heard. Admittedly, some of the Freiherr's new ordinances were not so very different than the rules that the villagers had long ago established for themselves, and some of the regulations and restrictions were similar to the informal rules they had lived with under the Freiherr's predecessor, the Freiherr von Oberdorf.

They could all agree on the restrictions meant to insure their safety, such as the prohibition against sending a child to borrow live embers, or the restrictions that protected property and income, such as the prohibition against cutting across cultivated fields. At one time or another, all of them had grumbled about being shorted by the butcher, baker, or innkeeper. But some of the provisions struck them as unreasonably intrusive, such as the requirement to obtain the lord's permission before marrying. And others, such as the prohibition against grazing their swine on acorns and beechnuts, cut squarely into their livelihoods. They were accustomed to fattening their pigs before the autumn slaughter. The prohibition would both curtail their income and reduce their already scarce supply of meat products to see them through the winter.

The former lord had prohibited the Hochfeld villagers from hunting large game, but he had looked the other way when they hunted small mammals or fished in the streams that fed the Neckar River. These losses also had a direct impact on the amount of protein available in the villagers' diets. Finally, many villagers lacked the extra money they would now have to pay for firewood, which could again endanger the health of their families over the cold, damp winter seasons.

But worse was yet to come. In short order, the Freiherr and his Amtmann began to squeeze the villagers for income through a variety of methods that kept many of them on the brink—and sometimes over the brink—of extreme poverty. The villagers had been accustomed to paying a Zehnt or tithe to maintain their local church and priest, and for the past century, part of that tithe had been owed to a priority in Wimpfen. Now, however, the Freiherr had purchased the priory's share and he controlled the disposition of the entire Zehnt. Over the next few years, the villagers watched as the Freiherr diverted the bulk of the Zehnt to enrich his own coffers, leaving less than ever to support the local parish priest and church. In addition, Caspar's Amtmann proved particularly ingenious in inventing new taxes, fees, and duties on every kind of income, life event, and transfer of property. And the unpaid labor services that the Freiherr's tenants owed him, which formerly had been fairly informal and relatively moderate, became formal, specific, and burdensome.

This unpaid labor, or Frondienst, included several categories of mandatory service. Most, but not all, of the Frondienst obligation derived from a villager's tenant status; however, there were separate requirements to support community public works projects, for example, for which all villagers shared a labor obligation. Frondienst categories included hand labor, carting labor, message carrying, hunt services such as beating the game into the open, fishing labor, building services, and field labor.

The Freiherr set his Frondienst requirements based on the resources available in each household, so that the households of the wealthiest tenants each owed 12 days of labor, which included provision of the villagers' own horses and carts. The middling tenant households who lacked horse and cart each owed 12 days of labor without horse and cart; if they could provide a horse and cart for their labor, they owed only 6 days. Only the very poorest villagers were excused from the labor requirement; they remained subject to Fron until 70 years of age.

Each person was required to bring his own tools when called to perform his Fron. The Freiherr could order villagers to discharge their Fron not just in Hochfeld but in any of his other villages. If the Freiherr ended up not needing his entire yearly quota of labor from one of his serfs, he instead

Figure 7. Woodcut of a peasant.

required that person to pay him a fee or *Frongeld*.[46]

The Frondienst requirement would survive in many villages until the mid-nineteenth century, and in some villages until the twentieth. Villagers so despised the demeaning Fron that the quality of labor they rendered was often as poor and as slow as the villagers could manage to make it. For the middling or poor villagers who sought to increase their family's income by performing day labor, the Frondienst also cut into the time they had available to earn wages.[47]

With regard to the financial burdens imposed on the villagers in the form of taxes, rents, fees, and tithes, one researcher has placed the overall rate of these obligations as high as one-half of the villagers' annual income. In addition to any rents, mortgages, and mortgage interest, there were three types of tithes due: the Great Tithe, taken as a tenth of the corn, oats, buckwheat, spelt, barley, and other cereals; the Small Tithe, a tenth taken of all cabbages, turnips, hemp, flax, fruits, and some livestock; and the Blood Tithe, which was calculated based on cattle ownership and was often taken in money rather than in kind. While these tithes were normally set at ten percent as implied by the name, some locales set different rates.

Other taxes and fees included, but were not limited to:

- *Laudemialgebühren*, the transfer fees charged parties in the transfer of a tenancy. The departing tenant paid a *Weglözin*, while the new tenant paid a *Handlohn*.

- *Erdschatz* or *Lehengeld*, the entry fee charged a new tenant or a receiving heir when he assumed a house or land holding; this was separate from the transfer fee.

- *Nachsteuer*, a supplementary tax owed on any mortgages held on any house, field strip, meadow, vineyard, or other real property.

- *Umbgeld*, a consumption tax on wine and beer.

- A variety of annual fees, assessed on the village bakers, butchers, smiths, and anyone who kept doves.

- *Schutzgeld*, protection fees, one assessed on Jews and another assessed on all male and female inhabitants.

- *Geflügelzinsen*, a poultry tax, assessed on all serfs as a sign of their subservience to the Freiherr.

- *Fruchtgülten*, the annual lease fee for property, paid in a fixed amount of wheat, rye, and oats.

- Perhaps most hated, the death tax, known variously as the *Hauptrecht*, the *Besthaupt*, and the *Todfall*. Most commonly, it required the payment from an estate of a man, his best cow, horse, or hog; and from the estate of a woman, her best dress. However, it could be set at an impossibly high level in order to force the heirs to yield their freehold property to the Grundherr. What most incensed the villagers was that Caspar demanded a third to a half of an estate as death tax even if the deceased was not his Leibeigene.[18]

Four years after Caspar imposed the Dorfordnungen on Hochfeld, the village experienced the wettest and coldest summer that any of them could remember. Planting had been late that year because the fields were too wet to plough, so the seeds had gone in late. A significant percentage of the seeds rotted before they could germinate, and those plants that sprouted remained yellow and spindly. By July, the villagers knew that there would not be enough food harvested in the autumn to feed themselves and their livestock over the winter. There was no recourse but to turn to the Freiherr for relief.

Figure 8. 1820 drawing of a village near fictitious Hochfeld. The village and its church (center) are dominated by the lord's castle to the right.

While Caspar recognized his obligation to assist the villagers through the difficult season ahead, he also saw the situation as an opportunity. He could use the crisis to further his goals of extending Leibeigene status and increasing his rental income. Through his Amtmann, Caspar let it be known that he would forgive the rent of any tenant who could prove his family's need during the coming winter, and he would insure that they received seeds to plant in the spring. Any free man who agreed to become a serf of Caspar would receive similarly generous terms. But for those individuals who were not tenants of his, Caspar offered to advance them food and seeds at a rate of repayment that would soon force them to surrender their lands.

Among the Hochfeld villagers, there existed an ever-shrinking group of Bürger who were both free and who were not tenants of any lord. Although they were still subject to the Grundherr's tithes and to many of the fees, they took great pride in their independence. They were determined to resist what they perceived as Caspar's extortion, and they threw themselves into the project of organizing resistance among the villagers. To the free men who were Caspar's tenants, these leaders talked about the tenants' impending loss of dignity and autonomy. To Caspar's serfs who owned part or all of their own property, the leaders emphasized the injury that the loss of property would cause to their children. And the leaders warned those villagers who were already bound to Caspar as tenants and serfs that if Caspar's maneuver went unchecked, his future tyranny would know no bounds.

It took the insurgents almost six weeks, but finally these leaders had won the support of a majority of villagers. The Schultheiss, who was trapped in his dual role of representing the interests both of the Freiherr and the villagers, refused to support the protesters, but they had been able to win the endorsement of over half the village court or Gericht. Their spokesman was Jörg Mann, whose ancestors had been farming in Hochfeld since the tenth century. Jörg and his deputation asked for a meeting with the Amtmann to state their grievances and present their demands.

The Freiherr's actions, Jörg informed the Amtmann, were coercive, illegal under the "good old law" of Germanic custom, and in violation of Caspar's duty to protect and support them. The majority of villagers were protesting Caspar's actions, and they respectfully asked him to reconsider his proposed actions. They were willing to work with the Herrschaft to find an accommodation acceptable to both sides. However, Jörg declared, the village was prepared to act if Caspar would not listen. In that case, the villagers would refuse to perform Frondienst. They would immediately begin to cut wood for firewood and lumber from the forest, and they would resume the practice of fattening their hogs on acorns and beechnuts. They would withhold the Small Tithe because the village families needed to conserve all available foodstuffs for the coming winter. And finally, despite the vow that the Freiherr had forced them to take four years earlier, the villagers were prepared to take their grievances to the imperial court. In violation of his responsibility to protect them, he was illegally pressing them into serfdom and he was stealing their lands.

In his study of the interrelationship between lord and peasant in Hohenlohe villages just a few kilometers to the east of Hochfeld, one scholar concluded,

> The authority and power of the [territorial lords] . . . appear less secure, less certain, than is sometimes supposed. This followed not simply from the poorly developed structures of . . . authority and domination in the countryside, but also from the fact that power rested, to a degree still not fully understood, on villagers sharing in the process of their domination. [T]he key to peasant loyalty and obedience was reciprocity. A lord could legitimately press his authority only by providing his peasants with 'protection' . . . Peasant loyalty was therefore a quality that no lord ever took for granted. Loyalty was evoked with a customary oath of loyalty, but then it had to be renewed repeatedly in peasants through concrete actions.[49]

Caspar was stung and angry at this revolt in his lands, and he toyed with terminating the leases and expelling the families of all the protesters. However, he knew that it would harm his own livelihood as well as theirs. He was also not interested in creating an angry and sullen populace that would find ways to sabotage his actions and income. He decided to bide his time; the plans he had put in place, especially his use of high death duties, would eventually bring most of the villagers onto his rent rolls and serf listing, anyway.

On 1 November 1493, Caspar signed an agreement with the Hochfeld villagers entitled the Allerheiligener Vertrag, in which he promised to extend rent forgiveness and to provide spring seeds to all villagers in need during the coming winter. More importantly, he rolled back some of the restrictions from his Dorfordnungen. In return, the villagers acceded to certain prohibitions in writing:

➢ For needed firewood and lumber, the Freiherr will allocate, from the Herrschaft woodlands, a half-morgen of woodland to each farmer and one-third of a morgen to each cottager. The lumber allotment will be without charge, but the firewood will require payment of a small allotment by the village of Hochfeld. [For an explanation of the land measure called a *morgen*, see this endnote.[50]]

➢ For the building and maintenance of the jurisdiction fences, the villagers may not take timber from the lordly woods. However, villagers may take hawthorn plants from the Herrschaft woodlands and plant them to form natural fences around their gardens.

➢ Villagers agree to plant three saplings for every tree taken from their allocation.

➢ Villagers may graze their pigs on acorns and nuts in the lord's oak and beech groves from 20 September until 21 December each year, upon payment by the village of 3 batzer.

➢ Villagers may hunt small predators such as wolves and foxes. They may also hunt hares found on community property. Fishing and hunting other game are forbidden.

➢ The villagers will place their best dogs at the Freiherr's disposal for the hunt.

➢ The villagers agree to provide up to 12 days of Frondienst each year in accordance with the current practice. The lord agrees to provide meals to all persons performing Frondienst.[51]

*   *   *

In 1784, a descendent of Jörg Mann, 30 generations removed, was born in Hochfeld—Johann Adam Mann, our protagonist. What is most noteworthy about the relationship between village and lord in the year of Johann Adam's birth was how little had changed since Jörg mounted his protest over Caspar's heavy-handed behavior. In 1784, the Freiherr von Steinweg was still the Grundherr of most of the village residents. The majority of villagers were still his serfs. They continued to pay him the tithes, rents, fees, and taxes that their ancestors had paid his ancestors for almost 350 years. Most remarkably, they continued to owe him Frondienst.

On August 6, 1806, the last emperor abdicated following a military loss to Napoleon and, with the stroke of his pen, the Holy Roman Empire ceased to exist. Napoleon had already occupied southwest Germany, and one month earlier he had consolidated the welter of small territories and principalities in that area into the Confederation of the Rhine. As the Freiherr's villages were absorbed, some into the Kingdom of Württemberg and others into the Grand Duchy of Baden, the independent rule of the Steinweg barons came to an end. Hochfeld became part of Baden.

Baden had abolished the institution of serfdom in the late eighteenth century. For its new territories, however, serfdom did not end with their incorporation into their new country. A difficult transitional period lasted into the 1870s as each former territory negotiated a new tenant-landlord relationship at its own speed and in its own way. In the Steinweg territories, serfdom or Leibeigenschaft finally ended in 1820.

In 1833, the same year that legislation ended the tithing system in Baden, the Grand Duchy converted the service obligation of Frondienst to an annual payment of 95 gulden. A family could liquidate their Fron requirement forever by a relatively steep payment of 1,140 gulden, payable over 12 years. Half of the payment was defrayed by the Grand Duchy, and the village of Hochfeld carried notes for the remainder at an interest rate of 4 percent. In October 1847, the Steinweg family agreed to a redemption agreement by which villagers could buy out the Freiherr's interest in their tenancies. The cost of the redemption plan averaged 1,270 florin—far beyond the financial capability of many villagers to pay.

This half-decade was a period of displacement and mobility as many tenants gave up their holdings, unable to afford their property redemption. The Steinweg family, however, allowed all their tenants to remain in place as leaseholders. The tithes, taxes, and fees did not go away just because the Freiherr was no longer the villagers' ruler. Over time, they simply converted to payments of various sorts to the Badenese government or its agencies.

In 1833, Johann Adam's financial situation was only marginally better than it had been in 1816. There was no hope that he would be able to buy himself out of the Frondienst system. And in October 1847, Johann Adam could not participate when villagers were offered the opportunity to assume clear title to the lands they had held, some of them for centuries; he had died in 1835. His son Jacob no longer lived in Hochfeld. By the time that *he* died, Jacob had achieved wealth and property beyond anything his father ever could have dreamed for him—but he had been forced to leave Hochfeld to find that better life.[52]

4

Religion

Father Jeremias, the *Pfarrer* or pastor of the Hochfeld church, was profoundly troubled. The year was 1521, and the Amtmann of the Freiherr von Steinweg had just ordered him to remove Our Lady from her alcove at the back of the parish church in Hochfeld, as well as the rack of candles that his parishioners lit when they prayed to Her. Of all the objects in the church, this statue of the Virgin Mary was the most beloved, particularly by wives and mothers. Father Jeremias had witnessed the devotion that Our Lady inspired on countless occasions, and indeed he himself had found comfort and solace many times when he sought her aid. He was a humble man, with just enough rudimentary education to be able to chant the Mass in Latin — certainly not enough to study scriptures on his own, had he been so inclined. But he was not the type of priest to seek after enlightenment and knowledge; he was satisfied with simple faith. He tried to lead his people through example, and to minister to their earthly and religious needs in as earnest and unassuming a manner as he could. He knew of several nearby priests who kept concubines and who had made themselves wealthy by earning extra money on the side; they were important men in their villages. Father Jeremias, however, had always tried to honor his vows of chastity and poverty.[53]

Eberhard, who became the Freiherr von Steinweg with his father's death in 1517, was one of the first nobles in southern Germany to convert to the ideas of Martin Luther, an Augustinian monk and theologian, and to Luther's new liturgy. The Freiherr was attracted to Luther's efforts to purify the Church and to return the act of worship to a simpler form. However, Luther also preached that humans could seek God and the remission of sins without the need for an intercessor such as priest or other ecclesiastical personage. Eberhard had only been the Freiherr for a few years, but he benefited from the counsel of his father's Amtmann, who pointed out to him that if Luther's reforms were successful, the ability of the Bishop of Worms to meddle in Eberhard's affairs and territory would be agreeably curtailed because Eberhard would control his parish church, not the Bishop.[54]

By the end of 1521, Eberhard had installed a new priest in the village church. Christmas services that year were conducted in accordance with the Lutheran reforms. There was still singing in the church, and the church itself was beautifully decorated with Christmas greens and candles, but the somewhat simplified worship service was conducted all in German. The

Lutheran reformer, Johannes Brenz, had recommended the new priest, Father Dieterich, to the Freiherr. Father Dieterich was only 30, having just finished his religious studies at the University of Heidelberg. He lacked Father Jeremias' cheerful and humble approach to ministry, but he was a good man, and over the years he would grow in pastorship as he lived with and learned from the people in the Hochfeld parish.[55]

Father Jeremias was gently but firmly dispatched to a Cistercian monastery in the Odenwald not far from Heidelberg, the Kloster Schönau, whose abbot was a cousin of Eberhard's. Although the monastery was dissolved in 1558 in the wake of the Reformation, it survived long enough for Father Jeremias to lead a happy life there, tending the monastery gardens and animals, before being buried beneath the stones of the cloister chapel in 1542. For the first few years after his departure from Hochfeld, some villagers grumbled about the changes in their church — the loss of their saints, the banning of the majestic albeit incomprehensible Latin mass, and even the abolition of the confessional. Over time, however, some of the parishioners came to appreciate hearing the word of God in their own tongue and learning about the empowering message of Luther's new doctrine.

*   *   *

And what was this new doctrine of Luther's? First of all, he preached that Christians did not have to atone for their sins. They did not have to suffer in Purgatory until they had paid for their sins or until their descendants had purchased enough masses or indulgences to release their souls to heaven. No person or institution — and that included the Catholic Church — could intercede on behalf of a sinner, and entrance to heaven was not based on good works or even penitence. Rather, Luther taught that Christians would be saved through their belief alone. The grace of God, his forgiveness and his salvation, were his exclusively to bestow; no acts by men or women could affect his granting of this grace. In addition, people could read and interpret the scriptures for themselves, guided by divine inspiration, and anyone could be called to preach the word of God, not just priests. Finally, Christians could and must speak directly to God concerning their personal salvation.[56]

It is questionable whether Martin Luther actually started this revolution against the established Church by nailing his 95 theses on the door of Wittenberg's Castle Church on October 31, 1517; after all, he held an appointment as the preacher and confessor at that very church. He was a young, ambitious theologian, and he had no interest in throwing away a promising career in the Church by being labeled a troublemaker. However, it is true that Luther did write a letter to the Archbishop of Mainz on that date, protesting the sale of indulgences.[57]

Figure 9. Martin Luther.

Indulgences were documents issued by the Catholic Church that offered people the opportunity to purchase full or partial remission of sins, either their own or those of a deceased loved one, in order to release them from Purgatory. Indulgences related to one of the Church's seven sacraments, penance. Penance consisted of several steps. The first was to be sorry for one's sins. The next was to confess them to a priest, who would mediate for the sinner with God. The next step was for the priest to absolve the sinner of guilt, and the final step was satisfaction, or the setting of a penalty or obligation. Indulgences absolved the purchaser of this final step. The original intent was that indulgences would be given to sincere penitents, who in gratitude would make a gift to the church; but in actuality, indulgences became a commodity to be bought and sold.[58]

A Dominican friar had recently been authorized to travel throughout the episcopate of the Archbishop of Mainz, selling indulgences for the purpose of funding the renovation of St. Peter's Basilica in Rome. Luther had parishioners who came to confession with these documents, claiming that they no longer needed to repent their sins because the document absolved them. Luther was so disturbed that people would take the easy way out, paying for an indulgence but not seeking the personal forgiveness and grace of God, that he was motivated to write his letter. Along with the letter, he included his 95 theses, which were statements of his viewpoints on indulgences, repentance, and the remission of sins.

In theses 42 through 44, Luther wrote,

> ➤ Christians are to be taught that the pope does not intend that the buying of pardons should in any way be compared with works of mercy.

> ➤ Christians are to be taught that he who gives to the poor or lends to the needy does a better deed than he who buys indulgences.

> ➤ Because love grows by works of love, man thereby becomes better. Man does not, however, become better by means of indulgences but merely freed from penalties.

Several of Luther's 95 theses were a direct challenge to the pope, such as number 52:

➢ It is vain to trust in salvation by indulgence letters, even though the indulgence commissary, or even the pope, were to offer his soul as security.

Even more pointed was thesis number 82:

➢ Why does not the pope empty purgatory for the sake of holy love and the dire need of the souls that are there if he redeems an infinite number of souls for the sake of miserable money with which to build a church? The former reasons would be most just; the latter is most trivial.[59]

In addition to his letter to the Archbishop, Luther sent copies of the letter and the 95 theses to some friends and to associates at a few universities. Apparently without Luther's knowledge or permission, the 95 theses were translated into German and published in Nuremberg, Basle, and Leipzig. Luther's document hit a nerve, both with churchmen and with the laity. Many had long been exercised by the corrupt behavior and lifestyle of many priests and higher officials, the formulaic nature of Catholic worship, and the greedy practices of the Church as embodied in the institution of indulgences. They complained that the pope favored political appointments of Italians to high-level posts in Germany for which the Germans must pay, but that many of the appointees pocketed their salaries, remained in Italy, and paid vicars a pittance to perform their German duties. In addition, the pope himself took kickbacks from these appointees equal to their first years' revenues from their German sinecures.[60]

After their publication, Luther's ideas raced across Germanic lands and into Scandinavia, Bohemia, and the Low Countries, spread by word of mouth as well as the printing press. Johannes Gutenberg introduced movable type in Europe about 1450, and the Gutenberg Bible was published in 1455. Now, with the clamor for printed sermons, pamphlets, and books on the new views of religion, the world experienced its first press campaign, and Lutheranism expanded along with the explosion in publishing. Luther chose to appeal directly to the people, publishing his *Sermon on Indulgence and Grace* in 1518. This document was reprinted at least 23 times over the next three years, and most of Luther's other writings were similarly popular. Luther was an extraordinarily prolific writer; his collected works include 60 volumes of treatises in Latin and German, 14 volumes of correspondence, and 12 volumes of his German-language translations of the Bible. By 1524, about one million copies of Luther's various publications were estimated to be in circulation.[61]

The widespread publication of Luther's writings also helped to establish the German language spoken in the central area from Mainz to Saxony as the standard for literary high German or *Hochdeutsch*. Of course, the local dialects persevered all over Germany and the Swiss cantons, and many of them still survive in the twenty-first century. The language of Luther, however, became the basis for standard written German.[62]

Unfortunately for Luther, the Archbishop of Mainz, to whom he directed his complaint about indulgences, numbered among the prelates who had paid Pope Leo X a princely sum for his 1514 appointment—although at least he was not Italian. Albrecht came from the powerful House of Brandenburg, he was in need of a living, and the archbishop position made him one of the Empire's electors. Albrecht wanted the position, Leo wanted to build St. Peter's basilica, and so the two men decided to mount an indulgence campaign to raise money, agreeing to split the profits equally. Albrecht would use the money to pay off the debts he incurred in order to buy his appointment.[63]

Understandably, Albrecht was annoyed to receive Luther's petition. Rather than responding himself, he forwarded Luther's documents to Pope Leo X in Rome. Luther spent the next 3 years defending his theological ideas, both in writing and in verbal disputations with papal emissaries. In 1520, a papal commission formally denounced Luther's position. A papal bull, *Exsurge Domine*, was issued, which declared that Luther would be excommunicated unless he recanted. All over Germany, authorities ordered their executioners to conduct public burnings of Luther's books. In response, Luther's supporters in Wittenberg gathered in December to burn volumes of canon law and books written by Luther's enemies. Luther himself added copies of canon law, his opponents' writings, and *Exsurge Domine* to the bonfire.[64]

On January 3, 1521, the pope issued the bull that excommunicated Luther. The papal delegate to the German Diet, however, delayed in publishing the document, concerned that the Germans might kill him because Luther was so popular. Likewise, the emperor was reluctant to proceed against Luther. Luther's sponsor, the Elector Frederick of Saxony, demanded that Luther be given an opportunity to defend himself in Germany to Germans. A decision was made that Luther should travel to Worms in April 1521 to appear before the imperial diet, the assembly of the estates, in order to be examined. Luther agreed, in return for a promise of safe conduct to and from Wittenberg. His trip to Worms ended up as a celebratory procession, with people lining the road to cheer him on.[65]

At the Diet, after an examination of Luther's writings and his statements before the assembly, the emperor issued the Edict of Worms. It declared that Luther was an outlaw, a statement that meant any person could kill him without fear of legal action. The Edict also banned the reading or possession of all Luther's works. Luther had been promised a safe conduct back to Wittenberg from Worms. Nevertheless, for his own safety, Frederick of

Figure 10. Luther appears before Charles V at Worms.

Saxony had him captured and taken to Wartburg Castle, where he remained for 10 months.

After the Diet of Worms, Emperor Charles returned to Spain, which was part of his Habsburg lands, convinced that he had dealt decisively with Luther and ended the heresy. However, he had miscalculated.

> The issue was not, as Charles assumed, a single monk with heretical ideas, but a phenomenon of increasingly widespread dimensions. Thus, neither the honoring of the safe conduct, nor even Elector Frederick's decision to 'kidnap' Luther, was the decisive factor. What did save the Lutheran cause was the increasing enthusiasm for Luther's message. In the months following the diet the *affaire* Luther became the German Reformation. Everywhere people began to take up Luther's slogans and to echo his sentiments. From the pulpits in Saxony, Nuremberg, Augsburg, Ulm, Strassburg, the Netherlands, and East Frisia came the new proclamation and from the pews, a response.[66]

Luther spent his months in Wartburg Castle translating the New Testament into German so that people could read the words of the Bible for themselves. From his emphasis on the Gospels came the church's new name, *Evangelisch*. Many persons also began to refer to the new church's followers as Martinians or Lutherans. Luther had not begun his campaign with a goal of establishing a new church; he simply wanted to reform the Catholic Church itself. However, he gradually came to accept that only the

establishment of a new church could sweep away what he considered to be
the Catholic excesses and return the people to the true religion. For a
generation or more following the publication of Luther's 95 theses, many
people, particularly the politically-minded nobles, kept an uneasy foot in
both the Catholic and the Evangelisch camps, while political and religious
developments drew and redrew the boundaries between Catholic and
Evangelisch territories.[67]

Luther was not the only reformer of his generation; he merely opened
the floodgates of change. In Switzerland, Ulrich Zwingli in Zurich and John
Calvin in Geneva, both of them Catholic priests, became leaders of their own
movements, collectively referred to as the Reformed churches. Their
churches spread to England, France, Germany, Hungary, and the
Netherlands. The Reformed approach to worship was decidedly more
drastic than Luther's. Luther continued to profess, as did the Catholics, that
the body and blood of Jesus were present in the sacrament of Holy
Communion, a doctrine called transubstantiation. The Reformed churches
declared that Communion was merely symbolic. Luther also continued
many of the elements of Catholic worship, such as vestments and chanting,
while the Reformed churches painted their churches white, banned any
singing except the Psalms, rejected the ancient orders of service, and
abolished the office of bishop. The Reformed theology was also sterner than
Luther's. While Luther held that humans would be saved by God's grace
alone, Calvin went further. Man was born in a state of depravity, incapable
of escaping his sinful nature. Only through God's election might the chosen
be saved. Christ's death offered a limited atonement to those whom God
elected; but for those whom God did not choose, there was no hope of
salvation.[68]

The division between the Lutheran and Reformed churches, both of
which called themselves Evangelisch in Germany, lasted until 1817, when
Frederick William III of Prussia united the two organizations into the
Evangelical Church of the Prussian Union. German immigrants to North
America brought this church with them, where it became the parent church
for the United Church of Christ.[69]

Another group of dissenters, the Anabaptists or *Wiedertäufer* in German,
arose in the sixteenth century. The origins of the Anabaptists are obscure.
During the Reformation, a group of Anabaptists were organized in Zurich,
and spread throughout Switzerland and into Germany, Austria, and the
Netherlands. Not all Anabaptist groups agreed on the exact tenets of belief.
However, they did share one practice, and that was the rejection of infant
baptism. They received the name "Anabaptist" from their practice of re-
baptizing new members who had already been baptized as babies. They
believed that a baptism was not valid until an individual was mature enough
to accept this rebirth into Christ. The tenets of Anabaptism are contained in
the Schleitheim Articles. In addition to baptism, included are the refusal of

oaths, the rejection of military service, and the belief in "the Lord's Supper as an expression of Christian community." Many Anabaptist groups committed to living separately in their own communities; they hoped to create a new, better society.[70]

Several modern churches have Anabaptist roots, including the Amish, the Mennonites, the Church of the Brethren, and the Baptists. Quakers are also occasionally grouped with the Anabaptists because of their shared emphasis on peace. Beginning with the Reformed theologian Ulrich Zwingli, Anabaptist adherents were persecuted as heretics by Evangelisch and Catholics alike. Quaker and Mennonite Anabaptists comprised the earliest wave of German immigrants to North America in the period 1683-1709, fleeing intolerance and repression.[71]

Inevitably, the Catholic Church finally responded to Martin Luther's charges of corruption, motivated by their losses of worshipers, territories, and princely allies. In 1545, Pope Paul III convened the Council of Trent to study the issue of indulgences, the corrupt practices of some bishops and priests, and the general need to reform and modernize the Church. The Council deliberated for almost 20 years. It upheld the basic organization and doctrines of the Church. Bishops, archbishops, monastic orders, and their properties and authorities would remain. The veneration of the Virgin Mary and the saints was affirmed, as was the communion doctrine of transubstantiation. The basic sacraments, including baptism, Holy Communion, marriage, and penance remained. The Council specifically declared that believers could attain salvation through both faith and good works — not faith alone, as the Lutherans and Calvinists had declared.

Despite its many conservative decisions, the Council of Trent also initiated a major period of reform within the Catholic Church. Corrupt practices were curbed in parishes, ecclesiastical palaces, and Rome. Bishops were required to take up residence in their appointed areas rather than employing vicars and living elsewhere. The Church followed the example of the Protestant churches and began to require better training and education for its parish priests. Perhaps most importantly, there was a renewed emphasis on the spiritual and devotional aspects of Catholic worship. It was the age of mystics such as St. John of the Cross and Santa Teresa of Avila. Ignatius of Loyola founded the Society of Jesus, or the Jesuits, in 1534, an order dedicated to discipline, obedience, scholarship, and expansion of the faith.[72]

Just as the Catholic Church sought to purify itself through the Counter-Reformation, so some seventeenth-century Lutherans sought a reformation of their religion. The founder of Pietism was Philipp Jakob Spencer, who studied theology at Strasbourg and Geneva. The movement's detractors were the first to call it Pietism, by which they intended to satirize its members' emphasis on devotion over form and doctrine. Pietists rejcted intellectuality in religion, instead embracing a simpler, heartfelt approach to God.

Although many Pietists remained members of their original churches, others separated themselves and established new churches, including the Moravians and the German Baptists.[73]

There was one last religious group in Hochfeld that did its best to stay out of the way of the Reformation's religious turmoil, and that group was the Jews. Germany and northern Italy were the only two areas in Europe where Jewish life and culture existed continuously from the medieval period until the Enlightenment. Despite the stereotype that the typical early modern Jew was a prosperous urban dweller, the vast majority of Jewish families were relatively poor, and over 70 percent lived in small towns or villages. Most of the Jews in the Holy Roman Empire could be found in an area stretching from Alsace and the Rhineland Palatinate in the west, across Baden, Württemberg, Hessen, and the Kraichgau, and on to Franconia and Bohemia in the east. They lived in tiny enclaves of two or three families, usually clustered together. Sometimes their isolation into one area was forced, but often it was voluntary. Many villages in the Hochfeld area still have a narrow street tucked someplace near the village center, called the *Judengasse* or Jewish alley, where its Jewish families formerly lived.[74]

Jews had suffered periodic expulsion and persecution ever since the Crusades, particularly in the wake of the Black Death peak in the fourteenth century. They were routinely denounced from city and village pulpits as the murderers of Christ. Since most territories and cities denied Jews the rights to own land or to practice most trades and crafts, the majority of them made their living through money lending, trade, and peddling. The limitations on their ability to earn a living resulted in a higher percentage of Jews than Christians functioning as petty criminals.[75]

In the relatively self-contained German villages, local trades- and craftsmen operated in an environment which was close to monopolistic; Johann Adam's license to set up as a cooper was an example. Villagers were pressured if not forced to patronize only the local trades- and craftsmen, so that village economies did not respond to the laws of supply and demand. In this environment, Jewish peddlers with their cheaper goods and their more aggressive approach to sales were deeply resented by the Bürger shopkeepers, who expected to wait in their stores for their captive customers. The irony was that the very limitations placed on Jewish ownership of village businesses tended to push them into itinerant, market-oriented practices with which the local businesses could not compete.[76]

* * *

The Holy Roman Emperor had not returned to Germany since the Diet of Worms in 1521. Charles V had little time for his German subjects, because in addition to his position as emperor, he was also the King of Spain, King of Naples and Sicily, Archduke of Austria, and ruler of the Netherlands. In

Spain, his primary concerns were the exploration of the New World and the three wars he fought against France, beginning in 1521. While Charles saw himself as the champion of the Catholic Church, his absence allowed the Evangelisch and Reformed churches to spread and become entrenched. In 1526, Charles' brother, the Archduke Ferdinand, convened an imperial Diet in Speyer in Charles' name to address the issue of the new churches. The Diet, with the concurrence of Ferdinand, ended by calling for a general council with emperor and papal representatives in attendance, with the purpose of reaching a decisive resolution of the religious question. In the meantime, the Diet members agreed that each ruler within the territory could choose his creed as his conscience saw fit and establish within his territory the religious church of his choice.[77]

In 1529, the Emperor convened a second Diet at Speyer. The purpose of this meeting was to deal with the threat of a Turkish invasion; however, it also became a religious battleground. At the Diet's conclusion, Charles cancelled the agreement of toleration that had been reached in the first Diet of Speyer, he forbade any further spread of the new religions, and he condemned the Anabaptists as heretics. The Evangelisch nobles in attendance rose in general protest, leading to their designations thenceforth as Protestants.[78]

Yet another attempt was made the following year at the Diet of Augsburg to resolve the empire's religious differences. The Protestant nobles presented to the Emperor the Augsburg Confession, which would become a fundamental manifesto of Lutheran beliefs. However, the Emperor could not accept this document, and gave the Protestants until April 1531 to return to the Catholic Church. In response, the Protestants formed the Schmalkaldic League, an alliance whose members pledged to protect one another if any was attacked for religious cause. During the 1530s, one territory and imperial city after another became Protestant: Württemberg, Hanover, Osnabrück, Dinkelsbühl, Bremen, Nassau, Anhalt, Pommerania, and Brunswick-Lunenburg joined the already Protestant territories of Saxony, Hessen, and Mecklenberg, among others.[79]

Meanwhile, Charles was distracted by his wars with France. When that conflict finally ended in the mid 1540s, he led a force of Catholic princes against the Schmalkaldic League. The Catholics won the first round of battles, the Protestants the second. Finally, Charles gave up his attempt to reunify the Catholic Church. The Peace of Augsburg, signed by the Emperor and representatives of the Schmalkaldic League on September 25, 1555, granted each ruler the right to establish his choice of religion within his own territory; in essence, each would become head of his own church. Any prince who had appropriated Church properties up to the date of 1552 would be allowed to keep them. However, any princely conversion to the Lutheran or Reformed churches that occurred after 1552 was to be considered a personal act; those lords' subjects and their parishes would remain Catholic.[80]

The Peace of Augsburg inaugurated what is called the confessional period. The term "Confessionalism" has been used both to describe the three German denominations as well as the doctrines, documents, and religious practices that defined each of those churches' beliefs—Catholicism, Lutheranism, and the Reformed church (Calvinism). By the time the Peace of Augsburg was signed, Southwest Germany was a patchwork of religious territories: Catholic, Evangelisch, Calvinist, former Protestant areas that had returned to Catholicism, and mixed areas. Many territories had changed their religious affiliations more than once. Over time, the relationship between neighboring villages of different confessions became rancorous or even hostile. As late as World War II, Catholic and Protestant villagers periodically came to blows; Protestant villagers ostentatiously worked on Catholic feast days while Catholic villagers marched their religious processions through the streets of Protestant villages.[81]

In general, the Rhineland Palatinate became Calvinist, Baden-Baden became Catholic, and most of Württemberg became Evangelisch. Wimpfen and the Steinweg lands were Evangelisch. However, from the roof of the church or the banks of the Neckar River, the villagers of Hochfeld could look across the river and see the small city of Gundelsheim, which was part of an independent entity owned by the Catholic Teutonic knights. Although Gundelsheim would become part of Württemberg in 1805 as a result of the Napoleonic reorganization, and Württemberg was primarily an Evangelisch kingdom, Gundelsheim and the surrounding countryside would remain Catholic. Its first Evangelisch church would not be built until 1895.

*   *   *

On the first warm day of spring in 1818, the year after his wife and children had died, Johann Adam Mann sat on the banks of the Neckar, gazing over at the church tower of Gundelsheim. The west bank of the Neckar where Johann Adam sat formed a high bluff over the river, while the east bank lay at the river's level, so Johann Adam could look down into the neighboring village as if he were God himself. He could see the men with their oxen, returning from a day of plowing the fields; the women hanging out washing to bleach in the sun; and when the wind was favorable, he could even hear the sounds of the children playing along the river. Breathing in deeply and deliberately, he did his best to absorb the sense of peace and order from the scene in front of him. Because Johann Adam was angry, angrier than he had ever been in his life.

Although he had of course attended church each Sunday all his life, Johann Adam had never been particularly religious; his faithfulness was habitual, not spiritual. Ironically, he had given more thought to God since he had lost his wife and children than in all his earlier years combined. And he had reached an inescapable conclusion: that if Luther's God really did exist, he wanted no part of him. Johann Adam could not accept that this supposedly loving, all-powerful being could allow — or even worse, direct — the deaths of innocents. He was not so naive about the ways of his village that he intended to announce his insight, but neither could he bear to attend church. So he had simply stopped attending.

His neighbors of course noted his absence. Some of them quietly remarked on it among themselves, but they chose to do nothing. They were certain that he would come around again, in time. A few weeks passed, then a few months. One Sunday in late March, Johann Adam's Aunt Praxedis looked out her window onto the alley and saw him working on a barrel in their common barn. Early the next morning, she sought out the Schultheiss and denounced him for his failure to attend church and, what was worse, for dishonoring the Sabbath by working.

Johann Adam had violated two village ordinances. Now that Praxedis had officially complained, the Schultheiss could no longer overlook Johann Adam's behavior. A transgression such as this by a village Bürger would inevitably lead to similar actions or worse on the part of others. The Gericht could not afford to invite a disregard of order and obedience in the village.

Figure 11. Elderly village woman in her home, the model for Praxedis.

The Schultheiss asked Johann Georg Kirstetter, Johann Adam's first cousin and a member of the council, to have an informal talk with Johann Adam. Johann Georg invited his cousin to the village tavern that evening. Over a beer, he told his cousin that his absence at church had been noticed, and he hinted that it was time to resume Sunday services. Johann Adam heard him out, drank his beer, but had little to say. The following Sunday, he could not bring himself to go to church.

Of course, Praxedis had been watching to see what Johann Adam would do. She was secretly pleased when he failed to appear in church because it allowed her to complain again. She knew it was only a matter of time before she would prevail, and she looked forward to the opportunity to humiliate her nephew. This time, Praxedis told the Schultheiss that if he did not take action, she would denounce Johann Adam publicly—as if she had not already done so at the baker's the previous day.

The next afternoon, the Schultheiss and Johann Georg Kirstetter paid Johann Adam a formal call. It was this visit that had resulted in Johann Adam's angry moments on the bank of the Neckar, just an hour later. Johann Adam must return to church, the two told him, and he must cease working on Sunday. If he did not, the council would take away his license to work as a Küfer.[82]

The following Sunday, inwardly seething but outwardly resigned, and solely for the sake of his son's future, Johann Adam Mann returned to church.

5

War

In 1521, the villagers of Hochfeld were, almost without exception, illiterate. Those who cherished the church had always approached their Christian faith through their hearts, not their heads. They were moved by the saints' statues, the stories of martyrs that were painted on the church walls, the candles, the chanting, the mysteries. They were superstitious people who had adapted many of their ancient Germanic superstitions into their notions of Christian worship. But when Father Dieterich preached to them in their own language about the grace of God and when he told them that they were each as valuable in God's eyes as the highest noble in the land, it was the first time that they could approach their religion with reason, not just faith. Father Dieterich and other Lutheran pastors were preaching a message that was more dangerous than they realized.

One Sunday in late February 1525, Father Dieterich read a sermon of Luther's to his congregation, something that the early Evangelisch pastors often did in order that their parishioners might learn directly from the words of the great teacher. Luther had taken as his starting point a passage from Luke: "The Lord hath filled the hungry with good things, and the rich he hath sent empty away." Luther continued, "Now all these things are written for the consolation and lifting up of them which be miserable, poor, needy, and oppressed with sin, that they may know to whom they may flee in all distresses, and where they may seek for help and safety: But see how Christ urgeth and inflameth faith in them . . . , whereby they may become stronger and more confirmed."[83]

The oppressed, made stronger and more confirmed in salvation. The poor, inflamed by God, who offers them his help and protection. And who banishes the rich, while he takes unto himself the poor. Surely then, the peasants reasoned, they were God's chosen people, unfairly subjugated. And just as clearly, Luther must be on their side.[84]

The Tuesday after Father Dietrich had read Luther's sermon to the villagers was one of their' favorite revels of the year — *Fastnacht*, the carnival celebration that took place on Shrove Tuesday, the day before Lent began. The village had been celebrating that day for as long as anyone could remember. There was music, dancing, wine, and even roast pork — a rare feast for many of the villagers who could not afford meat. But on Monday, the Amtmann to Eberhard, the Freiherr, paid a visit to the village Schultheiss. He informed the Schultheiss that Eberhard was hosting a hunt for some of the nearby nobles on Fastnacht. Eberhard had decreed that as part of their yearly Fron obligation, 20 of the male villagers must assist in the hunt by beating boars and deer out of the forests and driving them towards the waiting hunters.[85]

The Schultheiss assembled the villagers to deliver the bad news. To a man, they were incensed. The former Freiherr, father to this arrogant ingrate, would never have ruined a village festival day, they grumbled. Yes, he had demanded his rights and labor, and he had been strict, but he had treated the village customs with respect. But this young lord had demonstrated, in one incident after another, that he had no interest in his people other than as sources of labor and money. The injustice seemed particularly acute with the words of Martin Luther from the Sunday sermon still ringing in their ears.

Hans Mann, who was a great uncle many times removed from Johann Adam Mann, was the village hothead. He was a sturdy man with calloused hands and a neck thick from hard labor in the fields. He could be found many evenings in the village tavern, to the consternation of his wife, drinking and brawling. He was a cheerful, friendly man when he was sober, although he had a reputation as a dreamer and a braggart. From the occasional strangers passing through Hochfeld, Hans had heard that villages all over southern Germany were rebelling against their lords. He urged the men who were called to work the hunt simply not to comply. But his elder brother Georg, who was a member of the town council and a cautious man, urged restraint. Their burdens were heavy, but a rebellion might make them even worse. Georg recommended that they petition the Freiherr to change the day of the hunt, or to release the men from their Fron on that day. Up went the Schultheiss to Eberhard's castle to carry the message. Down came the Schultheiss with the answer: The Fron allotment had been increased from 20 to 30 men.

The 30 men reported for work on Fastnacht. The remaining villagers held the most subdued Fastnacht celebration the town had ever seen. And shortly thereafter, things on the Freiherr's lands mysteriously began to go badly: Grain trampled. Trees cut down and hacked so that they were useless for anything but firewood. When a prize horse was found with his tail cut off, Eberhard took action and assessed a steep financial penalty on the village. The next week, one of the Freiherr's barns burned to the ground, after which it was learned that Hans Mann had slipped away from the village with three other men. It was rumored that they had fled to join an army of six thousand peasants, led by a disaffected knight named Florian Geyer. Geyer's followers were one of the three most important peasant corps that formed in Franconia, and on April 18, they occupied Heilbronn, about 25 miles south of Hochfeld. The following day, the city of Heilbronn signed an alliance with the peasant leaders and made a troop of soldiers available to the peasant army.[86]

As Hans Mann had learned from the travelers, Hochfeld was only one of many villages in open rebellion. It was a movement that sprang up spontaneously in 1524 and 1525 in most parts of Germany—Franconia, Hessen, Brunswick, Baden, and Thuringia—but also in Bohemia and in parts of present-day France, Switzerland, and Austria. The only part of Germany that remained relatively untouched was Bavaria. The uprising reached a peak in the spring and summer of 1525, by which time about 300,000 peasants were involved. The uprising received only minor support from the working classes in the German cities, although miners in parts of Germany and some out-of-work mercenaries did join in. There were no imperial forces available to put down the rebellion because they were fighting in France and Italy. In its early stages, the spontaneous nature of the insurrection made it difficult for the lords to get the upper hand militarily. They never knew where or when an incident would occur; and of course, the villagers had the advantage of numbers.[87]

Figure 12. Rebellious peasants surround their lord.

One of the largest and most active areas of insurrection was centered in Swabia and in Franconia, where the Kraichgau and Hochfeld were located. The movement gained particular strength in those regions where partible inheritance was the custom, as it was in most of southwest Germany. Since parents' assets were divided among all the children in those areas, partible inheritance imposed acute economic pressures on offspring who held less land and property with each succeeding generation. People looked back nostalgically at earlier times, when villages governed themselves and set their own, unwritten rules, based on custom and common sense. They deeply resented the lords' imposition of village ordinances, such as the Dorfordnungen that the Freiherr von Steinweg had established when he first purchased the village of Hochfeld. They also feared the incursion of Roman law, which Germanic rulers had discovered was a useful tool to control and dominate their subjects. The peasants were accustomed to a system of justice in which an accused was tried in his home village by men who knew him and who were intimately familiar with the facts and circumstances of his life and his alleged crime. The Roman system of written statute and case law, the growing numbers of university-trained lawyers working for the territorial states, and the establishment of a system of higher courts all worked to erode village authority and autonomy. Also, Roman property law embraced a right to absolute ownership, while the German "good old law" was based on a concept of relative possession (see Chapter 2).[88]

The disturbances of 1524-25 were not the first peasant uprisings. The German territories had been dealing with increasing economic pressure ever since the onset of the Black Death in the latter half of the thirteenth century. As the income of the territorial lords dropped due to falling grain prices, they responded, as discussed in Chapter 2, by tightening the bondage conditions of their village tenants and squeezing them for ever-increasing taxes, duties, and labor requirements. As they reduced villagers' access to community pastures and woodlands, prohibited their freedom of movement, and restricted their right to marry outside their villages, the peasants responded with periodic uprisings. The most important of these movements had been the *Bundschuh* rebellion, which took place in the Upper Rhine Valley in 1493. But the Peasants' War of 1524-25 was the first time that peasants began to question the natural order of things — that they would and should always be subservient. The writings of Luther were simply the match dropped on the bonfire of peasant status, which was already set to burn.[89]

The typical progression of the 1524-25 conflict in individual villages would begin when the residents presented their lords a list of grievances. When the lords refused to address their concerns or attempted to stifle their actions, the peasants would respond by destroying lordly or ecclesiastical property. In some cases, the villagers used violence to force their lords into signing treaties with them. The final step in some areas was the forming of peasant armies.[90]

Hundreds of the lists of grievances that villages wrote during this two-year period are still in existence. In the south German city of Memmingen, a Lutheran lay preacher named Sebastian Lotzer condensed the demands from about 300 of these lists into a document entitled the *Twelve Articles*, which remains the most widely cited protest text from the Peasants' War. Lotzer converted the crude, ungrammatical writing of the peasants' lists into a more sophisticated statement of grievances, and he used his knowledge of scripture to develop a theological justification for the peasants' demands. The Twelve Articles demanded that:

➢ 1. Villagers should be given the right to select and to dismiss their own pastors.

➢ 2. The Great Tithe, paid by the villagers in grain, should be divided between their pastor, based on his need, and the poor. The Small Tithe, paid in fruit, vegetables, and livestock, should be abolished, because "the Lord created cattle for the free use of man."

➢ 3. Serfdom should be abolished, unless it could be shown to be justified based on Scripture. "It has until now been the custom for the lords to own us as their property," the third article declared. "This is deplorable, for Christ redeemed and bought us all with his precious blood, the lowliest shepherd as well as the greatest lord, with no exceptions. Thus the Bible proves that we are free."

➢ 4. The lords' prohibition on fishing and hunting by villagers should be abolished. Likewise, the lords must refrain from damaging villagers' crops by riding through the fields while hunting.

➢ 5. The lords must give up their exclusive right to wood from communal forests, which should belong to everyone in a village.

➢ 6. Fron (mandatory labor) should not continue to be increased in amount.

➢ 7. Fron should not be increased beyond the amount originally agreed to when the peasant first swore fealty to the lord.

➢ 8. The level of rents should be reconsidered.

➢ 9. The Roman system of law should not be substituted for the "good old law" of German custom, and punishments should not be assessed arbitrarily.

➢ 10. Any lords who had fenced in former common lands should remove their enclosures.

➢ 11. Death taxes would no longer be paid because they were an unreasonable burden on heirs and they were also used to confiscate villagers' lands.

➢ 12. The villagers were willing to withdraw any of these demands if they could be shown to be inconsistent with the Holy Scripture.[91]

By the spring of 1525, roaming bands of peasants were engaging with scattered mercenary troops and sacking the monasteries and castles. Numerous leaders rose up within the movement: in Franconia, Florian Geyer; in Rothenburg-on-the-Tauber, a preacher called Dr. Karlstadt; and in Thuringia in central Germany, a theologian named Thomas Müntzer. The leaders were successful in winning concessions from some towns and principalities, including Freiburg, Breisach, Offenburg, and other towns in Baden. The Margrave of Baden, for example, agreed that the Fron would cease, the small tithe would be suspended for the time being, and the great tithe would be held in trust until a final agreement could be worked out between lords and subjects.[92]

The peasant bands armed themselves with whatever they could find: axes, knives, and clubs. They also had a surprising number of guns, and even some cannons—although they seldom had enough men trained to use them. They were undisciplined, untrained, and just as interested in plundering the food and wine stores they found as they were in strategies and negotiation. The private secretary of the Bishop of Würzburg wrote of them, "More drunken, more full-bellied, more helpless folk, one had hardly seen together than during the time of this rebellion." They were massacres in the making.[93]

As a member of Florian Geyer's Neckar-Odenwald army, Hans Mann participated in the capture of the castle of the Teutonic Order in Heilbronn. He was among the cheerful group who hacked at the doors to the castle with their axes until it gave way—and he was also among the first to find the castle's wine stores. The band destroyed furniture, burned books, and terrorized the knights, but they inflicted few deaths or injuries. They did inflict humiliation, however. They forced the knights to wait on them as they feasted in the great hall. As Hans Mann ordered a knight to refill his cup, he crowed, *"Heut, Junkerlein, syn wir Teuschmeister."* "Today, little Junker, *we* are the knights."[94]

Luther had had no intention of inciting revolution when he began his Evangelisch ministry, and he was appalled to find himself in the center of a maelstrom. In April 1525, he responded to the Twelve Articles with a tract entitled *An Admonition to Peace on the Twelve Articles of the Peasantry in Swabia*. He did his best to be even-handed in response to the peasants, even though their insurrection horrified him. Luther's opening statement was drawn from the Twelve Articles, in which the peasants stated that they would cease their activities if such activities could be shown to be contravened by scripture. Luther cited Romans 12:19: "Dearly beloved, avenge not yourselves, but rather give place unto wrath: for it is written, Vengeance is mine; I will repay, saith the Lord." Luther agreed that many of the peasants' demands were justified and that the lords should be condemned for abusing their powers over the villagers. However, it was a mortal sin for the villagers to attack their rulers. They should follow Christ's teachings, turn the other cheek, and suffer as Christ had suffered on the cross. With regard to the article calling for the abolishment of serfdom, Luther reminded the peasants that slaves existed in the Bible. Christians were free and equal in the spirit, but this had nothing to do with their earthly bodies. Those who used their Christian faith to justify action on an earthly matter were endangering their own salvation.[95]

Shortly after completing this tract, Luther made two trips to investigate the rebellion first-hand. He saw looted monasteries, destroyed castles, and untended fields, and he heard stories of violence from observers. He may well have thought he could quell the rebellion, reasoning that if his writings had incited it, then his authority would be enough to end it. If so, he was rudely disabused. At Nordhausen, when he preached a sermon against the violence, he was booed and heckled—quite a shock for a man who was used to respectful adulation. Not surprisingly, Luther's next tract, *Against the Robbing and Murdering Gangs of Peasants*, was emotional and threatening—words which disheartened the rebel bands, and which continue to appall Luther's devotees even today.

> They raise up rebellion, rob and plunder with criminal violence cloisters and castles that do not belong to them, and so they deserve punishment of death in body and soul two times over as we punish robbers and murderers. For when we can establish that someone is a rebellious man, he becomes an outlaw before both God and emperor, and who ever can first kill that person does so legally and well . . . For rebellion is not merely murder; it is like a great fire that burns up and lays waste a land . . . So then anyone who can should smash, strangle, and stab, secretly or openly, remembering that nothing can be more poisonous, harmful, or demonic than a rebellious man, just as when one must kill a mad dog, for if you do not strike him, he will strike you and the whole land with you.[96]

Back in Hochfeld, it was clear to Georg Mann that things had gone too far. Despite the burdens of taxes, rent, tithes, and Fron, Georg held enough land that his family lived in relative comfort. He was a member of the Gericht and an important man. Since the population had begun to increase in the decades following the Black Death, village society had increasingly divided into the haves and the have-nots—the marginal farmers and landless cottagers. While the lower class of villagers had little to lose by inciting rebellion, Georg and his peers did. Georg had no illusions concerning the outcome of the insurrection. Lords and emperor would unite, troops would be mounted, and the natural order of things would be reestablished. It was time for the Schultheiss and the Gericht or local court to act in order to forestall disaster. They set up a meeting with the Amtmann to discuss the future.[97]

For his part, the young Freiherr was so incensed by the rebellion and by the damages inflicted on his property that he was lusting for revenge. But his Amtmann pointed out that not just the peasants stood to lose from this conflict. If he exacted harsh financial penalties on top of the villagers' existing heavy taxes, fees, and tithes, it would endanger their ability to prosper as farmers—which would hurt Eberhard's income as well as their own. The Amtmann had also begun to hear from nearby territories that some of their peasants were sneaking away to the empire's eastern territories, where more land could be had. For all these reasons, the Amtmann counseled Eberhard to temper his behavior. In the end, the Amtmann negotiated an agreement between village and lord. The village agreed to reconstruct the Freiherr's burned-out barn at village expense. Villagers would be paid for any unscheduled Fron duty if it fell on a Sunday or holiday, harvest season excepted. Eberhard delayed his most important concession for a few months, so that villagers would not directly connect his action with their revolt. At the beginning of the Christmas season, Eberhard's Amtmann quietly began to extend the right of Erblehenrecht to a substantial number of the middling-level peasants. Erblehenrecht allowed them to pass on their holdings to their heirs, and Eberhard's action was calculated to prevent the flight of his work force.[98]

On May 5, 1525, Frederick the Wise, Holy Roman Emperor, died. One of his last requests was that the princes treat their rebelling peasants with mercy. Two days later, cavalry from members of the Swabian League, a defensive alliance of lords and towns in the former duchy of Swabia, engaged a band of peasants near Wettingen, just north of Ulm, and slaughtered over one thousand of them. On May 12, over 7,000 lancers and cavalry engaged the 12,000-man peasant army of Württemberg near Böblingen. The peasants were routed, with estimates of their dead ranging from 2,000 to 6,000. On May 15 in Thüringen, Saxon and Hessian forces slaughtered another peasant army at Frankenhausen. Troops began sweeping through the countryside, burning villages, slaughtering peasants, and imposing heavy fines on the towns and territories that had capitulated to peasant demands. In Alsace, for example, peasants were slaughtered by the hundreds and thrown into a huge pile, left to rot; the place is still known as Blood Mountain, *Blutberg*, for the low hill that formed over the mass of skeletons. Although it took them until the middle of September, troops were able to stamp out the last pockets of rebellion. The total number of peasants who died was estimated by one contemporary at 130,000. Even if this number is inflated, it is unlikely that the final death toll was less than 100,000. Peasant rebels were executed by the thousands, hanged or beheaded in their villages, and their families were banished. A pamphlet published in 1525 stated, "Houses are burned; fields and vineyards lie fallow; clothes and household goods are robbed or burned; cattle and sheep are taken away."[99]

When Hans Mann's band of peasants was routed near Heilbronn, he escaped and fled to Hochfeld. There, in recognition of the truce that the town council had made with the Freiherr, and to save the village, the town council turned him over to the Amtmann. After he was found guilty of treason in a public trial, he was broken on a wheel set up in front of the church, his body was quartered, and the four parts were nailed to posts that had been erected on the village's busiest streets as a warning to malcontents. Half his lands and movable possessions were confiscated. The Freiherr had intended to take it all, but the Amtmann reminded the Freiherr that both Hans' brother and his wife's brother were members of the council. It would not do to alienate the village leadership. Harsh punishment they could understand and accept, given Hans' behavior; but the village would resent and remember any undue cruelty to Hans' innocent family.[100]

The immediate peasant revolt, the worst Europe would experience until the French Revolution, had been suppressed. However, the defeat of the peasant armies did not end the conflict between lord and village. All over Germany, scattered villages would continue to foment small rebellions and to challenge their lords in court over their treatment and living conditions. The revolt did have an impact on the lords' behavior. Despite the initial harsh treatment of the rebels, many lords ended up coming to the same conclusion that had motivated Eberhard to make some concessions to the villagers in Hochfeld. Fear of another major uprising as well as the potential flight of their peasants forced the lords to offer certain appeasing gestures. But princes and lords were also motivated to prevent a recurrence of armed conflict by strengthening their tools of governance. The domination of villagers and the tenuous power politics between ruler and ruled would continue, in some vestiges, into the twentieth century.[101]

*   *   *

In 1587, a great-great-grandson of Georg Mann was born in Hochfeld Hans Michael and his two siblings had each inherited enough land from their parents that they would be able to live comfortably. Hans Michael, however, was a driven man who was determined to become rich. He judiciously married a first wife who brought even more land into the marriage than Hans Michael had himself. His wife died bearing their third child, but because the first two children had survived, he was able to keep control of the land his wife had brought into the marriage, pending his children's majority. He immediately married again. His second wife's family owned one of the five largest farm holdings or Höfe in Hochfeld. He had achieved the most fervently held dream of most men in Hochfeld: he was a Hofbauer, with holdings of 63 morgen (about 56 acres) in fields and meadow.[102]

Over the years, Hans Michael worked harder than any other man in the village, and he earned money not only from farming but by making shrewd loans to other villagers. By 1620, he was one of the four wealthiest men in Hochfeld, a member of the Gericht, and he also held a powerful position as the *Almosenpfleger* or welfare administrator for the village church. He was respected, both by the villagers and his children, but he was not loved. It was not easy to love him. Whenever he fixed his gaze on a person or object, any observer could feel the automatic, mechanical accounting that took place behind his pale blue eyes. A look from Hans Michael reduced everyone and everything to the sum total of their monetary value.

One day in early March 1622, Hans Michael looked up from his plowing to see the current Freiherr riding out of Hochfeld on the Wimpfener Strasse, accompanied by three heavily armed retainers. The Freiherr was setting out to join an army being assembled by Georg Friederich, the Margrave of Baden-Durlach. The Margrave was preparing to retake the Rhineland Palatinate, just 60 kilometers to the northeast of Hochfeld, which an imperial army had confiscated from the Protestant Elector Palatine. The Hochfeld villagers had heard that a religious war was being fought far to the east, but now it had come to their doorsteps.

The distrust and animosity that had existed between the Holy Roman Emperor and Germany's Protestant princes ever since the Peace in Augsburg was signed in 1555 had finally erupted into war. The Peace of Augsburg and the 1552 Treaty of Passau had allowed German territorial lords to choose Catholicism or one of the two Evangelisch (Protestant) creeds, Lutheranism or Calvinism, as the official religions for their states. By 1600, however, alarmed by the continuing growth of Protestantism, the Emperor began to use his troops to force Protestant cities back into the Catholic fold. In 1608, the Catholic-dominated Diet of Regensburg ordered the return of any parish or bishopric office and property that had been converted subsequent to 1552.[103]

In 1618, the Emperor, who was also King of Bohemia, reneged on a pledge to allow his Protestant Bohemian subjects to follow their religion. In May 1618, the Bohemians overthrew the government, which caused Catholic forces to invade Bohemia. In August 1619, the Bohemians invited Frederick V, the Elector Palatine, to become their king. They selected Frederick largely because his father-in-law was James I, King of England; they reasoned that James would support the German Protestants by supplying money and troops to fight the Emperor's Catholic forces. However, when the English Parliament made clear that it had no interest in becoming involved in a protracted German war, James appealed to Spain to assist the German Protestants — an irony, since Spain was itself Catholic. Eventually, France, Denmark, and Sweden would also become involved in a war that dragged on for three decades and terrorized the German countryside. Effectively, the first world war did not take place in the trenches of Belgium and France in the twentieth century, but across the fields of Germany in the seventeenth. In addition to an almost unbelievable destruction of property throughout Germany, the Thirty Years' War was responsible for widespread famine, disease, and a death rate that some estimates placed as high as 50 percent of the population in parts of the Southwest; overall, the Empire's population dropped by about one-third.[104]

On November 8, 1620, a Catholic army, 25,000 strong, defeated a Protestant army composed of 20,000 Bohemians and mercenaries in the Battle of White Mountain, near Prague. The forces of the Catholic League bolstered the emperor's army led by Johann Tserclaes, Count of Tilly. As a result of this battle, the emperor retook Bohemia and also claimed the Palatinate. This confiscation motivated the Freiherr von Steinweg to join forces with the Margrave of Baden-Durlach. In the spring of 1622, the Freiherr crossed the Rhine from Alsace along with the rest of the Margrave's troops to join forces with Ernst, the Count of Mansfield, the supreme commander of the Protestants. The goal was to engage and defeat the Catholic troops, led by Tilly, which had moved west from Bohemia to secure the Palatinate.

On April 27, 1622, the Protestants defeated the Catholics at the Battle of Wiesloch, about 45 kilometers due west of Hochfeld. But on May 6, the two armies met again, this time outside Wimpfen, in one of the bloodiest battles of the Thirty Years' War. On the imperial side, Tilly commanded 15,000 men; on the Protestant side, the Margrave von Baden-Durlach and the Count von Mansfield fielded about 20,000. By the end of the day, the Catholics had won and 5,000 men were dead, including the Freiherr von Steinweg. The Protestants fled across the Rhine to the safety of Alsace as the Catholics occupied the Palatinate.[105]

Tilly had begun to move soldiers into Wimpfen as early as December 1621; by April, troops from both sides filled the entire Kraichgau, as the armies prepared to battle. Even after the theater of war moved north, Catholic troops continued to occupy Wimpfen and the surrounding villages. In Hochfeld, they torched the Evangelisch church, the Freiherr's castle, and most of the houses that they had not appropriated for their own use. They commandeered village men into the army; they murdered a few village leaders, including the Schultheiss; and they raped any woman foolish enough to come out of hiding. They confiscated all the horses, killing any that they determined were unfit for their use. They butchered the cows, pigs and poultry. They trampled the newly planted fields, and they consumed the grain stores that should have seen the villagers through to the harvest. The soldiers were like a swarm of locusts, consuming everything in their path and only moving on when everything that could be eaten, destroyed, or carried off had been consumed.[106]

The pastor of Hochfeld kept a diary of this period, beginning in May 1622 and continuing until his death from starvation about a year later. Some entries:

➤ June 15. A cavalryman beat a horse to death with a hammer because it could go no further. It was the first meat we had seen in over a month. We butchered and ate it gratefully.

➤ August 24. It is the feast day of St. Bartholomew. There are no animals left in the village except a few goats. Myself, I still have a dog, also two cats that no one has been able to catch.

> September 10. My parishioners have begged me for the love of God to give them my big dog, so that for once they can eat. I could not deny them this.

> November 18. Today I buried three more parishioners, dead from the plague. I fear the graves may not be deep enough to protect the bodies, but no one has the strength to dig.

> December 1. The people begin to look sickly white. They eat whatever they can find—groats, mill-tailings, horsehide—things that heretofore even the pigs would not eat.

> December 25, Christmas Day. Today I saw a neighbor catch a rat and try to make a stew of it using nettles. I heard a story from another pastor that a woman was driven out of a nearby village for trying to butcher her own dead husband.

> March 10. It is time to plant, but we have no seeds, no oxen, no strength. Today, I found a neighbor dead on the street, her mouth green from eating grass. Truly, the Lord God has deserted us.[107]

Of course, Hans Michael Mann suffered along with the other villagers. His house and barn were not burned, but only because the soldiers had confiscated them. His animals were all slaughtered, his grain supplies eaten. He still had his land, however, and since the Freiherr's family and staff had fled, for the time being, there was no one to demand rent and tithes. After his wife and youngest child died of the plague, he took what money he had left and moved to the walled city of Wimpfen with his remaining three children. Inevitably, Tilly's army consumed everything in the area and moved northward by the end of 1624, so Hans Michael moved back to Hochfeld to protect what remained of his property. His house and barn, although empty, were still standing. And from beneath one of his strips of field, he unearthed a small crock filled with the seeds of oat and spelt. He and his children started again.[108]

The village of Hochfeld remained untouched for ten years, during which Hans Michael was able to reestablish a modest living. In 1627, his only daughter died, leaving him two sons. In 1633, he married for a third time. He was 46, almost completely grey and arthritic, but he was still strong enough for field work. His new wife was only 25, but she was delighted with the union. Of the 48 families in Hochfeld before the Thirty Years' War, only 29 remained. Hans Michael might be old and much poorer than before the War, but he was still one of the richest and most eligible marriage prospects in the village.

On September 6, 1634, a Spanish army joined the Catholic imperial forces to attack the Protestant army, composed of Saxon and Swedish troops, outside the town of Nördlingen in Swabia. The battle was a disaster for the

Protestants, resulting in the rlight of the 16,000 Swedes northward towards Heilbronn and the area around Wimpfen. Ironically, while the Catholics had been responsible for the first destruction of Hochfeld, it was the Protestants who were responsible the second time. This time, Hans Michael was determined to protect his property. He had worked too hard reestablishing his wealth to let an army take it away again. He sent his new wife, pregnant with their first child, and the wives of his two sons to the safety of Wimpfen, but he kept his sons with him to guard the house, barn, and stock.

If anything, the 1634 destruction in Hochfeld was worse than in 1622. At least this time, far fewer people starved, because the death and destruction were so swift. Being good Protestants, the Swedes spared the church—but they burned half of the town, including Hans Michael's house and barn. The animals they did not butcher or confiscate, they killed and left dead. Two nearby villages were so completely destroyed that they were never rebuilt, and simply ceased to exist. Carcasses of humans and animals filled the streets and fields, awaiting the scavengers and carrion birds, because there were not enough people left in the ravaged villages to bury them.[109]

Figure 13. Soldiers muster for a battle.

The soldiers in Hochfeld had heard that Hans Michael was rich. They speculated that he had probably buried valuables, and they were right. When he refused to answer their questions, they tortured him to make him talk. But he was a stubborn man whose drive to amass property and to protect his life's work made him able to bear the pain. He continued to refuse to confess until they ran one of his sons through with a sword in front of his eyes and threatened to do the same with the other one. Then he told them that he had buried a crock of coins below the enclosure where he kept his one remaining animal, a brood sow. First the soldiers made his second son dig down to uncover the crock; then they killed him. As they prepared to take his pig away, Hans Michael saw his last chance to start again slipping away. Maddened by the death of his sons and the impending loss of the sow, he tried to wrestle it away from the lead soldier. He was cut down in a second, left dead in the muck.

In Wimpfen, Hans Michael's wife delivered a healthy baby boy, who would become the ancestor, many times removed, of Johann Adam Mann. This time, most of the surviving Hochfeld villagers remained behind the walls of Wimpfen until the end of the war in 1648. Almost all the children from old Hochfeld families who had been born between 1635 and 1650 were born in Wimpfen. When the Amtmann of the next Freiherr took an accounting of his Hochfeld villagers in 1648, there were only 9 families in residence, compared to 48 before the war.[110]

In the end, the warring parties did not resolve their religious issues so much as they simply agreed, from a great weariness, to cease the fight. On October 24, 1648, the Peace of Westphalia declared that Protestant and Catholic lands would be fixed as of their religious status in the year 1624. Calvinism was recognized to be a legal religion with equal status to Lutheranism and Catholicism. The imperial court was reorganized to include equal numbers of Catholics and Protestants to enhance the likelihood and the appearance of equitable treatment before the law. Most importantly, the agreement strengthened the position of the territorial lords so that the emperor became an even weaker central power than he had been before.[111]

While there is no doubt that the death and destruction wrought by the Thirty Years' War was enormous, the estimates of the death toll and property damage are controversial. Reports written in the years following the war are now considered to have exaggerated the losses. One report estimated the death toll at two-thirds of the German population, and it described enormous areas of the countryside as depopulated and devoid of standing villages. One reason for the exaggerated reports was propaganda, a desire to besmirch the reputation of the other side. But a more honest reason was the extrapolation of damage from the hardest-hit areas, particularly the southwest, to the entire country; in actuality, most of northeastern Germany suffered little or no damage. It seems likely that disease was responsible for the most deaths, followed by famine, and that no more than about 325,000 actually fell in battle or at the hands of the soldiers. The most generally accepted death toll is that Germany's population dropped by 30 to 45 percent, with between 5 and 8 million dead in total, out of a pre-war population of between 15 and 21 million.[112]

Never again would the Mann family in Hochfeld achieve the relative level of wealth that had represented Hans Michael's lifetime achievement. As the village began to return to normalcy after the war, it took very little time for the new Freiherr's Amtmann to update his *Lagerbuch*, in which he kept track of rents and debts. A 1654 decree of the Imperial Diet declared that old debts were still valid and payable, and the Mann family found itself obligated to liquidate part of their lands to pay back taxes, rents, and dues. Nevertheless, by the time that Hans Michael's sole surviving child was 30, he had achieved self-sufficiency as a farmer and he had been elected to take his father's place on the Gericht. While the enormous loss of population as a result of the war provided a brief window of mobility for peasants to improve their situations, the degree to which a village's oligarchic structure persisted after the war was astonishing. New families moved to Hochfeld, many of them from Switzerland, and the Freiherr recruited a few Mennonite families to the village to become his tenants; but the families who ran the village before the war, such as the Manns, continued to run it afterwards.[113]

6

Governance
and Community Power

On April 23, 1819, about two and one-half years after the deaths of Johann Adam Mann's wife and children, all the Bürger and many other villagers assembled in front of the Rathaus on a warm spring morning. It was St. George's Day, one of the three annual court sessions in Hochfeld. At the court session or *Ruggericht* on St. George's Day, the village Bürgermeister presented the annual accounting of village funds, the *Gemeinderechnung*, to the citizens.

While the duties of the Bürgermeister would change radically over the next two decades in Badenese villages, in 1817 in Hochfeld he was still responsible for management of the village's finances and assets. There were dozens of village officials who performed various duties for the community, but the Bürgermeister was one of the most important — so important that in some villages, two Bürgermeister shared responsibility, with one overseeing the funds and the other the village buildings and land. In Hochfeld, the sole Bürgermeister sat on the village council or Gericht. He collected taxes for the community, the local lord, and the Badenese government; he also collected pasture fees, fines, and payments for timber and firewood. He maintained the tax register, the account book, and the paper receipts for funds collected and loaned out.[114] The Bürgermeister functioned under the general supervision of the *Anwalt*, who in that time period served as deputy to the Schultheiss. He also worked under the general supervision of the Council of 24, called *die Vierundzwanziger* or simply *die 24ger*. This council was comprised of some of the most respected Bürger in the village, whose responsibility it was to make decisions about community business affairs.[*]

---

[*] The reader should keep in mind the confusing array of titles and duties that were assigned to officials in early modern Germany. Not only did these titles vary from one village, district, and principality to another, but the titles and duties also varied within each jurisdiction over time. Anwalt or *Anwaldt*, for example, evolved into the occupation of lawyer. In some locales prior to the early nineteenth century, he was an official appointed by the local lord to sit on the council and monitor financial transactions; in others, he was selected by the community (but of course was subject to lordly confirmation). In some locales, the Bürgermeister was the mayor, while in others, he was the village accountant. The description of titles and duties in this chapter is based on that found in several Kraichgau villages, principally Wollenberg, Ittlingen, and Fürfeld; however, even among these neighboring villages, there were

The Freiherren von Steinweg had rigorously controlled all village regulations and the appointment or confirmation of all village officials in Hochfeld since the mid-fifteenth century. Perhaps that is why Hochfeld was among the first villages in the Kraichgau to build a *Rathaus*, a building where villagers could meet to discuss local affairs away from the prying eyes of the lord and his officials. The first Rathaus, constructed in 1592, was burned down by Swedish troops during the Thirty Years' War and was

Figure 14. The Rathaus in Hüffenhardt, built in 1559, near fictitious Hochfeld.

replaced after 1648. Following the passage of a new, liberal constitution in Baden in 1818, the local lords were gradually forced to begin ceding most of their governing powers to Baden and the local community. Eventually, the Rathaus would become the seat of a true village council or *Rat*, also called a *Gemeinderat*. In the Hochfeld of 1819, however, the Freiherr had not yet lost his ruling prerogatives. The old institutions and offices and the ancient relationship between village and lord remained unchanged.[115]

The Bürgermeister in Hochfeld in 1819 was named Johann Martin Messner. He was 68 years old, and he had been Bürgermeister since his election at age 42 following the death of his father, who had served as Bürgermeister before him. He was known as one of the cleverest men in the village, possessed of a steel-trap mind that retained an up-to-date balance sheet of all village assets and liabilities. He had the ability to look at the village's three cultivated fields in July and calculate within a few florin what the income to the village administration would be the following October. He could perform the most complicated mathematical computations in his head. Some villagers had tried for years without success to catch him in an

differences in practice and terminology. Endnotes to the chapter also include references to customs in other villages of Baden and Württemberg. Concerning the 24ger, at least three Kraichgau villages (Ittlingen, Hüffenhardt, and Siegelsbach) had these groups, ranging in size from 14 to 24.

erroneous calculation. He also had a reputation for absolute honesty and fairness, so much so that the supervision exercised over his work by the Anwalt and the 24ger was nominal. Martin was cheerful, friendly, and always ready with a joke. The children loved him for his harmless pranks and his seemingly inexhaustible supply of riddles. Over the past year, however, the Schultheiss had been surprised to observe moments of irritation and bad humor on Martin's part. He caught Martin in a few errors of memory and even one in calculation. He had begun to wonder if it was time for Martin to retire, but he had reserved judgment until after the annual accounting.

The Schultheiss, Johann Bernhard Betz, convened the meeting and called on Martin to deliver his report to the assembled Bürger. Martin stood to face his fellow citizens and, instead of delivering an extemporaneous summary as usual, he pulled a paper from his pocket which contained his remarks, word for word.

> We began the year with a balance of 15 florin. The community's receipts were 242 florin. This included sales of wood and hay from the community's common lands; the community's share of harvest proceeds; and income from annual residency permits granted to Jews and other non-Bürger residents (*Beisitzer*). The community's expenditures this year totaled 251 florin. This included the salary of the schoolmaster, reparations assessed on the village from the war against Napoleon, and payments of various fees and taxes to the lord and to the Grand Duchy of Baden. The remaining balance is 6 florin. As you know, we planned to use any surplus from last year's funds to pay Hochfeld's share of repairs to the bridge to Gundelsheim, across the river, which we estimated would cost us 20 florin for materials and labor. It appears we will have to borrow money to cover this expenditure . . . [116]

But his comments were drowned out by a low rumbling of muttered comments, which grew more agitated and then erupted into loud comments and questions. Johann Bernhard struggled to keep order, and when finally he convinced the villagers to sit back down, he called on one of the men, known for his even temper, named Heinrich Bräuchle. "Martin," Heinrich asked, "how can this be? You told me yourself after the harvest last fall that it was our best in five years. And just last month I heard that our lumber sales were better than planned. How can our surplus this year be even smaller than last year?" The chorus of discontent rose again as Martin looked from his notes to his audience and back again, seemingly at a loss for words. What followed was a painful forty-five minutes in which it became clear that he could not answer their questions. As Martin became more confused and agitated, the Schultheiss finally adjourned the meeting. The Anwalt and the 24ger would meet with Martin the next day, he promised the Bürger, and he would insure that they would get answers to all of their questions.

The next day, when the officials went to Martin's home, they found him with his son Johann Christoph by his side, his records ready. Christoph had already gone through the records with his father, he told the officials. There had been an error. His father had neglected to record a loan made to a villager early the previous year, which had been approved by the 24ger. Martin had correctly balanced his cash with his lists of income and expenditures, but had forgotten to take into account the loan, which was due to be repaid before the bridge work would begin. Once the loan was repaid, the village surplus would be 22 florin, or just enough to cover the cost of the bridge repair. It was Christoph who answered the official's questions while his father sat mutely at his side. In a subsequent, private conversation between Christoph and the Anwalt, Christoph admitted that he had been helping his father more and more with the recordkeeping over the past half-year, watching while he recorded transactions and double-checking his figures. He had been unaware of the loan, which had been made before he began to work with his father; however, after the debacle of the meeting, Christoph had found the promissory note for the loan among his father's papers. His father seemed to have days when he was forgetful and irritable, Christoph said, although other days Martin seemed to be fine. After the Anwalt briefed him, the Schultheiss convened the Gericht in a special meeting. Johann Martin was gently retired, and Christoph was subsequently elected as Bürgermeister. A newly vigilant Anwalt scheduled regular monthly meetings with Christoph to go over the records together.

*   *   *

Although the Steinweg lords had long ago promulgated the village ordinances or Dorfordnungen by which the villagers lived, there was another authority, at least as influential and pervasive, which governed the villagers' daily lives—the community structure itself, made up of all the Bürger and their families, and called the *Gemeinde* in German. In English, the simple term "community" is most commonly used to denote a town or neighborhood and its inhabitants. The German term Gemeinde, however, is more complex. In addition to referring to the physical village, the term Gemeinde also referred to its residents, its administrative organization, and the community's decision-making processes. It was not a formal administrative council such as the Gericht or the 24ger; rather, it was simply the sum total of all a village's or town's citizens. Perhaps it could be compared to an American town's roster of registered voters, although in the early modern German village, the Gemeinde carried more responsibility and its male members were much more involved in village life than in colonial America.

The manner in which German villagers organized their community lives in medieval and early modern times was one of the purest examples of self-government that can be found in the history of public administration. Before the fifteenth century, when noble landlords tightened their direct control over their tenants in order to squeeze the maximum profit from their labor, the Gemeinde was close to a perfect example of autonomous organization. Even after the lords became more involved in villagers' lives, however, the Gemeinde retained many aspects of their former independence.[117]

> Actually, landowners usually seem to have permitted their villagers a great deal of autonomy in managing their communal affairs. Seigneurs saved themselves time, trouble, and expense by allowing the peasants to provide services for themselves which the lords would otherwise have had to furnish. This was especially true of estates in which the lord himself did not engage in direct production [i.e., in which he rented to tenants and took part of their proceeds rather than farming his own land directly using bonded labor], but even when the proprietor had demesne land and animals he allowed the community to share his authority.[118]

The Gemeinde performed all the functions of modern government for its inhabitants but within a uniquely personal system, one in which the inhabitants—or at least, those with voting privileges—helped to determine policy and practice. In addition, many of the citizens served on boards and councils or held part-time offices within the village administrative structure. The Gemeinde operated as an economic entity, collecting and dispensing funds for community projects and expenses; it was a collection agency, gathering the tithes, fees, and taxes owed to the local lord, the Badenese government, and the community itself. It functioned as an administrative unit, which ruled over and on behalf of all residents and served as the first-level court, dispensing justice and resolving local conflicts. The Gemeinde also operated a mutual-assistance system, providing loans to its members and dispensing alms to its needy members. It insured peace and safety within the Gemeinde's boundary through its policing and firefighting functions, and it supervised the morals of community members, both in public and in private.[119]

One of the Gemeinde's most important activities was the regulation and coordination of farming activities within a village. In areas of partible inheritance such as in Hochfeld, where one farmer might own or rent strips of land in each of the village fields, decisions about crop selection, planting and harvesting dates, and rotation of the fields to a fallow status were made collectively. Most villages controlled common woodlands and meadows as well, so the Gemeinde set rules about how much and when wood could be taken from the forest, and how many sheep and cattle each community member would be permitted to graze on common pastures. In Hochfeld, the

Gemeinde owned one bull, which all villagers shared to service their cows. The Gemeinde employed three herdsmen for the community, one each for the cattle, hogs, and geese. It also assessed labor and monetary dues on its members for common public works projects, including repair of community buildings, the church, bridges, pathways, and roads. For the past five years, the Hochfeld Gemeinde had sponsored an ongoing project to drain a boggy area near the community boundary. As the village population grew with each generation, the need to reclaim any marginal land in order to support community families had grown ever more acute. Some villages also owned various businesses, such as mills, community ovens for baking, or smithies, both to provide services for its residents and to earn the community some additional income. In Hochfeld, the Gemeinde owned the butchery and employed the local butcher as a community employee.[120]

Figure 15. Community repair of the village boundaries.

The village residents survived by sacrificing a certain degree of individual liberty and choice in order to pursue common, collective interests. Community members adhered to a strict standard of behavior or they risked ostracism. The community also frowned on blatant commercialism or ambition. There was enormous pressure on villagers, often supplemented by local ordinances, to insure that they bought and sold their land, goods, and services within the community itself. This practice meant that an individual who aggressively maximized his profit by lowering prices, increasing his output, or cutting deals with his customers was a threat to the *status quo*. For example, in a village where its inhabitants were dependent on two village cobblers for all their shoes and boots, one of the cobblers would have become impoverished if the other was able to corner most of the available business. Such a move would destroy a part of the village's delicate economic balance and would increase the village's charity obligation.

Personal ambition hurt the stability of hometown life, and so the home town suppressed, excluded, or expelled it. Ambition made for inequality, and the home town worked against inequality among its members, whether it threatened from above or below, from outside or within the community. There was a real egalitarianism to hometown life, but it was not an equality of open opportunity but rather equal subjection to limits placed both on opportunity to rise and upon liability to decline. Of course the community knew clear gradations of wealth, influence, and social standing within itself. It expected different things of different people. But it did not tolerate too wide a spread or too rapid a shift . . . The home town maintained a steady pressure on all members toward the median . . . Hometownsmen liked money as much as anybody else, and maybe more than most, but their circumstances and their neighbors kept them from getting very much, and they fiercely resented anybody who did get very much.[121]

Although the Gemeinde was communitarian, it was anything but egalitarian. Not all inhabitants shared in the full citizenship of Bürgerrecht — only those individuals who were born into the community as the child of a Bürger or those who had applied for citizenship, paid a substantial entry fee, and were accepted by the Gericht on behalf of all Bürger. And while women could also hold Bürger status as a result of birth or marriage, they had no rights to vote. If a Bürger woman's husband died in Hochfeld, she became the head of household and was able to vote as a Bürger; she paid an annual widow's fee of half a florin, compared to the male Bürger who paid twice that amount. Hochfeld also permitted some individuals, such as a few Jewish families, to live in the village without obtaining Bürger status; these *Beisitzer* were required to pay an annual fee and could be banished from the community at any time. The Beisitzer did not share in collective decision-making, nor were they permitted to share the village common assets (such as grazing rights) and benefits. The larger the population became, the more concerned villagers became about their dwindling resources and the need to exclude new people from the village, lest the newcomers become charity burdens on the community. The Gericht, and later the Rat, in an effort to control internal population, continued the strict controls on marriage approvals that had originally been instituted by the local lord. An unintended result of their marriage control policy was a rise in illegitimate births (See Chapter Seven).[122]

Custom insured that no one exceeded a certain, undefined level of wealth, but nevertheless each village was divided into the well-to-do, the middling, and the desperately poor inhabitants. In Hochfeld, 43 of the 139 households on the tax rolls owned or leased 77 percent of the property in the village. Of those 43 households, the top six — each of which held at least 20 morgen in land — controlled 54 percent of the land. This meant that 96 of Hochfeld's households lived with the daily and desperate chore of earning enough income to forestall starvation. In 1816-17, the year that Johann Adam Mann's family died, 70 families received alms; in a year of good harvests such as 1819-20, about 34 families typically applied to receive alms. These poorest households included individuals whose holdings were too small to feed a family, cottagers who owned their own houses or part-houses and perhaps a small plot for vegetables, and individuals who did not even own their homes. All three of these groups were dependent on the availability of wage labor to make ends meet. Thirty-seven households, the middling households such as Johann Adam Mann's, were able to feed and clothe its members as long as they evaded illness, injury, an inadequate harvest, or other disaster such as the death of their animals or the destruction of their house by fire. Meanwhile, the top six households had few money worries and were generally able to put away additional savings at the end of each season. While they might owe rent to the lord on part or all of their holdings, these few wealthy households were also landlords themselves for the poor, landless workers. At some point, however, the number of households needing to rent houses outstripped the ability or willingness of the Gemeinde and the wealthiest villagers to construct enough homes, with the result that houses began to be divided into halves, quarters, or even smaller sections.[123]

The class distinctions between rich and poor villagers had of course always existed. In fact, some scholars believe that this division was one of the causes of the 1525 Peasants' War; these scholars conclude that intra-peasant discontent was at least as important as the peasants' unified grievances against their noble lords. But regardless of whether this hypothesis is correct, there is no doubt that any sixteenth-century conflict was exacerbated by the growing population of the seventeenth and eighteenth centuries. The majority of the poorest individuals were not newcomers to the village, but were children of Bürger whose property had been split so many times over the generations that the resulting pieces could no longer support a family. Between 1770 and 1860, 27 percent of children from Bürger families would inherit no land and become propertyless tenants; no wonder so many of them emigrated.[124]

Not surprisingly, the wealthiest peasants formed an oligarchy that controlled the community. Five of the six richest Bürger, including the Schultheiss, were either members of the Gericht or the 24ger. The six controlled these councils through their own votes and their relationships with the other members, but they also exerted influence over elections and other decisions made by the entire Gemeinde because the poor and middling Bürger depended on them. The less fortunate villagers were the elites' tenants, day laborers, and seasonal farm hands; they turned to the elites when they needed a loan or to rent a farm animal or tool that they could not themselves afford; they also counted on the elites to haul their harvest for them in the carts that only the wealthier Bürger possessed.[125]

People in Hochfeld used the term *Vetter-Gericht*, or Cousin-Council, to describe the ties of blood and marriage between its members. From the frequent occurrence of village domination by ruling groups that shared blood and marriage relationships came a modern German term for nepotism — *Vetterleswirtschaft*. Although the Hochfeld ordinances forbad the election of first-degree relatives such as brothers or sons to either the Gericht or the 24ger, there was nothing to prohibit the simultaneous office-holding of brothers and sons on each of these two separate bodies. Cousins typically sat in the same councils, as did brothers- or sons-in-law. The oligarchy further cemented its influence by arranging marriages between their children and by giving one another preferential treatment in any land transfers. These cozy arrangements lasted in Badenese villages until communities were forced to comply with a 1821 Badenese statute that prohibited fathers, brothers, sons, and sons-in-law from sitting on councils together and also required the establishment of a citizen's committee comprised of one-third each of the poorest, middling, and richest taxpayers. Despite the reduction in nepotism, however, old habits died hard. As late as 1893, the Bürgermeister in Hochfeld was a descendant of one of the six elite families from 1819.[126]

While some villages had been granted the privilege of selecting their own village leaders, in Hochfeld the Schultheiss and the Gericht members or *Richter* were appointed by the Freiherr. This is not to suggest that the local Bürger had no say in their selection. The lord made his selections based on the suggestions of his Amtmann, who carefully evaluated possible candidates and solicited the opinions of the Bürger themselves. With few exceptions over the centuries, Hochfeld's Richter had been well-respected leaders in the community. They were also generally among the richest by village standards. The lord controlled the selection process so that his interests would be protected but also to insure that the peace and stability of the village would be maintained. An unpopular selection might arouse the anger of the villagers and make them rebellious; therefore, to a large extent, the villagers' own preferences were reflected in the Richter selections. But the fact that the Richter were among the wealthiest members of the community meant that they were unlikely to encourage rebellion against the lordly authority. The Richter would have had everything to lose in opposing the lord and nothing to gain.

How did the elites manage to survive in a village that resented excessive wealth? First of all, any village inhabitant whose family had been in Hochfeld since the end of the Thirty Years' War was related to one or more of these six wealthy individuals. Besides the kinship ties, the elites had probably stood as sponsors for the births of the other villagers' children. There also was a sense of mutual obligation between the classes; just as the poorer villagers needed the jobs offered by the elite, so the elite needed the labor of their less-fortunate neighbors. Finally, those members of the richest families who failed to serve the interests of the entire Gemeinde did not stay long in leadership positions. In Hochfeld and many other villages during the early modern period, the local lord appointed the Schultheiss and the Gericht, but only after his Amtmann had carefully consulted the villagers concerning their preferences and opinions of each candidate. In other villages, candidates for the Gericht, the 24ger, and the top village offices were first elected for a specific term, most typically four years; if incumbents were elected a second time, they then served for life unless they chose to retire. Individuals who failed to gain the respect and trust of villagers were not elected for a second time, regardless of their wealth.

> The base of a hometown leader's influence was with the community, and depended in the end on the possession of qualities — family tradition included — that his fellow townsmen respected and needed more than they envied or mistrusted them . . . It was a regime not of oligarchs but of communarchs, a regime of uncles. For the hometown leader was a Bürger, and could not think of his place in terms other than those of his own town and its Bürgerschaft. The Bürgerschaft were his acquaintances or his relatives . . . Social, political, and economic relations intertwined, giving the community great strength even as it gave great local power to the uncles . . . [The villagers] had to get along at birthday parties, weddings, and funerals, and then there was the disposition of the family bakery to think of . . . And so there was no serious dissent, and the community worked very smoothly on the whole.[127]

*   *   *

If one examines the number and distribution of public offices in villages such as Hochfeld, one can see clearly that the Gemeinde was self-government at its most elemental level. In 1819, over one-quarter of the heads of household in Hochfeld had received appointments to one or more of the 38 available posts, not including the Gericht and the 24ger. If one also factors in membership in these councils and then subtracts those households headed by widows — who were not eligible for any appointment other than the village midwife — then between one-third and one-half of Hochfeld's Bürger were holding at least one office. In addition to the Schultheiss, Bürgermeister, Anwalt, the 9 members of the Gericht, and the members of the 24ger, the other posts were the *Gerichtschreiber* (village scribe and clerk), *Lehrer* (teacher), *Heiligenpfleger* or *Kirchenpfleger* (church warden), *Almosenpfleger* (charity administrator), *Ruggerichter* (responsible for moral regulation), 3 *Vormünder* (guardians for orphans), 2 *Waldhüter* (forest custodians), 4 *Nachtwächter* (night watchmen), 3 *Feldschützen* (field guards), 3 *Feldrichter* (who adjudicated boundary disputes), and the three herders (*Viehhirt*, *Schweinehirt*, and *Gansehirt*). Finally, there were inspectors for numerous entities, including the school, mill, tavern, bakery, butchery, wine, cattle, fish, horses, roads, and buildings. There were no appointments to firefighting positions; in case of fire, the village bell was rung and everyone turned out to fight any blaze, which represented an enormous threat to all villagers' homes and property in such a contained village. With regard to police functions, the night watchmen handled those duties; their occupation would eventually transition into a modern law enforcement organization.[128]

*   *   *

Our cooper, Johann Adam Mann, was not a wealthy or important man in Hochfeld; he did not sit on the Gericht or the 24ger. His family had once been prominent in the village, but during his generation, Johann Adam had struggled, not very successfully, to eke out a living for his family. Nevertheless, he was considered an honorable man, and it was a mark of the high opinion that villagers held of him that they had elected him to the important post of Feldrichter or field judge. The Feldrichter commanded enormous respect within the community, and the incumbents had to be men of unimpeachable integrity and good judgment.

In this post, Johann Adam and his two fellow Feldrichter monitored the *Grenzsteine* or boundary markers that delineated each villager's land holdings. In case of dispute between two villagers, the judgment of any two of the Richter was binding. This was a more complex task that it might seem if one keeps in mind that there was no uniform land survey system or land registry in place until 1856. Also, land measurements were not uniform, either between villages or even within a single village over time. In Hochfeld, two separate measurement systems had been used interchangeably over the decades: the *Speyerer Mass* (Speyer measure), equal to 2.77 meters, and a measurement system from Württemberg, in which 10 shoes were equal to 2.86 meters. Given the lack of uniform measurement, the records in the Lagerbuch or land book were, at best, guides subject to considerable interpretation.

When he received his appointment, Johann Adam also received the uniform of his new office—a long coat, once blue but now grey-black from decades of use, and a large, broad-brimmed hat. While on duty, always paired with one of the other Feldrichter, Johann Adam and his counterpart would walk the boundaries of the fields, woodlands, and meadows, measuring as necessary, checking against the Lagerbuch, and making notes. But shielded by their long coats and large hats, they secretly completed another task: the surreptitious burying of small clay disks, called *Zeugen* or witnesses, along the boundary line. Only the Feldrichter knew the exact location of their *Zeugen*. But in case of a dispute or an allegation that the *Grenzsteine* on the surface had been moved, the Feldrichter, their actions again hidden by their long coats, would locate their "witnesses" and verify the true boundaries.[129]

* * *

Figure 16. Leadership and consultation.

No matter what the village headman was called—and he had a variety of titles in different locales—he occupied a sensitive and difficult position in his village. He represented and led the people, but he was also responsible for communicating and enforcing the edicts of the lord and, later, the higher levels of government, such as the district office or *Amt* of the kingdom (Württemberg) or duchy (Baden). These higher authorities held the headman, who was called the Schultheiss in Hochfeld, accountable for the timely and complete collection of all fees and taxes due from the village. Both the higher authorities and the villagers themselves expected the headman to be a god-fearing, moral, and honest official, a role model that all could trust and look up to. He was expected to carry out his duties equitably, insuring equal justice for all villagers, regardless of their wealth or lack thereof. He supervised the church administration and the school system as well as the work of the Bürgermeister, Heiligenpfleger, and other officials. In Hochfeld, he sat in on and ran the meetings of the Gericht and 24ger. He saw to it that villagers attended church on Sundays and holy days, he insured that they kept their homes and buildings in good repair, and he verified that merchants' products—particularly wine, meat, and bread—were of good quality and proper weight. He also had the authority to impose fines, ranging from 15 kreuzer up to 1 gulden or florin, for small offenses or infractions.[130]

The Hochfeld Schultheiss who dealt with the Bürgermeister issue in 1819 was the same man who had arranged for Johann Adam Mann to be licensed as a cooper following the death of his family. Johann Bernhard Betz was a quiet and thoughtful man, a listener rather than a talker, who managed better through behind-the scenes negotiation and facilitation than as a public speaker. At 78, he was the oldest member of the ruling elite. His sandy hair had long since turned white, but the grey-green eyes that peered out at villagers from below his bushy eyebrows were kind. His many years of service had rendered him wise in the ways of humankind, and he kept close the many secrets he had learned about his fellow villagers.

The Schultheiss was assisted by the Gericht, the village's most important and powerful deliberative body. During the sixteenth and seventeenth centuries, the Gericht performed what today we would consider to be both administrative and judicial functions. It acted as a first-level court for minor infractions, disputes, and local matters that were not of interest to the local lord. It also considered and ruled on a wide variety of issues: citizenship applications, annual crop selection and harvesting schedules, usage of common lands and assets, and public works projects to name just a few items.[131]

The Schultheiss was also aided in his oversight role by the Amtmann, also called the *Vogt* in other villages or areas. This official's title is variously translated as district official, bailiff, or magistrate. He was not part of the Gemeinde, and typically his responsibilities included oversight for several towns or villages. He supervised the actions of village officials, insured adherence to all regulations, and acted as the Freiherr's eyes and ears. The Amtmann worked directly for the Steinweg family. The Steinwegs continued to employ an Amtmann to look after their affairs even after their villages became part of Baden—in particular, to insure that they received their full due of rents, fees, tithe, taxes, and in-kind labor. As Baden began to exercise authority over its new territories, it appointed its own Amtmänner to supervise activities within their assigned districts. For a period of some decades, therefore, the village administrative system had to answer to two separate and sometimes conflicting higher authorities.[132]

*   *   *

For his time, Karl Friedrich of Baden was an enlightened ruler, even though his rule was absolute. From his father, he inherited the Margraviate of Baden-Durlach. In 1771, he inherited Baden-Baden from a Catholic branch of the family, doubling his holdings. In 1783, he abolished serfdom, freeing the vast majority of villagers in Baden-Durlach and Baden-Baden. He even attempted, but failed in the face of lordly resistance, to abolish tithes and ground rents. He maintained a precarious relationship with his many non-noble civil servants, whose goals were to reform the duchy, create a constitution, and establish a limited government subservient to law rather than absolute rule.

The French revolution had a substantial impact on Karl Friedrich's fortunes. In 1796, France forced tiny Baden into an alliance and made Karl Friedrich cede to France all his territories west of the Rhine River. In return for this alliance and for Karl Friedrich's agreement to allow French soldiers free passage across his lands, Napoleon quadrupled the size of Baden in the first decade of the nineteenth century and elevated Karl Friedrich to Grand Duke.[133]

In 1806, Napoleon split the independent territories of the former Imperial knights in the Kraichgau between the Grand Duchy of Baden and the also newly elevated Kingdom of Württemberg. After a brief period of tussle between Baden and Württemberg over the Kraichgau spoils, they finally agreed on a division of the territories. In the process, the holdings of the Freiherr von Steinweg were divided between the two, with Hochfeld becoming part of Baden. The Freiherr, formerly an independent ruler, became a *Standesherr* or mediatized lord—in other words, he was demoted to the status of noble subject to the Grand Duke, since his home was actually in Badenese territory. He was far from alone in his new, reduced status; an 1833 summary of Badenese subjects identified 100 Grundherren, which included 13 Grafen (counts) and 55 Freiherren (barons), ruling over as few as 19 subjects. Steinweg was still landlord or Grundherr for his villagers, both those in Baden and in Württemberg, but theoretically, he no longer had the right to establish and enforce village regulations or to administer village justice. Nevertheless, to the extent possible, the Freiherr simply ignored his new status and continued to treat the villagers as his subjects.[134]

The Freiherr von Steinweg was not alone in his unhappiness with the new state of affairs; the Gemeinde of Hochfeld was also suspicious. In such a deeply conservative community, any change that threatened the *status quo* was a negative development. The villagers may have had their issues with the Freiherr, but at least they understood how to deal with him. Their pessimistic attitude was exacerbated when tax assessors from the Badenese district office (or *Amt*) in Mosbach showed up and began to collect information about income and assets for the Gemeinde and the individual taxpayers. The first round of Badenese assessments, coming on the heels of the Freiherr's continued demands, motivated the Bürger to send a delegation of Schultheiss and Gericht representatives to Mosbach for discussions. The result was that the Amt officials in Mosbach informed the Freiherr, politely but firmly, that he no longer had a right to many of his former taxes and fees.[135]

By 1817, the Grand Duke considered a proposal from his senior civil servants, who urged him to establish a modern constitution. The reformers were particularly interested in creating a legislative body that would be made up of representatives from the towns, the noblemen—and even from the villagers themselves. It was the last straw for the mediatized lords. The Freiherr von Steinweg and 32 of his fellow noblemen from northern Baden met and signed a protest over the actions of the Badenese government; they accused the government of having destroyed the relationship between lord and subject. The lords earned a brief reprieve while Karl Ludwig, Grand Duke since the death of his grandfather in 1811, procrastinated on the subject of a constitution. Ultimately, however, he signed off on it in 1818. The new constitution guaranteed equal rights and equality in taxation, and it established uniform military conscription for all except the nobles. It recognized religious liberty for all subjects and established the right of due process in the courts. Finally, it established a two-chamber legislature, the upper chamber for lords and princes, the lower chamber from towns and districts.[136]

In 1821, Johann Bernhard Betz, Hochfeld's venerable old Schultheiss, died. The Badenese Amtmann took advantage of this transition to implement an 1809 edict that dealt with municipal administration. From henceforth, the new head of the village government was called a Bürgermeister. He was elected by the entire Bürgerschaft, subject to confirmation by the Badenese government, and subjected to reelection every 6 years. The Gericht was replaced with a body empowered to pass village ordinances, replacing the legislative powers of the Freiherr; this group was called the *Gemeinderat*. The 24ger was replaced with a new council with similar responsibilities, whose size was based on a ratio of 1 member for every 40 Bürger; this new council was called the *Bürgerausschuss*.[137]

In 1831, after many years of discussion and negotiation, a citizenship law passed the legislature.This new law had a substantial impact on Badenese villages. The goal of the "Law on the Rights of Communal Citizens and on the Acquisition of Citizenship" was to offer an easier and more equitable process for individuals to gain citizenship or Bürgerrecht in their current village or to acquire it in a different place. It was a step on the path to equal citizenship for all, to a future state in which one's citizenship would derive not from his village but from his nation, to a time in which individuals would be permitted to move freely from village to city or back again.

The 1831 law established a standard and reasonably affordable property qualification for applicants of 300 gulden in villages, rising to 1,000 gulden in the largest cities. The entry fee for villages was set at a maximum of 80 gulden. The result was that 80,000 *Beisitzer* or *Schutzbürger*, second-class residents who were denied full citizenship rights in their towns and villages, applied for and received Bürgerrecht across Baden. Now only the Jews continued to be excluded from the right to Badenese citizenship. Of course, towns and villages protested this incursion into their right to exclude applicants as they saw fit; but as a tradeoff, another 1831 law, the "Baden Community Ordinance," also strengthened the authority of village Gemeinde to govern themselves.[138]

The community had been able to function as it had by careful selection of who its members should be, by the imposition of . . . long scrutiny to make sure of a candidate's conformity and familiarity with community ways. But now an outside civil servant armed with general laws took over the Bürgerrecht and admitted citizens by the book: as taxpayers, as state subjects, or because they chose to live there, and admitted them freely; or else he applied laws giving all residents rights equivalent to citizenship. The bias of state administration was to bring new citizens into the community; they were after all state subjects and had to be located somewhere, and the fewer the distinctions among them the better . . . Sometimes the communities grumbled and resisted; in some places there was violence, military intervention, and imprisonment; but mostly they seem to have drawn in closer unto themselves.[139]

Old habits die hard. The Freiherr continued to think of the villagers as his subjects, and they continued to defer to him — at least in public. As late as 1844, when the villagers elected a candidate for Bürgermeister who was known to have participated in political demonstrations in Ludwigsburg, the Freiherr intervened with the Badenese Amt to successfully block the candidate's selection. Nevertheless, the villagers of Hochfeld continued to practice self-government and to promote the civic responsibilities of its citizens — knowledge and experience which some of them would take with them to the New World.[140]

7

Law and Order

In November 1817, the nine members of the village's governing body, the Gericht, convened the Ruggericht, a court session open to all the Bürger, in the largest room of the city hall or Rathaus. Hochfeld had become part of Baden during the Napoleonic reorganization in the first decade of the nineteenth century, but until the 1830s, the Badenese government would continue to tolerate certain aspects of the absolute rule exercised by the Freiherr von Steinweg and other local lords. In 1817, therefore, the Freiherr was still writing Hochfeld's laws, hearing all criminal and most civil cases, and deciding punishments, as he had done for centuries. However, there were many local matters that he permitted villagers to resolve on their own—disagreements between neighbors, for example, and some morality violations—and these cases were the responsibility of the Gericht. (In earlier centuries, morality violations were the responsibility of the parish council or *Kirchenkonvent)*.

The Gericht was composed of Hochfeld's most esteemed men, eight village elders plus the Schultheiss as the presiding official; the members of the Gericht were known as Richter. Each of their court sessions was called a Ruggericht—a word derived from the German word *ruegen*, which means to censure or admonish. The Ruggericht institution, through which Hochfeld's leaders had heard local complains and dispensed home-grown justice, predated even the imposition of law by the local lord. The earliest session for which documentation existed had taken place in 1593, but the tradition itself was centuries older.[141]

Hochfeld convened three sessions of the Ruggericht each year: on St. George's Day (April 23), St. Bartholomew's (August 24), and St. Catharine's (November 25); weather permitting, it was held outside in front of the Rathaus, where the entire community could witness the administration of justice. The Ruggericht was an opportunity for each Bürger to raise any concerns or complaints. Each man could also use the Ruggericht sessions to make the court—and the community—aware of any misdoings on the part of someone else in the village. While today we might consider this practice to be snitching, each Bürger was obligated, based on his annually renewed Bürger oath, to report any violations of Hochfeld's ordinances and community standards. This self-policing insured the stability of the community; everyone knew what to expect, how to behave, and the penalties they would incur if they violated village norms.[142]

On November 25, 1817, Schultheiss Johann Bernhard Betz brought the Ruggericht session to order. As was customary, Bernhard opened the session by reciting the most important obligations of all Hochfeld citizens. No Bürger should inflict any dishonor or damage on another, nor should he permit any other person to do so without bringing it to the attention of the Ruggericht. He should strive always to live in Christian fellowship and harmony with his family members and neighbors. Bernhardt then reminded the villagers that they were required to remove the remains of their summer gardens and any other trash from the village alleys if they had not already done so; not only were the remaining piles unsightly, they were fire hazards. He also informed them of an upcoming village work detail to repair the boundaries between the farming parcels.

Next, Bernhard and the other Richter swore in two Bürger who had been appointed to village posts since the last Ruggericht. Then he summoned all the sons of Hochfeld's Bürger who had turned sixteen since the last Ruggericht. As a group, the young men shuffled to the front of the room, raised their right hands with three fingers extended and, for the first time, repeated the citizenship oath as Bernhard read it aloud to them. He admonished them to be good citizens and neighbors, to be hard-working and honest, and to be loyal to the Grand Duchy of Baden. The Ruggericht members then welcomed them as new Hochfeld Bürger. As the boys swaggered self-consciously, proud of their newly acquired adult status, a representative of the Badenese district government led them away to be registered for possible future military service.

After the swearing-in, the Ruggericht took up the business of appointing guardians (called *Pfleger* or *Vormünder*) for seven minor children who had lost a parent since the last court session. These individuals were often a male relative of the deceased parent, but even if the new guardians were relatives, they were required to be approved and appointed by the Richter. Once appointed, the Pfleger would be required to appear frequently in a specialized guardianship court, the *Waisengericht*, to account for the management of their wards' expenditures and assets. This court was staffed by three of the Richter from the larger village court.[143]

Four Bürger now rose to take their place in front of the Richter. Together, they lodged a complaint about the tavern keeper. They asserted that three times, they had been served spoiled food at the tavern. In addition, they alleged it was common knowledge that the tavern keeper watered down his wine. At that point, the tavern keeper rose from his seat and shouted that the men were liars. The four were trying to take revenge on him because he refused to serve them any more. They were disorderly, and often they could not pay for their drink.

A general uproar ensued in the room, as men took sides and began to bellow at one another. As a man, the Richter rose from their seats and ordered all to cease their arguing. When order had been restored, the

Schultheiss asked the four if they had any proof of their allegations, which they did not. To conclude the matter, Johann Bernhard reminded them that the tavern keeper had the right to admit or not admit anyone to his establishment. If, on some future occasion, they were admitted to the tavern and then served spoiled goods, they should bring a sample to a Richter and reinstate their complaint. Fixing his gaze sternly on the tavern keeper, Johann Bernhard reminded all the village merchants of the serious fines and penalties that would be assessed against them for selling shoddy, spoiled, or adulterated goods. He then asked for the next case.

The local bricklayer, Heinrich Hoffmann, testified that for the past few months, the Bürger Johann Künzel had been working as an unauthorized bricklayer, even though he had never earned his master bricklayer license. Asked to respond, Künzel admitted that the charge was true, but he begged leniency because without this income, he could not feed his family. The Gericht responded that while it was sympathetic to his plight, the employment rules and restrictions were there for a reason; his unauthorized work was taking food out of the Hoffmann family's mouths. To the annoyance of Hoffmann, the Richter declined to assess a fine out of its concern for Künzel's financial situation, but they warned him never to be caught bricklaying again.

Johann Adam Mann and his fellow cooper in Hochfeld then raised a similar complaint about Johann Christian Horsch, a Bürger and apprentice cooper from the nearby village of Heinsheim, who was pursuing unauthorized work commissions in Hochfeld. Johann Adam pointed out that Horsch was neither a licensed cooper nor a Bürger of Hochfeld. There was not even enough barrel-making work in Hochfeld to support the village's two authorized coopers, let alone someone from outside Hochfeld. The two coopers asked the Gericht to prohibit further such actions by Horsch. Horsch was not in court to defend himself, but the Richter promised the coopers that they would refer Horsch to the trade licensing authority for punishment, with a recommendation that Horsch be banned from the trade if he made any future attempts to undercut Hochfeld's craftsmen. Since the Hochfeld Ruggericht had no jurisdiction over a Bürger from another village, the Richter also told their coopers that they would refer the complaint to the Gericht in Heinsheim for any action which that court might deem appropriate.

Among the complaints brought forth by one villager against another, there was one man who complained about the drunken and disorderly behavior of his neighbor, who often came home late from the tavern. Frequently, the drunken man's wife began screaming at him upon his arrival, and the ensuing altercations between husband and wife woke up everyone on the street. The Richter assessed a fine for disturbance of the public peace, and warned the man that another such incident would earn him time in jail. One *Taglöhner* or day laborer complained that a local farmer had failed to pay him for a week's work; in response, the farmer claimed that the Taglöhner came late, left early, and broke two tools while in the farmer's employ. The Richter ordered the farmer to pay one-half of a normal week's wages to the laborer. Another man failed to repair the door to his barn, so his cow had escaped and damaged the garden of another; again, the Richter assessed a fine. Finally, the wife of a villager known for his explosive temper had recently beat her so hard that she had lost two teeth; that transgression brought a stern lecture from the Schultheiss and 2 days in the village jail. While it was accepted that a man had a right to discipline his wife and children, the village would intervene in extreme situations; such behavior was not tolerated.

One final category of cases remained to be dealt with before the Ruggericht was concluded. Bernhard called on the village pastor, Christoph Ulrich Pringsauff, as the villagers inwardly groaned. This pastor was nothing like the simple, humble man who had ministered to the Hochfeld villagers at the beginning of the Reformation. Christoph Pringsauff was not from Hochfeld. As was common for German pastors in the seventeenth through nineteenth centuries, he was born into a pastorship family and received a theology education at the University of Tübingen. Pringsauff was widely considered to have wrung every bit of joy out of Christian life and worship in the village. His sermons focused on sin and punishment, seldom on salvation and mercy. He was an Old Testament pastor, the villagers agreed, the servant of a wrathful god. He watched the villagers constantly, kept track of their failings, and liberally employed their transgressions to illustrate his weekly homilies. The only villager who seemed to approve of Pringsauff's approach was Johann Adam Mann's spiteful aunt, Praxedis, since she enjoyed punishment and retribution as much as the pastor himself.[144]

Paper in hand, the pastor took his place in front of the Gericht and began to read aloud the list of villagers who had desecrated Sunday by failing to attend church. Next he read out a list of men who had been overheard cursing and blaspheming. Since at that time the village school fell under his jurisdiction, he also named those parents who had kept their children out of school to work in the fields or around the house. Bernhard offered those who had been named to defend themselves, and he also invited the villagers to offer their observations before the Richter issued judgment. Few of the accused had anything to say, except for a few parents who pled poverty and the need to work their children in order to feed their families. After a brief, private consultation, Bernhard read out the list of small fines that the Richter had assessed for these transgressions.

Prior to 1813, Pastor Pringsauff sometimes used the Ruggericht sessions to denounce unmarried women who had delivered illegitimate children. The authority to deal with adultery and fornication cases actually belonged to the Freiherr prior to the village's incorporation into Baden, but he generally left it to the village to decide punishment in these cases. Typically, the unmarried mothers would have been assessed a *Bastardstrafe*, a fine of about 5 gulden, for a first illegitimate child, perhaps more for subsequent children. The practice officially ended in 1813, when the Badenese government passed an ordinance that unwed pregnant women could no longer be punished merely for fornication. In truth, however, the practice of punishing women for illegitimate births had begun to die out in many villages before its official abolishment.[145]

The only morals case brought before the court that day involved adultery between two married villagers. As a result of the affair, the husband of the accused woman had left her, and she had brought an illicit child into the world. The Richter fined both of the adulterous individuals 15 gulden and ordered that they be placed on the pillory in the front of the Rathaus for two hours, where all could view their shame.[146]

At long last, after two exhausting days of discussion and deliberation, the Schultheiss adjourned the Ruggericht.

*   *   *

Had the woman delivered her illegitimate baby 100 years earlier, her sentence might have been far harsher. Before the sixteenth century, she might even have faced the death penalty. Among the crimes that could result in a death sentence in this early period were larceny, fraud, murder, infanticide, adultery, whoring, other sexual offenses, fraud, sorcery, and blasphemy. Besides the death penalty, the punishment of mutilation was common before the sixteenth century. The nature of the mutilation was frequently chosen to reflect the guilty party's offense. Someone who had stolen, for example, was likely to have his hand cut off. A man who had blasphemed, perjured himself, or insulted authorities might have his tongue cut off or slit. Also common was branding, having an ear cut off, or having one's eyes put out. Combined with banishment from one's community, these visible signs of guilt were usually death sentences because no other community would admit an individual who bore these marks.[147]

By the sixteenth century, mutilations and death sentences had become less common, as had the use of torture to elicit confessions. They were generally replaced with less extreme forms of corporal punishment such as flogging, loss of village citizenship, and banishment—itself potentially a death sentence, since with banishment one lost one's livelihood and entitlement to community assistance in times of need. Also increasingly common were the imposition of fines and monetary compensation as well as various types of punishments designed to humiliate the guilty party. Although laws and punishments varied from jurisdiction to jurisdiction across the German lands, all the systems of justice had two goals: recompense for injured parties and revenge against those who had committed a crime or violated a community standard.

An individual's position in a community was dependent on the degree to which he or she was considered an honorable person. A woman who acquired a bad reputation or who became the topic of racy gossip was unlikely to find a husband, which could doom her to a life of poverty or dependence, or both. Men who were considered dishonorable forfeited their right to practice their trades and to be members of guilds. They might be refused access to taverns and public baths or denied honorable burials. Often they were ostracized by their neighbors. Depending on the basis of their dishonorable status, it might even be inherited by their children and grandchildren.

> Every station in life was apportioned its appropriate form of honour. Substantial peasant farmers were "honourable", a fact which allowed them to defend their position in lawsuits brought against grasping feudal lords who attempted to force on them labour dues and services not laid down in custom or law . . . Even those townsfolk who worked with their hands had an appropriate degree of honour. Artisans such as silversmiths, carpenters, . . . and the like, were organized in fixed corporations which exercised a tight control over the provision of the relevant goods or services. The possession of honourable status was crucial to the members of guilds, especially guild master . . . For women, much more than for men, honour was a product of sexual propriety and conformity; and here, too, infamy could mean the end of marriageability and the threat of poverty and destitution.[148]

Dishonorable status was not only earned, but could result from practicing certain occupations or belonging to certain social groups. The ranks of the dishonorable included anyone who performed distasteful occupations, particularly executioner and skinner or *Knacker*. Jews and gypsies were considered dishonorable, as were bastards and those conceived before marriage. Anyone who was found guilty of a crime in a town or village might permanently join the ranks of the dishonorable, depending on the severity of their offense. The mere act of associating with a dishonorable individual could taint another person and endanger that person's own standing in a village or town. Those persons from a permanent dishonorable group, either by birth or occupation, could never expect to marry an honorable person. Instead, they formed informal clans. An executioner, for example, married the daughter of another executioner, and his son would follow his father into the occupation, because he had no other choice.[149]

If a villager was found guilty of a minor transgression such as disturbing the public peace, drunkenness, marital disputes, or gambling, the village officials generally resolved the infraction with a fine and a punishment designed to shame and humiliate the guilty person. However, the honor of the individual was not permanently damaged. Neighbors and other observers would do everything they could to resolve a problem such as drunkenness or disorderly conduct without bringing it to the official attention of the village. Only when villagers continued to act in violation of community standards after being warned and perhaps privately reprimanded could they expect to be brought before the Ruggericht or the local lord for punishment.[150]

Sometimes a decision to administer a shaming punishment came not from the lord or the Gericht, but from the community members themselves. Such incidents were not administered uniformly; for example, not all men who beat their wives nor all women who acted in a provocative manner could expect to receive a shaming punishment. Rather, community members, particularly the women in a village, might decide to shame another villager whose acts had been particularly provocative—perhaps someone who had been warned several times to no avail, or someone who committed a particularly public or offensive act. Sometimes these community-initiated punishments were used to shame individuals to resolve their conflicts; other times the punishments were used to enforce village norms of behavior. These shaming punishments helped to discourage other villagers from committing similar acts. The use of shaming as a tool of social control was not unique to German territories; it was a feature of village life throughout early modern Europe. This category of social control is often referred to as "rough music" because the shaming incidents often involved the singing of rude songs or the banging of pots while an individual was paraded through the village streets. One historian writes,

> The rites of rough music were . . . employed with intelligence and wit on occasion, and on other occasions with prejudice (against innovators, 'deviants', outsiders) and rancour . . . There is nothing automatic about the process; much depends on the balance of forces within a community, the family networks, personal histories, the wit or stupidity of natural leaders . . . . The decisive factor may be whether offenders are already unpopular [in the village] for other reasons.[151]

Throughout the early modern period, Hochfeld and other German villages had employed a variety of shaming punishments for individuals who had committed sexual offenses. Sometimes the women had been sentenced to dance with the local executioner—the lowest of dishonorable occupations—in the village square, while offending men had been obliged to dance there with prostitutes. If a woman committed adultery, the other women in the village might cut off her hair, and she could expect to be paraded through the streets of the village to the accompaniment of banging pots and catcalls. Other times, she was forced to drag a dung cart through the village streets. If a woman was known to be pregnant on her wedding day, she was denied the privilege of wearing the traditional bridal wreath of flowers and greenery; instead, she wore one woven of straw. If a village traditionally celebrated weddings on a certain day of the week, it might designate a different day for the marriage of couples already expecting a baby.[152]

Early Modern German villages often owned one or more devices used for shaming punishments. One category of these devices were the *Schandmasken* or shame masks, which were hinged metal cages that were locked around the head of a guilty person before he or she was placed in the pillory or paraded through the village streets. The different forms of Schandmasken symbolized various transgressions; for example, a pig's head with its long snout represented gluttony; a bear's head might signify brutish behavior. Hochfeld owned one Schandmaske, which had long donkey ears and an exaggerated tongue and was used to punish malicious gossips.

Figure 17. Schandmaske with pig snout.

Another punishment, called a *Steintragen*, forced guilty parties to drag a heavy stone or block of wood, often attached by rope or chain to their necks, through the streets of the village as their neighbors mocked and insulted them. Quarrelsome women might find themselves paraded through the village in a *Schandgeige* or "shame violin," a hinged wooden implement in which the head and hands were locked into holes in the implement before the women were paraded through the streets. There were also *Doppelgeigen* or double violins, in which argumentative couples might be imprisoned in the same implement, facing one another, to shame them into reforming their relationship—at least in public.[153]

The center for shaming punishments as well as for some of the more serious offenses—fraud, theft, blasphemy, perjury, adultery, or other sexual crimes—was the pillory. Hochfeld's pillory stood next to the church, and it took the form of an ancient stone post with iron manacles for the neck and hands, attached to the top of the tall post. The first pillory in Hochfeld was set up before 1500, and was still standing and in use during the first half of the nineteenth century. Rough carvings of monkeys and pigs, considered unclean animals, covered the pillory. Both the lord and the Gericht used the pillory for punishments; in some cases, time spent in the pillory was followed by banishment or other punishments such as flogging. One of the worst aspects of time in the pillory was the mockery and ridicule to which guilty persons were subjected by their neighbors.

The Hochfeld couple who were found guilty of adultery during the November 1817 Ruggericht served their time in the pillory the day after the court adjourned. The following day, the villagers learned that the man had fled the village. The humiliation of the stock had been more than he could bear, and he feared that his neighbors would never forget his sin. The woman, with her ties to her children, had no choice but to remain in Hochfeld, and in the end her husband allowed her to remain in his home. But the man with whom she had strayed was never heard from again. It was rumored that he had fled to America to make a new start.

*   *   *

In the centuries leading up to the demise of the Holy Roman Empire in 1806, the Freiherren von Steinweg enjoyed a close-to-absolute right to establish laws and sit in judgment over all the residents in their territories, whether they were his serfs or were free. This legal jurisdiction was known as *Gerichtsherrschaft*. Nevertheless, territorial lords from the German dukes and kings down to the independent knights were still subject to the authority of the Holy Roman Empire. Theoretically, the villagers in Steinweg villages had the right to appeal their lords' decisions in the imperial courts. Occasionally, villagers who were very brave or very stubborn actually dared to appeal a Steinweg decision, but they risked retribution at the hands of the lord if they did so. They had all sworn in their Bürger oath never to seek judgment outside the Steinweg territory. While Hochfeld remained subject only to the justice of their Steinweg lords until the early 19th century, nearby villages that were already part of Baden or Württemberg were afforded appeal rights within those larger territories. When Hochfeld became part of the Grand Duchy of Baden, the villagers gradually acquired similar rights of appeal as the power of the Freiherr waned.

Despite their legal authority, territorial lords did not hold the power of life and death over their residents unless the Emperor had granted them the right of *Hochgerichtsbarkeit* or High Jurisdiction. Crimes covered by High Jurisdiction included murder, infanticide, theft, rape, homosexual sex, sorcery, and witchcraft. Hochgerichtsbarkeit (also referred to as *Blutgerichtsbarkeit*) was commonly known as the *Blutbann* or Blood Ban because the punishments for these crimes — death and mutilations — were bloody. Lords who possessed this authority gained the right to erect stocks and gallows and to sentence accused persons to death and torture. Caspar von Steinweg had been granted this authority by Emperor Frederick III in 1487. He erected a gallows near one of his other villages, just outside the village boundaries. Unlike the pillories, which were useful for public humiliation, the gallows were considered so dishonorable and polluting that they were always located away from the centers of population. Seldom did a year go by that the reigning Freiherr failed to execute someone from one or more of his villages for their criminal offenses.[154]

Given the dozens of territorial entities in the Empire, each with its own set of laws and punishments, the administration of justice in the German lands was a tangle of inconsistencies. There was imperial law, church law, territorial law, and manorial law. Some jurisdictions still depended almost exclusively on legal practices from the old Germanic tradition, but by the sixteenth century, most German territories were in various stages of adopting the Roman legal system.

In southwest German villages, inhabitants were not simply subject to the lord's justice and the court system staffed by their own village leaders. The lord's primary administrative official, the Vogt, also held regular sessions called *Vogtruggerichte,* in which he questioned every Bürger in the village to see if he knew of any violations of the lord's rights or the village ordinances. In Württemberg, parishes were required to conduct their own "courts" to investigate lapses in morality or religious correctness. These courts were run by the Kirchenkonvente or church consistories (councils). In Württemberg, this court was the venue for such issues as failure to attend church, working on Sunday, instances of blasphemy, marital discord, village quarrels, and accusations of magic. The activities of Württemberg Kirchenkonvente were subject to annual review by officials from the higher-level territorial church office. One scholar has written, "No area of village life, however intimate, remained immune to clerical snooping." Since Hochfeld was not part of Württemberg, it was not subjected to a Kirchenkonvent. Nevertheless, as the behavior of Pastor Pringsauff demonstrated during the 1817 session of the Hochfeld Ruggericht, local villagers were just as subject to moral scrutiny as their Württemberg neighbors.[155]

In 1532, the lords and princes of the imperial Diet adopted a new imperial code, the *Constitutio Criminalis Carolina.* The purpose of the Carolina was to establish greater uniformity in the law and in legal practices. After the adoption of the Carolina, lords and princes continued to administer their own laws and legal practices within their individual territories, but at least a first step had been taken toward creating a single system of justice in the German lands.[156]

The Carolina introduced certain modern concepts into German law. Traditionally, judges had based their decisions on the accusations presented in court by an injured party. The Carolina initiated the practice of independent judicial fact-finding before an imperial court could reach its decision. Hearsay and circumstantial evidence were deemed inadequate for conviction. If two eyewitnesses could not be found to testify concerning the crime, then a confession was required. The court employed torture to gain the information it needed. The purpose of the torture was not necessarily to extract a confession, but to uncover information about the details of the crime which only the perpetrator could know. The Carolina contained detailed guidance on the use of torture; for example, it forbad the use of leading questions in the torture chamber.

The use of torture as specified in the Carolina actually represented a step towards modern justice. Earlier, in the medieval era, guilt and innocence were determined by ordeal. The prosecutors, after praying to ask for a sign of guilt or innocence from God, would throw the accused into water. If the accused floated, God was considered to have shown his guilt; if the accused sunk, he was considered innocent and was fished out of the water.[157]

One category of crime that particularly affected women was witchcraft. There had been witch hunts and trials in Europe since the middle ages, but the Carolina set out specific instructions on how charges of witchcraft should be handled. While men and even children were also convicted of witchcraft, an estimated two-thirds of those found guilty were women. A woman who stood out as "different" in a village was subject to suspicion and fear, and might find herself charged as a witch. Such a woman might be targeted merely because she was a single woman or widow, living alone and without the supervision of a man. Earning her own living gave her a degree of independence that could be viewed as threatening to the social order. Some women were targeted for their outspoken natures, short tempers, or poor relations with their neighbors. Women with special knowledge, for example of herbs or of childbearing, could also be perceived as a threat.

Figure 18. From the *Carolina* title page, a wood-cut depicting punishment devices.

There was also a sexual aspect to the fear of female witches; the authors of the most important early modern treatise on witchcraft, *Malleus maleficarum*, stated that it was women's lustful nature that drove them to seek a union with the devil. Women were either tried singly or in mass trials of up to 300. Across Europe, one conservative estimate of the number of women executed for witchcraft was about one hundred thousand. There were more witch trials in Germany than in any other part of Europe; in southwest Germany, witch hunting reached its hysterical height during the seventeenth century.[158]

The last Hochfeld resident to be accused and tried for witchcraft, Anna Maria Wagemann, was accused and tried in the village in 1716. Frau Wagemann's initial accuser was her daughter-in-law. It is not known what led her daughter-in-law, Anna Margaretha, to start her campaign. Perhaps she sincerely believed she had seen her mother-in-law practicing witchcraft. More likely, her charge arose out of hostility between the two women. Perhaps Frau Wagemann had opposed the marriage of her son to her daughter-in-law, or perhaps Anna Margaretha felt that Frau Wagemann had prevented the couple from receiving a larger financial settlement when they married. For whatever reason, Anna Margaretha began to tell her neighbors that she had witnessed her mother-in-law perform many acts of witchcraft, including using dark magic to kill a goat. The more Anna Margaretha accused her mother-in-law, the more the villagers began to talk among themselves. Frau Wagemann earned a small income by making a tea from cabbage, which she sold to many people in the village, claiming that her special tea prevented sickness. As the power of groupthink swept over the villagers, they realized that Frau Wagemann's tea was undoubtedly bewitched. In the trial, villager after villager came forward with eyewitness accounts or stories of the spells that Frau Wagemann had placed upon their animals or themselves. No one came forward to defend Frau Wagemann, and everyone believed her guilty as charged.

After an examination by the Freiherr von Steinweg, the Hochfeld Schultheiss, and the Gericht, the men determined that there was enough evidence to send her case to the law faculty at the University of Tübingen for final disposition. The faculty reviewed the case transcript, concurred in the decision of the local court, and ordered that Frau Wagemann be executed for witchcraft. On February 5, 1717, Frau Wagemann was burned at the stake.[159]

*   *   *

Although the Hochfeld Bürger had burned their last witch in 1717, the power of superstition, fear, and tradition survived in the village. One last incident occurred in 1817, one hundred years later, before the shaming instruments were put away forever.

Johann Adam Mann's first cousin Anna Sabina, the retarded daughter of his shrewish Aunt Praxedis, had long been a target of mischief by the village children. They loved to tease her whenever they found her outside her house—a rare occasion, since Praxedis was so protective of her. But one day while Praxedis tidied up their bedroom, Anna Sabina opened the door and went out to sit on the stoop. When Praxedis came downstairs, she heard the jeers and laughing of a group of children outside the house. She opened the door to find Anna Sabina crying as the group spun her in a circle. In her anger as she rushed to retrieve her daughter, she screamed at the children. "I curse you one and all! May you never live to have children or to know a happy day! If I ever catch you tormenting my daughter again, I will come after you myself!"

The next week, one of the children fell ill, and then another one. Both recovered, but their illness was enough to start the mothers in the village talking. They had despised and avoided Praxedis for years, so it was not too surprising that they began to consider the possibility that she was a witch. After a period, one of the women approached the Schultheiss with their suspicions, but he told them to hold their tongues. Praxedis was indeed meddlesome and ill-tempered, but that did not make her a witch, he told the woman. It was clear that the male village power structure would do nothing to deal with Praxedis. The women were still angry about her frightening

Figure 19. Woodcut of woman in a Schandgeige.

their children, however, and more than a little afraid of Praxedis themselves. They decided to take matters into their own hands.

The next morning, Johann Adam Mann was awakened by the sounds of shrieking in the other half of the house he shared with Praxedis and Anna Sabina. He dressed hurriedly and ran out of the house to find that several women in the village had dragged Praxedis out of her home. They had fetched the Schandgeige from storage in the village Rathaus and had locked it around the neck and wrists of his aunt. By the time he arrived, the women had hoisted Praxedis on top of a dung cart and were beginning to lead the oxen and cart through the village streets. Praxedis, weeping from rage and humiliation, attempted to get down, but a woman on each side of the cart kept her firmly in place. The village children followed, banging pots and chanting over and over: *"Schreckschraube, Zankteufel, Haarige Hexe! Schreckschraube, Zankteufel, Haarige Hexe!!"* —"Battle axe, termagent, hairy witch!"

The women tormented Praxedis for almost an hour, after which they let her go. Praxedis retreated into her house and shut the door; thereafter, she emerged only to purchase food and other needed items, using only those words that were absolutely necessary and never looking her neighbors in the eye. She even gave up church—but the villagers and Pastor Pringsauff decided to overlook this transgression. The villagers had achieved their goal of getting even with her, not just for threatening their children but for her years of spying on them and reporting them. But for the first time since he himself had discovered her nasty temperament while still a young boy, Johann Adam felt heartily sorry for Praxedis, and believed that the village women had gone too far

8

Marriage and Inheritance

In September 1818, almost two years after he lost his wife and most of his children to illness and malnutrition, Johann Adam Mann married again. His bride, Anna Barbara Wagenbach, was from Hochfeld and about ten years younger than he. She had been widowed for just over a year, and was the mother of two sons and a daughter. Life without a husband in this patriarchal culture was difficult, so Anna Barbara was motivated to seek a new husband immediately in order to provide a home and some income for her children. A quick marriage was a frequent solution to the problem of widowhood.[160]

The marriage was not a love match in the sense of romantic love, but the two were well matched. They had known one another their entire lives, and had similar expectations from the relationship. Johann Adam sought a partner who would cook for him, take care of his home, and help to rear his remaining son, Johann Jacob. Anna Barbara needed the protection of a husband, a home, and a father for her young children. The two began with mutual respect and understanding for one another, which would grow into a solid affection during their years together.

The couple did not arrange their own marriage. Anna Barbara's brother, who acted as her spokesman in legal matters since as a woman she could not represent herself, began looking for a new spouse shortly after her first husband died. He had already suggested another man before contracting the marriage with Johann Adam. The first candidate was wealthier than Johann Adam and in many ways a better match, but Anna Barbara had heard that he had regularly beat his first wife. She could accept that a husband might occasionally cuff his wife in a moment of anger, but she was not willing to endure a life of violence and fear. Her first husband had treated her with respect, and she sought a second husband who would do the same, so she refused to consider her first suitor.[161]

It was not unusual for prospective marriage partners to have a say in the selection of their future spouses. As early as the fifteenth century, parents began to acknowledge and accept that mutual attraction and emotional affinity were important to a successful match. Therefore, the prospective bride and groom were consulted, and their opinions were a factor in most matches. While this consultation no doubt led to some love matches, romance was not as important as similar upbringing, social standing, and economic status. As one German scholar has noted,

Physical attraction and emotional love were not viewed as essential conditions for marriage, although few doubted that they played a role; the love that drew husband and wife together was a mutual willingness to make sacrifices for one another, hence a duty that developed within marriage. Such love emerged most readily between spouses who at the outset found one another worthy of respect and trust. Not "Do I desire and want this person?" but "Do I find this person honorable and companionable?" — that was the central question for a successful marriage.[162]

Anna Barbara had a reputation as a stubborn woman, but she was also known as a hard worker and a thrifty wife. Her economy and her sage suggestions to her first husband about money management had resulted in a significant increase in their net worth. The attribute of Anna Barbara's that most appealed to Johann Adam, however, was her good nature. She found humor everywhere in the daily events of life, and her hearty laughter gradually began to melt the ice that had formed in Johann Adam's heart when his family had died. For her part, Anna Barbara was attracted to Johann Adam's kindly blue eyes, his shy smile, and his obvious affection for his son Jacob.

Johann Adam and Anna Barbara were distant blood relatives — not unusual in small villages where families intermarried for centuries. They were actually related in numerous ways, but their closest relationship was what a modern genealogist would call third cousins, which meant that they shared one set of great-great grandparents. In German tradition, this meant that they were related in the fourth degree of consanguinity or *Blutverwandtschaft*.

The marriage ordinance for the Steinweg villages closely followed that of neighboring Württemberg, under which the couple would not have been able to marry had they been more closely related. The marriage ordinance was based on the incest prohibitions from Leviticus, chapters 18 and 20, as expanded by canon law and the Germanic method of computing blood relationship. It forbad marriage between persons related in the second or third degree of consanguinity (blood relationship) or affinity (the marriage tie). While a modern genealogist distinguishes between consanguinity and affinity, the early modern German did not. Incest was based not just on birth, but on sexual relations between spouses, which was considered to have mingled their blood. A spouse's blood relations became one's own blood relations when a marriage was consummated. Therefore, even if Anna Barbara and Johann Adam had not been related themselves, they could not have contracted a legal marriage if Anna Barbara's first husband had been a first or second cousin of Johann Adam, or if Johann Adam's first wife had been the same to Anna Barbara.

This did not mean that marriages between closer relatives never occurred in southwest German villages; there were simply too many blood and marriage ties within the small communities to preclude cousin marriages altogether. Different villages enforced the incest provisions with varying degrees of consistency and diligence. Couples could also obtain dispensations from church authorities; for example, in some cases dispensations were granted if the couple shared a grandfather or grandmother, but descended from different spouses of that ancestor. Keep in mind as well that the specific ordinances described in this book were not in force across Germany; each principality, duchy, or independent territory had its own set of marriage ordinances.[163]

Anna Barbara and her family members held detailed discussions about potential spouses, and sought advice from close friends in the village before settling on Johann Adam. Likewise, Johann Adam's relatives were involved in evaluating possible new wives for him. The discussions within the two families led to a meeting between Johann Adam and Anna Barbara's brother, Michael, who was acting as her representative or *Kriegsvogt*. The two men agreed to the marriage and shook hands on the agreement, after which Johann Adam gave him a single coin as a symbol of his pledge. The giving of a single coin had symbolized Hochfeld marriage agreements since medieval times.[164]

*   *   *

The following week, Johann Adam and Michael went to the Rathaus together, where they publicly signed a betrothal document and registered the upcoming marriage. The signing was followed by a small gathering of friends and family at Michael's home, where the guests and the bride and groom shared a glass of wine and *Lebkuchen*, a traditional cookie similar to gingerbread. The couple also publicly exchanged gifts. Johann Adam gave Anna Barbara 25 florin and a pair of tiny gold earrings, while she gave him two shirts and two handkerchiefs, which she had sewn herself. Her gifts were symbolic as much as they were useful. One scholar has noted that a prospective bride's hand-sewn gifts "represented her skill as a seamstress and housekeeper worthy of the control of the household stocks of linen, and prefigured the emotional investment of time and care that she would make in household tasks."[165]

Before the Reformation, the above rituals constituted the entire marriage ceremony. However, the Evangelisch or Lutheran Church required that a public marriage service be conducted, with a pastor in attendance, before the marriage was legal. In 1563, the Catholic Church followed the Evangelisch lead when the Council of Trent also required that marriage vows be recited in the presence of a priest.[166]

During the Sunday church services in the three weeks leading up to the marriage ceremony, Pastor Pringsauff read an announcement of the couple's intent to marry. This was the *Aufgebot* in German, or the banns in English, which in both languages refer to the act of summoning. It was an opportunity for anyone who knew of any impediment to a legal marriage to come forward and prevent the marriage. Such impediments might be a prior, secret commitment that the bride or groom had given to another person, the discovery of a kinship that violated the incest prohibition, or a lack of consent to the marriage by either the bride or groom. [167]

Figure 20. Wedding procession.

The day of the marriage, Johann Adam walked to Michael's home, where Anna Barbara waited for him, dressed in her best clothes. He gave her a bouquet of flowers and, followed by their children, relatives, and guests, conducted her to the church. Pastor Pringsauff greeted them at the door and blessed the couple; at the end of the regular Sunday service, he performed the marriage ceremony. The wedding party then walked together to Johann Adam's house, where the couple was to live with their four children. Female relatives from both families had worked for a week, scrubbing and cleaning the house inside and out in preparation for the marriage feast. The house was filled with greens and spring flowers, and a table had been set up outside, groaning with wine, beer, and the best food that the family could afford to offer their guests: duck, capons, fish, sausage, fresh fruit from the hillsides, and several pastries. The party was a noisy and boisterous gathering that went on late into the night. As the couple slipped away to their marriage bed, a group of half-drunk male guests posted themselves directly below the bedroom window and tormented the couple with pot banging and ribald songs, bellowed at the top of their lungs. The guests continued to sing and dance until festivities ended in the early hours of the next morning.[168]

One purpose of the marriage ceremony in early modern Germany was to demonstrate a family's generosity and financial standing. As was common, Johann Adam spent far more on his wedding celebration than he could truly afford, but nevertheless the festivities were relatively modest. If he had been able to afford a more elaborate feast and celebration, he might have run afoul of the village ordinance that limited excessive expenditure for weddings. The ordinance read, "No one is allowed to spend too much money on a wedding. Even when rich people marry, they may not invite more people than can be seated at four tables, unless they have special circumstances and the approval of the lord."[169]

This restriction fell into a category of prohibitions called sumptuary laws. Every community had sumptuary laws, and they were not unique to early modern Germany. Greece, Rome, even oriental cultures had them. Their purpose was to enforce distinctions between groups or classes of people, as well as to discourage the immoral expenditure of funds on frivolous items. The first imperial police ordinance in Germany to establish sumptuary restrictions was issued in 1530. In addition to setting limits on how much people of various classes could spend on events such as weddings and funerals, it also dictated who was allowed to wear certain colors, fabrics, headgear, and jewelry. It mandated that certain groups of dishonorable people, for example executioners, prostitutes, and Jews, must wear special clothing or symbols that set them apart from honorable citizens. In the case of the Jews, they were required to wear a yellow circle sewn to their clothing or hats.[170]

Writing about German cities, one scholar stated, "Townspeople lived on preassigned streets, according to their trade or profession, and they dressed in clothing appropriate to one's social class. To reach above one's station in life or to act contrary to it unsettled one's neighbors and was viewed as a threat to public order." [171] Villages like Hochfeld were too small to set up designated neighborhoods for various trades, but they were not too small to frown upon excessive consumption—particularly if it appeared an individual was attempting to rise above his ordained life station.

After the wedding, the couple and their children started the process of learning how to become a family. Johann Adam adored children and loved playing with them, and his stepchildren were eager for a father figure, so that part of the transition was easy. The adjustment for his son Jacob was more difficult. Jacob was twelve years old when his father remarried. He and his father had grown extremely close in their two years alone together.

Between them, they had managed rudimentary cooking and bachelor-style housekeeping. They had spent long hours together as Johann Adam started to teach his son the barrel-making trade, and he had begun to speak to his son as a young man who would soon be ready to assume adulthood. Jacob did not feel threatened by his father's new relationship with the much younger children, although the children's constant chatter and activity often annoyed him. The single sleeping room was once again crowded, and Jacob missed having time alone.[172]

Anna Barbara treated Jacob with businesslike kindness, and for this Jacob was grateful. He had assumed it was inevitable that his father would marry again, and he had heard many horror stories about the cruelty or indifference of stepparents, the extreme favoritism they showed their own children. Jacob had adored his mother, had vivid memories of her, and was too old to long for mothering for himself, so all he wanted from his stepmother was fair and courteous treatment, which she gave him. On balance, he was glad to give up his exclusive relationship with his father in order to enjoy a clean house and clothes and decent food on the table again. When he observed how happy his father was in his new marriage, he was more than willing to share his father's heart.

*   *   *

Johann Adam's family had not always been as poor as they were in 1816, when he lost his wife and children to malnutrition and disease. His paternal grandparents, Jörg Mann and his wife Maria Schneider, had owned a house and outbuildings as well as land holdings of 42 morgen under cultivation, 2 morgen of meadowland, and a 1-morgen garden plot. They were comfortable, even prosperous. But they also had five children who survived to adulthood. In Hochfeld, as was common across most of the southwest German lands, all children shared equally in their parents' estates.

As his share of his parents' inheritance, Johann Adam's father, Georg Adam, received 10 morgen under cultivation, one-half of the garden plot, a cow, two pigs, and some tools and equipment. Georg Adam's wife, Maria Magdalena Lymbach, brought house linens, cooking pots and utensils, and money to the marriage. The only real property she received was the outbuilding and the half-house in which Johann Adam now lived; her parents' field strips and garden plot went to her brothers. Maria Magdalena bore ten children, but half died, and there were never more than five children alive at any given point during the marriage. Therefore, Georg Adam and his wife were able to rear their family, securely if not lavishly, on the land they controlled.[173]

When it came time to settle the estate of his parents, for his share Johann Adam received the half-house and its outbuilding, some of the house's furniture, some tools and equipment, and the half-morgen garden plot. His brothers received one-third each of the cultivated land and half each of the livestock while his sisters shared one-third of the land, some of the furniture, and a little money. Johann Adam's wife brought to the marriage 2 morgen of cultivated land and household items such as linens, pots, and utensils. The negligible land holdings of Johann Adam and his first wife were the reason that in addition to growing vegetables and cultivating his wife's field strips, Johann Adam had been forced to hire himself out as a day laborer. But as he began his second marriage, Johann Adam hoped for a more secure economic life as a result of the modest income he now earned as a barrel-maker and the assets that his new wife brought to the marriage.

Anna Barbara's parents were both still alive when she married for the first time, so she had not yet received her inheritance portion. Instead, she received what most about-to-be married children received from their parents: a *Heiratsgut*, or an endowment with which she could begin her adult life. (In parts of Württemberg, this advance of part of a child's inheritance was called a *Voraus*. The modern equivalents are *Aussteuer* or *Mitgift*.) A Heiratsgut might include land, dwellings, money, livestock, equipment, tools, and household goods. As her Heiratsgut, Anna Barbara had received clothing, household goods, linen, a sow, a milk cow, and 165 florin. Anna Barbara did not receive another endowment upon her second marriage, but she brought with her the initial Heiratsgut.

A Heiratsgut was considered to be a temporary distribution of assets; technically, the adult children returned this property to the estate of their parents before a final distribution was made at the parents' deaths. In most but not all cases, the final distribution would be larger than the Heiratsgut since it also included the assets with which the deceased parents had supported themselves. Anna Barbara's only surviving sibling was her brother Michael, so she could anticipate eventually receiving half of her parents' estates. Anna Barbara's father had died before her second marriage, but her mother was entitled to use his real and personal property during her life, so there would be no final distribution until after the death of Anna Barbara's mother. Overall, Anna Barbara and Johann Adam brought approximately the same net worth to the new marriage.[174]

*   *   *

Because of the extreme importance that early modern Germans attached to inheritance and to the accounting for individual and marital assets, it was the custom in some southwest German territories or villages for a marriage contract to be negotiated. The marriage contract would typically detail the real and personal property each partner brought to the relationship and how these possessions would be allocated when the death of one partner ended the marriage. The drawing up of a marriage contract was most common when one or both of the couple had been married before, due to the tangled web of inheritance rights for his children, her children, and their children. If one of the two new partners brought significantly more property to the marriage, a contract could protect both of them. The poorer partner, for example, might ask for protective financial provisions if widowed, or specify that the small amount of property that the poorer partner brought to the marriage would not be reduced in case of the couple's future financial losses. The richer partner might have been urged by existing children or other relatives to insert provisions that would prevent the poorer partner from walking away with some of the family wealth. Despite the potential protection of a specific marriage contract, marriage contracts were rare in many villages because the couple expected to abide by the existing intestate inheritance ordinances in force in their kingdom, dukedom, or territory. In the absence of a will, these ordinances dictated how a deceased person's estate was to be divided between children and a surviving spouse.[175]

In Hochfeld, marriage contracts were seldom negotiated because most couples abided by the local ordinance and customs.[176] However, whether couples negotiated a contract or not, all of them were required to prepare a detailed inventory (*Inventarium* or *Inventur*) of the possessions of the bride and the groom. The drawing up of the Inventur was a laborious, often time-consuming process that could last months, particularly if it was a first marriage and the two families involved were in the process of negotiating exactly what real and personal property they would give their children to begin their married lives. Because the Inventur was the basis of subsequent taxes, fees, and rental charges, it was also of significant interest to the lord, the local officials, and the district officials if the village was part of a larger territory. Many men might sit in on the sessions in which the Inventur was negotiated or drawn up: the Schultheiss; two members of the Gericht, who also sat on the orphan's court or *Waisengericht*; the lord's Vogt or his representative; the father or guardian of the bride; any future heirs; and the guardians (*Pfleger* or *Vetreter*) of any children from prior marriages. In the case of Johann Adam and Anna Barbara, fifteen persons attended each session. Besides the village's and the lord's officials, Anna Barbara's brother was there as her *Kriegsvogt*, her daughter had a Pfleger, her sons shared another one, Johann Jacob had one, and a brother of Johann Adam attended to safeguard the Mann family assets.[177]

An Inventur, particularly one drawn up for a first marriage, divided the property of each person into two categories: *Heiratsgut*, or the endowment that each of them had received from their parents, and *Eigenes*, or their personal possessions. The Eigenes included any personal property, such as clothes, linen, household goods, or tools that the bride and groom had acquired on their own. It also included any savings that the individuals had put aside. It was common for late teens or young adults to spend a few years working as a servant to amass some savings before beginning their married lives. In the case of a widow or widower, the Eigenes could also include that individual's share of earnings from the first marriage, in accordance with the spouse's will or with agreements made at the time of marriage.[178]

When completed, the Inventur of Johann Adam and Anna Barbara covered several pages. Each of them had a separate section under which everything they owned, down to the last handkerchief, was listed. Below the two general headings of Heiratsgut and Eigenes, the possessions of both were divided into several categories, including immovable property (*Liegenschaft*), which included land, houses, and outbuildings; moveable property (*Fahrnis*); and any cash, debts, or credits. Each segment of land was described in detail: its value, its exact location, its size, its use (cultivated, meadow, woodland, garden), and any obligations on each piece (mortgage or lease arrangements). The moveables were divided into categories such as cash, linen and bedding, clothing, cooking pots and utensils, foodstuffs, livestock and poultry, and farm equipment.[179]

The only asset from Anna Barbara's listing that was not part of her original Heiratsgut was her half of the nest egg that she and her first husband had saved; it was listed as part of her Eigenes. The other half of these savings could be used by the newly married couple, but they could not deplete its value without the concurrence of the Pfleger of Anna Barbara's three children, because it was part of their future inheritance. When the first wife of Johann Adam and the first husband of Anna Barbara died, death inventories had been conducted of the marital funds at the time of death. This death inventory, called a *Teilung*, allocated all of the assets and debts between the two spouses. The portion that fell to the deceased spouse was now the property of the children, according to the inheritance ordinance. Therefore, this property was not included in the marriage inventory of the new couple.[180]

Once the married couple's Inventur was agreed upon by the interested parties, all the listed assets were available to be used jointly, regardless of which person brought them into the marriage. With certain restrictions, the inheritance portions that belonged to their children, which were listed in the deceased spouses' Teilungen, were also available to be used. As the man and head of the household, the husband controlled and managed all marital funds, as well as the future inheritance portions of their children. However, just as surviving spouses could not sell the assets of their children and use the proceeds for their own gain, a husband could not dispose of or mortgage the property of his wife without her permission. A man had the right to control his family's finances, but there were many other individuals interested in how he handled his responsibilities—his wife's Kriegsvogt, his children's and stepchildren's Pfleger, and the village administrators. If a husband misused his financial rights, he could find himself declared *Mundtod* or legally incompetent. He would be stripped of his privileges as an adult male to represent himself in court and to manage his family finances;

the local court might even assign him his own guardian. Losing his right to manage the family funds was the ultimate emasculating humiliation.[181]

* * *

The rules and customs that governed the disposition of property in Hochfeld were based on a system called partible inheritance. It was one of the two basic systems that were used in the German territories, the other being impartible inheritance. Under the impartible system, one heir alone inherited a family's property and possessions. Under the partible system, the parents' estates were inherited more or less equally by all of their surviving children. In Germany, impartible inheritance was called *Anerbenrecht*, while partible inheritance was called *Realteilung*. Partible inheritance was the predominant system through most of southwest Germany, including the Kraichgau (northern Baden and Württemberg), the Swabian Alps, the Rhineland, Hessen, southwest Westphalia, and limited parts of central Germany (Thüringen, southwest Saxony, and southern Hanover). Impartible inheritance was practiced in most of northern Germany, Bavaria, and some areas of the Black Forest.[182]

In the regions that practiced Realteilung, each territory developed its own set of rules and customs, which can be grouped into three basic systems:

➤ *Fallrecht*: A surviving spouse was allowed the lifetime use of the deceased partner's estate. Eventually, the estate would be inherited by the children or other family members of the deceased partner. It was not shared with the surviving spouse.

➤ *Teilrecht*: A surviving spouse divided the deceased partner's estate with the deceased's children. If there were no children, the surviving spouse inherited it all.

➤ *Verfangenschaftsrecht*: A surviving spouse inherited non-fixed assets and the children inherited the real property such as land and houses. However, the surviving spouse received lifetime use of the real property, even in case of remarriage.[183]

The villages in the Steinweg territory, including Hochfeld, followed the Fallrecht system. This meant that Johann Adam's son Johann Jacob, as the only surviving child of his first wife, was the sole heir of his mother's estate. However, Johann Adam had the use of that property until he chose to pass it on to Johann Jacob. To protect Johann Jacob's interest, a maternal uncle acted as his guardian or Pfleger, and Johann Adam was required to appear in the orphan's court at least annually to account to the Pfleger and members of the orphan's court for his management of his son's funds. If Jacob had died along with his other siblings in 1816, then his first wife's estate would have returned to his wife's blood relatives, either when she died or more likely after the death of Johann Adam.

The Realteilung system had a number of implications for the territories that practiced it. For example, no family had a particular attachment to any parcels of land. All the field strips were subject to shuffling with each new generation, and many families held some land in each of a village's cultivated fields, so there was no nostalgia for a birth farm. The dispersed property resulted in a great deal of trading or inter-village sales as the Bürger attempted to aggregate their tiny holdings into larger pieces. Another implication was that half-siblings who formed a blended family might look forward to vastly different inheritance expectations. They shared inheritance from their common parent, but different inheritances from their deceased parents. Obviously, this situation could result in tensions and jealousies within a family unit, and made the challenge of forming a successful new family even more difficult.[184]

*   *   *

Beginning as early as the late seventeenth century, as villages began to recover from the ravages of the Thirty Years' War, population increases in each generation reduced the average size of inheritances. It became harder and harder for villagers to pay their taxes, fees, and rent, let alone feed their families. At this point, landlords and government officials became alarmed, and began to place restrictions on the continued partition of property. The result was that in some areas of southwest Germany, partible inheritance began to resemble impartible inheritance if a family was unable to split its property among several heirs. The resolution was that one heir inherited the property, but he owed his co-heirs, called the yielding heirs, an equivalent amount in cash or other moveable goods. This meant that the heir who held the family property started his life under an enormous burden of debt— sometimes so much that he was unable to make a living from his property, and he was forced to sell.[185]

One scholar has studied a village located in northwest Germany, which also followed the practice of partible inheritance. This village had adopted the same mechanism of selecting one heir to take over the property, with the obligation of compensating his siblings in cash or other goods. The scholar noted,

> [P]arents with large holdings were unable to provide all their surviving children with social positions equivalent to their own. Some thus experienced downward mobility. For the generations marrying between 1771 and 1860, 37% of the surviving children from large farms could secure the status their parents had had neither through inheritance nor marriage. Only 10% were able to acquire some real property by marrying into a small

farm; 27% became *Heuerlinge* [i.e., renters dependent on wage labor] for the rest of their lives. Downward mobility was more extensive for daughters than for sons: 45% of surviving daughters experienced declining fortunes while only 26% of the sons shared this fate. Downward mobility increased to some extent from the late eighteenth through the early nineteenth century, even though there was some modest recovery after 1830. In this period, some of the disinherited children may have preferred emigration to America to becoming a *Heuerling* at home . . . [186]

In addition to prohibiting the continued partition of land, some governments or village officials began to place restrictions on the formation of new households. A young couple who lacked sufficient resources to support themselves and their families could possibly become a welfare burden for the village, so if they were unable to demonstrate that they possessed resources and income above some designated minimum amount, they were be denied permission to marry. The result was that,

> [i]n many cases, the poor were forced to be flexible—forced, that is, to postpone weddings or to forgo marriage altogether. Custom and law prevented the formation of unions that would be unable to support themselves at an acceptable standard of living . . . . The offspring of [well-off villagers] faced few economic barriers to marriage and so wed in their early twenties, and occasionally even younger. By contrast, the children of [the less fortunate] were compelled to wait several years longer. These postponements were especially lengthy in hard times.[187]

There is little wonder that illegitimacy increased in the late eighteenth and the nineteenth centuries. Marriage restrictions became common all over Germany, not merely in the areas that practiced partible inheritance, but their impact on the illegitimacy rate was particularly severe in the southwest.

> It is almost certain . . . that one effect of blocking communal entries by prohibiting marriage was to increase the rate of illegitimacy, wherein [German territories] at the end of the fifties led western Europe . . .

> In Württemberg there was a survey to find out what effects the marriage and membership laws [i.e., the restrictions on admission to village citizenship] actually had on the marriage rate. The figures showed that about one formal application for marriage in thirty was refused by the communities in 1847-51, and that in 1852-1856, . . . about one in fifteen was refused by communities and state in combination. Neither figure takes into account the effects of informal community pressure, and neither takes into account the number of marriages delayed or prevented by the presence of the law without its formal invocation against the applicants.[188]

By around 1840, there was one illegitimate birth for every 5.61 legitimate births in Baden, one for every 7.69 legitimate births in Württemberg, and an astonishing one for every 3.98 births in Bavaria. In comparison, the rate was 6.15 in Saxony, 6.5 in Mecklenburg-Schwerin, and 9.62 in Hanover.[189] Another set of sources put the illegitimacy rates at the end of the 1850s as 22.6 percent in Bavaria, 16.9 percent in Baden, 16.3 percent in Württemberg; comparatively, the rate in Prussia was 8.3, France was 7.5, and Great Britain was 6.5.[190]

By the late fourteenth century, it had become increasingly common for noble rulers, local communities, and Catholic Church officials to legislate against premarital sex. With the Reformation and the introduction of Protestant doctrine, the pressure to remain chaste until marriage increased. Before the Evangelisch church decreed that a marriage was not legal until a ceremony had been performed in church, it had been common practice for engaged couples to become sexually active. Yet there was no consistent treatment of unmarried pregnant women in early modern Germany and, in fact, many localities preached chastity while they simultaneously condoned premarital sex between future marriage partners.

Writing of one Catholic community in the late sixteenth and early seventeenth century, a researcher noted, "The custom of pre-marital (though post-spousal) sex was broadly tolerated, with only the occasional prosecution to keep up appearances. On the other hand, if something went awry in the two to five weeks between engagement and wedding day, the *Offizialat* [regional church official] might be visited by an abandoned (and often pregnant) woman, desperately hoping the ecclesiastical court would enforce the marriage promise she was sure she had been given."[191]

The toleration of premarital sex did not extend to illegitimate births; a woman who was unable to legitimize her baby by marrying before the birth could expect severe treatment. She might be drummed out of the village at worst, or subjected to fines and shaming punishments at best. In the local church book, the record of her child's birth would be recorded in red ink, or upside down, or perhaps would be recorded in a separate section so that the child's birth was marked as shameful for as long as the records survived. In some communities, illegitimate inhabitants were prohibited from inheriting land. The unmarried mother, if employed, usually lost her job. Her child might be barred forever from most occupations, so that both of them became dependent on income as laborers or servants. Most trade guilds refused to admit illegitimate members. The guilds placed such a high value on honor that they even expelled a married member whose wife delivered a child after less than nine months of marriage.[192]

The extreme sanctions for illegitimacy lasted until the mid-nineteenth century, when proto-industrialization increased employment options and legislation passed in Württemberg and Baden to abolish citizenship based on village of birth. Pregnant women without husbands now had more employment options available to them, as well as increased mobility to escape village punishment. With the rise of weaving as a cottage industry in the southwest, large families became desirable because children could be put to work at a young age, thereby increasing the family income. Poor couples who turned to weaving or other industrial employment could now marry and establish families even without land, reducing the temptation to engage in sex outside marriage. This is not to say that public opinion in the southwest German village became forgiving of unwed mothers and their illegitimate children; the sting of bastardy and dishonor continued to be felt in the countryside into the twentieth century.

*   *   *

In 1835, a woman preparing to emigrate to America with her husband wrote to her brother, "How many parents sigh as they stand beside the cradle and wonder how they can raise their little ones?" For families whose ancestors had known better days, for fathers who longed to own their own farm and give their children the hope of a bright future, it is not surprising that population pressures, lack of land, and problems in gaining permission to marry led so many to emigrate. The rate of emigration was highest in the German southwest—and the practice of partible inheritance, which on its benign face was so egalitarian, was a primary factor that caused so many to desert their village and homelands forever.[193]

Family Roles and Relationships

Over the next decade, Johann Adam Mann and his wife Anna Barbara labored side by side to rear their children and earn their daily bread. For the most part their marriage was harmonious and affectionate. Thanks to Anna Barbara's thrifty housekeeping practices, a period of better-than-average harvests, and the steady if small income from Johann Adam's barrel making, the family enjoyed a modest prosperity. The only dark period for Johann Adam followed the death of the couple's first baby. The little girl was born early, struggled to breathe, and quietly died in her mother's arms a few hours later.

Johann Adam and Anna Barbara worked as partners in a joint endeavor, but there was no doubt who the head of the household was. They lived in a patriarchal society, and both law and custom favored the *Hausvater* or "house father" over the *Hausmutter*. Even their clothing symbolized this relationship. Adult males wore leather money pouches and carried knives, signifying their physical and financial powers. Adult females kept their heads covered with scarves or hats as symbols of their modesty and subservience; around their waists were their white, black, or brown aprons, while hanging from their belts were usually found the keys to the household.[194]

Scholars have debated how unequal the power distribution was between husband and wife in early modern Germany. Before the women's movement of the 1970s introduced a new perspective on family research, historians had generally viewed the evolution of the wife's position as one long, unbroken climb towards equality. In the 1970s, however, feminists applied a different lens to the topic and reached different conclusions. In their view, medieval women who entered the convent had experienced independence from men, built careers for themselves, and acquired power within their cloistered world. After the Black Death wiped out thirty to sixty percent of the European population in the thirteenth and fourteenth centuries, the newly-formed trade guilds opened their doors to women because of a dearth of male workers. The feminist scholars concluded that prior to the early modern period, there had been no sharp line between men's and women's work, either in the workshop, the fields, or the home. According to them, women's status changed for the worse after the Reformation. Luther and his followers closed convents and monasteries, denounced the celibate clerical life, and established the primacy of marriage as the holiest and best lifestyle. As the population grew, guilds began to ban women from the trades and crafts. Women found their new and subordinate place by the hearth and the cradle while men took over primary responsibility for earning the family income and speaking for the family in village society. In the division of responsibilities that characterized the relations of husband and wife in the early modern period, production was assigned to the man, reproduction to the woman.[195]

Women were considered to be emotionally unstable creatures who lacked the mental faculties of their husbands. Legally, they were *Vogtbar*, which meant that they were subject to the control and guidance of a man, who spoke for them in court. The exceptions were those rare women who earned their own money and ran their own businesses. In general, a woman's father represented her until her marriage, her husband thereafter. Local officials or her family appointed a Kriegsvogt or spokesman for a widowed woman. A woman could not buy, sell, or mortgage property, or otherwise litigate, without a man to represent her. She could not make decisions concerning her children's education and property without the concurrence of her husband or her children's Pfleger. However, the law also protected a woman. Her husband could not sell or mortgage her property without her consent. Creditors could not go after her property to satisfy her husband's debts. Also, barring specific language in their marriage contract to the contrary, any debts or obligations after marriage were paid out of her husband's assets, not her own, as long as her husband still had assets to liquidate.[196]

A man was expected to control his wife, and he was held responsible for all aspects of her behavior. A husband with an outspoken wife might become an object of village ridicule; both he and his wife could find themselves subjected to shaming punishments. In extreme cases, the couple's roof would be stripped from their house as the symbol of a marriage relationship turned upside-down, or the woman's stove—the heart of her home—would be smashed. Village women were as likely as village men to be behind any shaming incidents, since many felt that a domineering wife was a threat to their conception of their own role.[197]

Because a man's honor within the community was largely dependent upon his wife's behavior, a man who could not control his wife was deemed unable to act responsibly in other areas of his life and thus he was ridiculed in the language of popular culture. Ballads and songs depicting the 'struggle for the breeches' were designed to reaffirm a husband's claim to authority by laying bare the dysfunctional marriage . . . [In the nineteenth century], "[p]ersonal relations were [still] built upon an economic and sexual hierarchy that . . . continued to regard a woman's independent sexual power as destabilizing."[198]

If a man could not control his wife's behavior through reason, he was expected to use physical force to curb her inappropriate actions. If he did not, then the village would censure him, not her; his failure to exercise effective authority was deemed worse than her actual behavior. German law and custom accepted physical punishment as an appropriate control tool. Villagers even overlooked instances of marital rape or severe beatings, if rare, because of their unwillingness to interfere with a man's authority within his family. A woman thus treated had no recourse in the village courts. On the other hand, a man who severely and regularly beat his wife could expect to face censure in his village. "Among neither Protestants nor Catholics was the ordered and disciplined home a tyrannized home," wrote one scholar.[199]

Following the establishment of the Protestant churches in the sixteenth century, German territories passed ordinances that permitted divorce for a limited number of reasons. Both Luther and Calvin wrote that a troubled couple should pray to God for guidance and earnestly seek to mend their relationship. If they could not, however, then divorce might be permitted. Württemberg was one of the first German territories to adopt a divorce ordinance. In 1522, Luther listed the justifications that he could accept for divorce: adultery, impotence, desertion, or a refusal to engage in sexual relations within the marriage. Calvin's list of reasons was similar. Calvin specifically rejected antipathy, incompatibility, cruelty, and rough treatment as inadequate justifications. Subsequent theologians, however, broadened the acceptable grounds for divorce to include extreme incompatibility. One of them, Martin Bucer, wrote that God never intended for partners in an irreparably broken relationship to live out their lives in misery.[200]

Frequently, the local pastor became involved in attempting to mediate marital problems. Sometimes he was able to use his considerable local power and the threat of village censure to bring a couple back together. When he was unsuccessful, however, the couple could take their case into court—the church court or consistory, the local court, or a district court in larger territories. Based on the records of one Württemberg village, which began to keep records of the marital conflict cases in 1730, women were far more likely to bring complaints to the court's attention, to request a legal separation, or to sue for divorce. The tally of cases showed that women were most likely to complain about physical and verbal abuse, drunkenness, adultery, and deceit. Men complained about stubbornness, laziness, refusal to have sex, witchcraft, and bad cooking.[201]

Even among cases that reached a court, divorces were an act of last resort, and they remained rare in Germany well into the nineteenth century. Despite the extreme cases that reached a court and left behind records of marital misery, early modern marriages were at least as likely to be successful as modern marriages. Some were happy, some unhappy, some cold, some argumentative, some dominated in all aspects by the husband, some more equal, and in some the woman held the balance of power— usually in a covert manner that did not attract village disapproval. Since the vast majority of couples expected to remain together until separated by death, marriage partners were more likely to accept and tolerate their spouses' shortcomings than partners of today. The marriage of Johann Adam Mann and Anna Barbara, in which the couple consulted jointly on marital decisions and in which an initial respect and compatibility matured into love and devotion, was ideal, but certainly not unique.[202]

One historian who has written several books on the development of the German family concluded,

> Family archives compellingly document the folly and hubris of assigning quintessential spousal and parental love only to modern or recent times. Such high qualities prove to be specific to family life itself and not to time and place — this notwithstanding the very different public faces that time and place always affix to particular ages and cultures. From this point of view, the evidence suggests that the 'modern sentimental family' exists as far back in time and as widely in space as there are proper sources to document it.[203]

* * *

Following the Reformation, a series of books and pamphlets called the *Hausvaterliteratur* became popular throughout Germany. This "house father literature" dispensed technical advice to the German man on a variety of topics including child rearing. It described the ideal lord of a territory or husband of a family as a benevolent ruler, loving yet firm, over his subjects or his family. The most widely read of the Hausvater books in the seventeenth century, *Oeconomia ruralis et domestica*, described the model husband as "god-fearing, wise, understanding, and experienced, who has God ever before his eyes, prays and works diligently, does harm neither to his neighbors nor to the members of his household, and is able to maintain the love, friendship, and good will of all around him."[204]

As late as the mid-nineteenth century, almost every family in Württemberg still owned or leased some farming land, even if the husband also practiced a trade or was a day laborer or cottager working someone else's plots. His farming and laboring work usually brought the majority of cash into the family coffer, and most men kept a *Hausbuch* or housebook that detailed family income and expenditures. On behalf of the family, the man appeared at local court sessions, perhaps served in a village office, participated in work details, negotiated land or other deals, paid the tax bill, paid the mortgage or lease, and took out loans. While village women worked alone on most of their tasks, men were much more likely to spend significant portions of their day in the company of other men. They planted, plowed, worked the fields, harvested, chopped wood, and went to market with other villagers. At the end of the day they spent time together in the tavern, drinking, discussing village affairs and farming conditions, and gossiping.

Those who worked in the construction trades spent weeks or months away from their village, again spending their working and free time with other men.[205]

Parenthood was considered too important to be left solely to the woman. Fathers were encouraged to be actively involved in caring for their children from birth. No less an authority on moral behavior than Martin Luther wrote, "When a father washes diapers or performs some other mean task for his child, and someone ridicules him as an effeminate fool, . . . God with all his angels and creatures is smiling." Once a child reached the age of six or seven, most fathers took over the primary responsibility for discipline. About that same age, most boys began to spend time working with their fathers, either in the fields or the workshops.[206]

One historian cites two German poems of the early modern period that describe and contrast the life cycles of the man and woman. In the poem about the man, he is described as "at twenty a young man, at thirty a man, at forty well established, at fifty at his peak, at sixty the onset of old age . . . " The poem views man in terms of his vitality and mastery. The poem about the woman, in contrast, views her in terms of her child-bearing capacity and her relationship to her family. While the man reaches his peak at fifty, the woman at that age is already old.

> At ten a child,
> At twenty a maid,
> At thirty a wife,
> At forty a matron,
> At fifty a grandmother,
> At sixty age-worn,
> At seventy deformed,
> At eighty barren and grown cold.[207]

It was not surprising that women aged more rapidly than men. The life of the Hausvater was hard, but that of the Hausmutter was doubly so. A man's work required bursts of extreme strength and effort, but usually was punctuated with periods of inactivity or even leisure. The woman's life was one of never-ending labor in her every waking moment: cooking three meals over an open hearth, baking, tending the children, hauling water from the village well, feeding any animals, milking a cow or a goat, sowing and weeding vegetables in the family plot, washing and mending the clothes, and keeping the house. In the eighteenth century, it became more common to keep horses and oxen in stalls instead of pastures, and it was generally the wife's job to walk to the family plots, gather the clover or hay, and haul it to the animals' stalls.

Many women also worked in the fields by their men, particularly during planting and harvesting seasons, performing all but the heaviest tasks. Poor women hired themselves out as day laborers as well as tending their home and family. Better-off women might have servants to supervise, and most had daughters to train. In the winter, women worked at the spindle making thread and at the loom making cloth, and they sewed and knitted most of the family's clothes. Many women earned money selling eggs, milk, butter, cheese, vegetables, cloth, or clothing, and it was often their income that paid the family's tax bills.[208]

On top of her unremitting life of labor, the Hausmutter spent most of her adult life pregnant or recovering from a recent birth or miscarriage. On average, a woman experienced five to seven successful pregnancies (i.e., those producing a live child) every two and one-half years, up to the age of about 38-40. Pregnancy was dangerous to a woman's health, even more so if she was malnourished or weakened from a recent pregnancy. Instead of improving, mortality from childbirth increased in the nineteenth century. Between 1655 and 1724, the rate of death from childbirth was 2 to 3 percent, but it increased to 5 to 6.5 percent between 1760 and 1829.[209]

Many Lutheran homes owned a copy of one or more devotional handbooks, which wives could use in praying for God's protection during pregnancy and childbirth. Of course almost all of them were written by male theologians. These handbooks placed a heavy emphasis on the fundamentally sinful nature of woman as well as her need to labor in pain in order to atone for the Fall of Eve. For those women who could read, it is unlikely that these texts offered much hope or comfort. One such devotional, however, was written by a well-educated woman, who was the countess of a small principality in eastern Germany. Aemelie Juliane von Schwarzburg-Rudolstadt was a mother herself, and her prayer texts were quite different than those written by the male theologians. While the males focused on reminding women that their labor contractions were punishment for their essentially sinful natures, Amelie focused on reassuring and comforting women through their pains. They reflected the thoughts that all women, in all ages, have shared about their approaching labor. Many of the prayers were designed to distract women during the labor itself, similar to the breathing exercises and other Lamaze techniques that some women use today. Few if any women in southwest Germany would have owned Aemelie's handbook, but they would have shared her fears, her hopes, and her love for the growing child:

> O Lord, continue your goodness
> to me, and have mercy on me and on the fruit of my womb.
> Protect us from all bad things, fear, terror, anxiety, and suffering.
> Protect my body and my soul, my comings and goings, that I
> might carry the fruit of my womb successfully until the correct
> time for birth, with your gracious protection, and that I might
> bring it into the world healthy and without any damage. Prepare

and form the fruit of my womb according to your fatherly
desire, give it an intelligent soul, protect it like the apple of your
eye, and bring it to the light of day in joy, and without defect,
adopt it then through holy baptism as your own child and
heaven's heir, and establish it under your blessing for eternity.
Then we will want to spread the word that you are helping us,
And we will praise your name, O God, forever and forever . . . Amen.[210]

*   *   *

Fourteen months after Anna Barbara lost her first baby with Johann Adam, she became pregnant again. The couple was overjoyed. Anna Barbara was a young, healthy woman; all of her children but the last one had survived into at least infancy, so she had every reason to hope that this pregnancy would turn out well. As for Johann Adam, no man in Hochfeld loved his children more. Johann Adam proceeded to pamper his wife as much as his limited resources would allow. He bought her fish and other special foods, and even hired a servant to help her as her time approached. A few weeks before the birth, Anna Barbara's friends and relatives began to loan her swaddling clothes for the baby. Many of them brought in meals for the family so that Anna Barbara could rest and prepare herself.[211]

Although many German men did all they could to support their wives during pregnancy, the process was an essentially feminine experience in which a woman's female relatives, friends, and neighbors gathered around to support her during her pregnancy and labor. Midwives, the only women to receive appointment to a village office, helped to prepare expectant mothers and to deliver their babies. By the nineteenth century, male doctors in some cities had begun to deliver babies, but in the rural villages they attended childbirths only in the most difficult cases — and not always even then.[212]

Pregnancy remained as much a mystery as any other physical condition during the early modern period; medical treatment had more to do with myth and guesswork than science. A person's health was believed to be based in the four humors, a concept that dated back to the Greeks. The four humors were phlegm, blood, black bile, and yellow bile; sickness resulted when these four humors were out of balance. If someone exhibited signs of having too much blood, leeches or lancets were used to remove the excess. People believed that when a pregnant woman stopped menstruating, the blood that remained in her body became polluted and could endanger her health. Anna Barbara was lucky enough to remain healthy during her pregnancy, so no one attempted to bleed her so as to remove her bodily impurities.[213]

People believed that everything a woman saw, smelled, and tasted, as well as the emotions she felt, would affect the growing baby. If she became angry, her blood would heat up and harm the delicate baby. If she suffered a shock or fright, her blood would drain away, causing miscarriage or deformation. One sixteenth-century Hausvater book, which continued to be updated and sold into the nineteenth century, urged women to pray regularly while pregnant so that their children would develop high moral character. The author of this book assured women that seeing animals while pregnant would not harm their developing child — although a woman who craved rabbit, or who was frightened by one, would probably bear a baby with a hare-lip.[214]

Another Hausbuch author advised the seventeenth- and eighteenth-century woman of steps she should take to prevent miscarriages. She should

> . . . regularly eat fresh young capons, deer, lamb, veal, partridges, or hazel hens, avoiding, however, gluttony . . . She should seek a physician's counsel for persistent coughing, vomiting, diarrhea, tenasmon, and nose or vaginal bleeding (these latter conditions indicate that she has become too ripe with blood and should be bled to remove the excess). She should also avoid heavy exercise and work, running, and jumping, excessive standing and walking, and situations that frighten or terrify her . . . In the last weeks of pregnancy the expectant mother [should eat] non-constipating foods that moisten but do not fatten, like fried apples with sugar wine, sweet apple juice, and figs, and avoid baked and fried foods, rice, hard-boiled eggs, and millet, which dry, stop up, and constrict . . . The expectant mother should regularly drink broth made from fat young hens or capons and should lubricate [her] privates with chicken, duck, or goose grease, or with herbal oils.[215]

About three weeks before the baby was due, Johann Adam and Anna Barbara selected tentative godparents — two women if the baby were a girl and two men if he were a boy. Villages followed a variety of practices in the selection of godparents. In some, it was customary to ask village leaders or the wealthiest men — their wives if the child was a girl — to be a baptismal sponsor. A sponsor became the *Gevatter* or, for women, a *Gevatterin* to the baby's parents. Parents who selected these important individuals were cementing valuable relationships with the village power structure; they could usually expect a valuable christening gift, and they would hope that the Gevatter relationship might result in future business deals or employment offers.

By the nineteenth century, however, it had become just as common to select relatives as village leaders. In many villages, couples selected the same individuals to serve as godparents for all the male or female offspring. For the coming birth, Johann Adam had asked his son Jacob's godfather to sponsor his baby if it were a boy. Jacob's godfather was Johann Adam's first

cousin, Johann Georg Kirstetter, who was a member of the Gericht. The other
sponsor would be Anna Barbara's brother, who had been the sponsor for her
two older sons. If the new baby were a girl, Johann Georg Kirstetter's wife
would be one of the godparents. The other would be the same woman who
had sponsored Anna Barbara's daughter by her first husband.[216]

Because of the high rate of child mortality, it was customary to baptize a
child quickly so that it could go to heaven if it died within a few days of its
birth.[217] Johann Adam and Anna Barbara therefore had two names ready
before their baby's birth. If it were a boy, he would be named Johann Georg
after Johann Adam's cousin, who would be the boy's baptismal sponsor; if a
girl, she would be named Maria Magdalena after her paternal grandmother.
Johann Adam had already given these names to two children of his first
marriage, both now dead.

Naming practices varied from territory to territory. In Württemberg, for
example, the names Eberhard, Ludwig, and Ulrich were common because
they were the names of Württemberg dukes. In Baden, Bernhard, Philipp,
and Friedrich were common for the same reason. Before the middle of the
seventeenth century, a child born in southwest Germany was likely to have
only one Christian name. For boys the most common included Johannes (or
Hanß/Hanss), Georg (Jerg/Jörg/Joreg), Martin, Christoph, and Jacob, while
for girls some of the most common were Maria, Margaretha, Anna,
Elisabetha, and Barbara. Catholic and Protestant villages shared all these
names, but there were some saints' names, such as Xaver or Franz, which
were much more common in Catholic areas.

By the end of the seventeenth century, most children in southwest
Germany were given two names, while in northern and eastern Germany, it
was not uncommon to give three baptismal names. Both Catholic and
Protestant families generally chose a saint's name for the first baptismal name. The
second and third names were also often saints' names. The second or third name was
called the *Rufname* or "called name"; it was the name by which the child was actually
known in the village. In Hochfeld, the villagers generally referred to Johann Adam
simply as Adam, and they always referred to his son Johann Jacob by his Rufname of Jacob.
Hochfeld parents were as likely to name their children after their godparents as they were
to name them after a parent or grandparent.

Anna Barbara's labor began early one frosty spring morning. By the afternoon, the
midwife and several other women had

Figure 21. Woodcut of a woman in labor

arrived and had established themselves in the sleeping room. Jacob and the smaller children had been sent away for the day, but Johann Adam stayed nearby in case he was needed. The women sat with their sewing and distracted Anna Barbara with gossip and jokes. Evening came, and the women took turns sitting with Anna Barbara while the others went home to tend their own families.

The midwife had already checked the position of the baby in the birth canal and determined that it was in the optimal, head-down position. As the hours went by, she coached Anna Barbara through her labor pains and periodically urged her to walk around the room. Anna Barbara labored on into the night, growing more tired with each contraction. A little before midnight, the midwife determined that the time was near. She lubricated Anna Barbara with chicken fat, massaged her stomach, and urged her to take slow, deep breaths. She placed Anna Barbara on a folding birth chair, which she carried with her to all birthing rooms. The chair supported Anna Barbara's back and provided footrests that functioned as stirrups; the seat had a cutout which provided easy access for the midwife to the birth canal. With a series of final pushes, Anna Barbara delivered a healthy, squalling son.[218]

While the women washed Anna Barbara and put her into a clean bed, the midwife bathed the baby in warm water, cleaned its nose, wiped its eyes with a daub of olive oil, and swaddled it tightly before handing him to Anna Barbara. Then she called up Johann Adam from downstairs to greet his new son, Johann Georg. Johann Georg, who looked very much like his elder sibling and namesake who had died in 1816, was the joy of Johann Adam's remaining years. Johann Georg experienced the normal round of childhood illnesses as a child, but he was to survive them all. He grew up to marry in Hochfeld and become the father of four children himself.

Two more babies would be born to Johann Adam and Anna Barbara. To their parents' deep distress, neither child lived beyond infancy. Together and with their first spouses, Johann Adam and Anna Barbara lost a total of seven children during their married lives. In addition to the newborn Johann Georg, those who survived to adulthood were Jacob from Johann Adam's first marriage and three of Anna Barbara's children from her first marriage. This survival rate of only one-third of their children was worse than the average family experience. Child mortality rates varied significantly from one southern German village to another, but in general, data suggest that between one-third and one-half of children died before their fifth birthdays.[219]

Some modern scholars have concluded that early modern parents protected themselves from the heartbreak of so many children's early deaths by holding back their feelings; if they did not become too attached to a child, his or her loss would be more bearable. But other scholars roundly dispute the contention that parental love was an invention of the industrial age. As evidence, they point to the loving letters between parents and children at school, and to the tone of child-rearing advice contained in the Hausvaterliteratur, "setting forth remedies for every conceivable affliction of infancy and childhood, quite obviously in the belief that parents would spare no effort to secure the health and well-being of their children. The very detail in which [the Hausvaterliteratur authors] discussed these matters is itself a positive commentary on parental love in Reformation Europe."[220]

*   *   *

After the birth of Johann Georg, Anna Barbara remained abed for a couple of weeks, while the temporary servant whom Johann Adam had hired took care of the cooking, cleaning, and the other children. All of Anna Barbara's friends and relatives dropped by during this happy break to congratulate her, admire her baby, leave the baby a gift, and enjoy a glass of wine with the new mother.

While Anna Barbara gradually began to resume household management, she kept her baby comfortable, clean, and safe while she was busy with other chores by swaddling him. Two or three times a day, she would remove the cloth bindings, wash the baby, and then rewrap the baby in clean cloths. He remained in swaddling for the first four months. Mothers believed that swaddling prevented deformity and insured straight limbs. As was common, Anna Barbara nursed her new baby for almost a year. After a few weeks, she also started to feed him a thin gruel to supplement her breast milk.[221]

Forty days after Johann Georg's birth, Anna Barbara left her house for the first time and went to church. Traditionally, a mother's first outing after a birth was to the church for the ceremony of churching. Churching was an ancient Christian practice with its roots in the biblical passage of Leviticus 12, which declared that a woman who had given birth was unclean; a woman could not be accepted back into the village community until she passed forty days at home and had then gone to church, offering in hand, to be blessed by the priest or pastor. By the fifteenth century, churching had lost most of its association with uncleanliness and had become a joyous ritual. The midwife and her other attendants, all of them dressed in their best clothes, accompanied Anna Barbara to the church. After the pastor delivered his Sunday sermon, he called the women to the altar, where the mother knelt before him. He instructed the congregation on the miracle of children and the import of childbirth, after which he led everyone in prayer before blessing the new mother. Following church, the group of women returned to Anna Barbara's home, where they celebrated with cake and wine.[222]

Whenever her baby experienced a rash, fever, or other illness, Anna Barbara was his nurse. She relied on folk medicine and tradition that had been passed down from generation to generation. Lacking knowledge of the causes of sickness, the early modern woman knew only how to treat symptoms: fevers, coughs, swelling, bleeding, rashes. As with pregnancy and childbirth, medical practice reflected superstition as much as it did a knowledge of the healing properties of blossoms, herbs, and roots. Sometimes their knowledge turned out to be accurate—for example, brewing tea from willow, which is the source for aspirin—but other times it was a fallacy—for example, wrapping a spider in a ball of dough to treat fever.[223]

In the poorest families, children were pressed into labor while still toddlers, particularly in weaving families where every pair of hands was required to insure the family living. While he insisted that all his children begin to perform chores from an early age, Johann Adam was determined to provide them some happy years of play before he began in earnest to prepare them for adult life. The diversions in the early modern village did not differ much from those of early twentieth-century children throughout Europe and North America.

There had been a school in the village of Hochfeld since a Freiherr von Steinweg established the first one following his adoption of Luther's theology in the early days of the Reformation. Luther had promoted education as a useful tool to train children in religious precepts. Württemberg passed its first schooling law in 1559, contemporary with several other Evangelisch territories and principalities. Catholic territories followed suit shortly thereafter. In its earliest centuries, the Hochfeld school ran for one hour daily during the winter months, beginning after the harvest

Figure 22. Village boys at play.

and ending before planting, and even some of the girls attended for a few years.[224]

The early church schools had a simple goal: to teach children about their religion. This did not mean that they were taught enough reading so that they could read the Bible for themselves. Of course, children who were destined to become pastors studied the Bible, and well-to-do children in the Latin schools also mastered reading. But sixteenth-century church authorities did not believe that peasant children could or should be taught how to read the Bible themselves; in fact, they thought such a skill could be dangerous. The semi-educated peasants might draw different conclusions from their studies than those which the church wished them to hold. So the Württemberg ordinance of 1559, as well as those in most other German states, declared that it was enough for children of villagers to learn to pray, to recite their catechism, and to sing the psalms. They might also learn rudimentary reading and writing. In Catholic territories, particularly across Austria, schooling did not include instruction in reading; it was enough that the children memorize what they needed to know about religious doctrine.[225]

Most large towns and cities had a larger variety of schooling alternatives than in the villages. Wealthy city parents placed their boys in municipally sponsored Latin schools where they could receive a college prepatory education. Middle-income parents had other municipal schools available, where their sons could receive education appropriate for a career in the trades and business. For poor parents who could scrape together the tuition, so-called *Winkelschulen*, or "corner schools," sprang up to educate children in the practical skills of reading, writing, and basic math. These schools were open to girls, unlike many of the municipal schools. The church authorities denounced these unsanctioned schools because they deemphasized religious training in favor of useful skills.[226]

Schooling changed in the early nineteenth century, when territorial lords including the King of Württemberg and the Grand Duke of Baden embraced schools as an important tool to improve the productivity of their workers. At that point, the Hochfeld school extended its daily hours and its school season; it even ran a short session during the summer, and it enforced attendance rules. The schools now taught children reading, writing, and simple math in addition to singing and religion. Even though few children attended past their thirteenth or fourteenth birthdays, the villagers received enough education that most village adults possessed a rudimentary ability to read and write. By the nineteenth century, most Hochfeld families also owned and used a Bible, and some even owned hymnals.[227]

When Johann Adam's eldest son Jacob reached his thirteenth birthday, his father decided it was time for him to leave school. Although Jacob had been assisting his father to make barrels ever since Johann Adam had been granted the right to set up as a cooper in Hochfeld, Jacob would never have been allowed to take over his father's business unless he served a formal apprenticeship, worked as a journeyman, and was granted master status. Johann Adam therefore found him a place in the workshop of a master cooper in the nearby city of Heilbronn. The apprenticeship fee or *Lehrgeld* cost Johann Adam 10 florin, or the equivalent of about five months' wages for the apprentice. Jacob spent three years as an apprentice before receiving his *Lehrbrief* or apprenticeship certificate. He then took to the road, working as a journeyman cooper wherever he could find employment. He knew he could not attain master status in his home village until his father or the other cooper there died or retired—and then only if granted the license by the village elders. His only other options to become a master were to save enough money to start his own business—an almost impossible feat—or to marry a cooper's widow, who needed a journeyman to run the family business.[228]

Anna Barbara withdrew Maria Rosina, her daughter from her first marriage, from school when she turned ten, or a few years earlier than Johann Adam had withdrawn Jacob. Anna Barbara kept her daughter home with her for two years, teaching her the domestic skills she would need as a wife. Then she arranged for Maria Rosina to become a domestic servant to a well-off family from a nearby village. For the next twelve years, Rosina worked for several different families while she saved the money that would permit her to marry. The family all recognized that the Heiratsgut it could afford to provide to this daughter would not be enough for her to attract a marriage offer and set up an independent home. This decade or so of work was a common life passage for late teens, girls as well as boys.[229]

* * *

A year after Anna Barbara's first marriage, her brother Michael married. Anna Barbara's parents were still both alive then, but were ready to enter semi-retirement. Anna Barbara was settled in her husband's house so her parents decided that as his Heiratsgut, Michael would receive part of the family house and one of the family's cultivated strips. One strip was not enough to support a married couple, but Michael's wife had also received a cultivated strip as part of her Heiratsgut. As they began to have children, they would need to acquire more land; either Michael would need to purchase some additional strips, or their parents would need to turn over more of the family land to the young couple as they moved into semi-retirement.

It was unusual in southwest Germany for three or more generations of the same family to form a household. Retiring couples did everything they could to maintain their independence from their married children. When they turned over the family house or the bulk of the family farming land to their children, retiring couples negotiated detailed written agreements (*Leibgedingen*) concerning the resources that they would keep for themselves. If they were turning over the family house to one of their children and they had nowhere else to go themselves, then the agreement would delineate how the house would be divided. The retired couple might keep some rooms for their exclusive use or, in more crowded conditions, specify that they had the right to the corner of the Wohnstube or living room that was closest to the hearth.[230]

Anna Barbara's parents wrote into their agreement with her brother that they were reserving spaces in the shed and barn for their remaining animals and possessions. They held on to all the family's farming tools so that Michael would continue to be dependent on their good will. They reserved part of the garden plot for themselves, and they required Michael to supply them each year with a specified amount of wine, flour, salt, lard, and pork. Finally, the parents stipulated that if the two families could not get along in the same house, Michael would pay for separate accommodations for them elsewhere in the village.

After Anna Barbara's father died, her mother turned over the garden plot and the farming implements to her son. She was no longer able to cook for herself, but she specified in a new written agreement that Michael's wife was to feed her the same food that his family ate at each meal. She also required Michael to agree that his wife would nurse her, should she become incapacitated. The old lady continued to maintain a separate corner for herself in the Wohnstube and to eat separately from her son and his family until her death.[231]

*   *   *

One spring day in 1835, two men who were working near Johann Adam out in the fields heard him call out and then fall to the ground, clutching his chest. They carried him home and helped Anna Barbara to get him onto his bed, where he lingered for a few hours before dying of a heart attack. He was forty-six. Besides his widow and stepchildren, he left behind two sons, Johann Jacob and Johann Georg. He had been a loving husband, a kind father and stepfather, a good friend to his neighbors, and a man who had worn himself out trying to insure his family's welfare. Anna Barbara mourned him deeply, but nevertheless, she was only thirty-five when he died, and she still had to worry about her family's livelihood. She married again one year later; her new husband brought some land to the marriage, but no house, because his former home remained in the family of his deceased first wife.

Jacob, who was 23 years old, was not in Hochfeld when his father died. He was still on the road, working as a journeyman cooper and saving as much money as he could. He still hoped to settle in Hochfeld and marry some day, however. Two years earlier, he had fallen in love with a Hochfeld girl two years his junior. Maria Sophia's father, Georg Philipp Schramm, was a member of the Gericht and had been a good friend of Jacob's father. The couple had not approached their parents about a match because there was no point in doing so until Jacob could support her. He was now of an age to marry, and he hoped that he might inherit enough so that he could contract a marriage.[232]

After Johann Adam died, a Teilung was prepared to inventory his property and allocate his estate among his heirs. His assets consisted of the half-house, the outbuilding, furniture and household items, a cow, the half-morgen garden plot, and his share of the savings from the years he and Anna Barbara had scrimped along. The 2 morgen that he had farmed his entire adult life had come from his first wife's Heiratgut. They were the property of Jacob, Johann Adam's first wife's only heir, even though Johann Adam had enjoyed their use through his lifetime. Johann Adam's other assets were duly allocated between his two sons—at least on paper. In actuality, they remained under the control of Anna Barbara as the surviving spouse, even though she soon married again. The most valuable of Johann Adam's assets were the half-house and its outbuilding. At some point, it would have to be sold to satisfy the inheritance rights of the two children, unless one of them kept it and paid the other one for his equity in cash. However, until her last child reached majority, Anna Barbara had every intention of continuing to live in Johann Adam's house.[233]

Johann Jacob saw this moment as his best chance to make a match with Maria Sophia Schramm. He asked his uncle, who acted as his Pfleger, to negotiate a Heiratsgut with his stepmother out of his future inheritance so that he could approach Maria Sophia's father with a marriage proposal. But Anna Barbara was loathe to give up any of her husband's assets. She reluctantly agreed to release the 2 morgen of land that was Jacob's from his mother, but she refused to relinquish the half-house, and she pled an inability to pay Jacob a settlement out of her existing cash. She pointed out that he had already received his apprentice fees from his father, and that this Lehrgeld counted as part of his inheritance.[234]

His uncle did his best, but he was unable to negotiate a Heiratsgut that would permit Jacob to marry. It seemed clear that the amount of cash his stepmother would be able to advance from the family's small cash reserves was inadequate to buy a home and establish a household. The only way she could have raised enough cash to permit Jacob's marriage was to sell off the family half-house which was part of Jacob's eventual inheritance. But since his stepmother enjoyed use of marital assets until her death under the form of inheritance practiced in Hochfeld, Jacob knew that he could not force his stepmother out of the home. The only good news his uncle had to offer was that the Schultheiss had agreed to reserve Johann Adam's cooper license until Jacob was ready to set up his own shop. Defeated and disappointed, Jacob arranged for his uncle to farm his land in exchange for a share of the proceeds. Jacob returned to the road to earn more money, hoping he could save enough before his intended bride's family found her another husband.

Work

When Jacob Mann became an apprentice to the master cooper or Küfer in Heilbronn, he entered the powerful world of the German guilds. Although the guilds performed the same basic functions and operated in similar fashions across the German territories, they went by different names in different areas: *Zunft, Innung, Amt, Handwerk, Gilde, Gewerke, Gaffel, Bruderschaft, Zeche, Einung,* and *Mittel.* The legal authority of the guilds came from the city, territory, or principality in which they operated. By the time that Jacob became an apprentice in Heilbronn, his guild operated under the statutory guidelines of Württemberg.

The systems of guilds in China, India, and the Islamic world were already ancient when the first European guilds formed during the medieval era. Guilds continued to control trades and crafts in most German territories into the nineteenth century. They were associations of craftsmen who organized to regulate members, establish trade practices, dictate rules for entry into the guild, and discourage competition from outsiders. Membership in the guilds was limited to the masters. While guilds regulated the entry, training, and behavior of apprentices and journeymen, the non-masters were not actually members of the trade guilds. In some locales, the journeymen formed guild-type organizations of their own.

Guilds gained their start in the cities, where they became powerful political players. Out in the countryside, some guild organizations began to organize themselves following the Thirty Years' War. However, the rural and regional guilds never attained the same degree of political and economic power as the urban guilds.[235]

In one ecclesiastical territory in southern Württemberg,

> rural guilds sprang up in virtually every conveivable trade, including . . . Potters (1623) and the Butchers (1631); . . . those of the Teamsters, Blacksmiths, and Locksmiths (1668), Tailors (1672), Shoemakers and Tanners (1675), Bathhouse-keepers and Barber-surgeons (1685), Cabinetmakers, Glassmakers, Coopers, Painters, Gunsmiths, Cutlers, and Ropemakers (1689), Bakers (1690), Beerbrewers (1695), Millers (1698), Carpenters, and Masons (1700). To be sure, all of these trades had already been practiced for centuries, but their organization into guilds suggests an enhanced importance of rural industries, and a greater ability to compete openly (and effectively) with their urban counterparts.[236]

The rural guilds were organized into district *Laden* or guild lodges, which had jurisdiction over all the villages and any larger towns within the district. Until 1828 in Württemberg, these *Laden* controlled not just the trades and crafts, but almost all forms of economic activity, including sheep herding, wine making, fishing, chimney sweeping, working as a sailor, painting, even making music. The Laden also regulated shops that sold such products as cloth, garments, hides, leather, spices, dyes, chemicals, metal, and foodstuffs. In Württemberg, merchants and shopkeepers remained under the control of guilds as late as 1862.[237]

Guilds had several sources of income such as membership fees (*Meistergeld*) on new masters, fines on members for infraction of guild rules, and the interest on guild funds. From these funds, they provided a variety of social services to their members. They offered relief to their poorest members during illnesses, and they paid for their burial. They paid relief to the families of deceased members. They handled legal expenses for members and for the guild itself. They also subsidized the travels of journeymen during their *Wanderjahr*, the year after craftsmen finished their apprenticeship and took to the road to work in the shops of one or more masters.[238]

Guilds scrupulously guarded the honor of their organizations, both by carefully controlling membership and by regulating the behavior of their members. They attempted, not always successfully, to protect the guild's reputation by establishing quality standards for guild products, employing inspectors to review the work of guild members, and occasionally fining or expelling members who failed to meet these standards. Guilds also policed the morals of their members. Masters who deserted their wives or were caught in adulterous acts were thrown out of the guild. They were enjoined from associating with dishonorable individuals such as executioners or skinners, and they were forbidden to marry women whom the guild deemed not honorable or who had been born out of wedlock. They were also not allowed to accept apprentices who lacked documents to prove their legitimate births.[239]

As the population grew and competition made it more difficult to earn a living, guilds identified and brought charges against non-guild members who attempted to compete in a guild's territory. They also made it almost impossible for outsiders to be accepted as apprentices; for example, applicants whose fathers were not themselves masters were charged exorbitant entry fees.

Once apprentices completed their training years, they were required to take to the road, working in the workshops of other masters to learn new methods and to perfect their craft. This period of travel is the basis for the term "journeyman"; it referred to a man who had completed his training, spent his time journeying on the road (the *Wanderjahr*), and was qualified to become a master. It was expensive for a journeyman to become a master, and usually his best opportunity was in his own home village—assuming there was a master vacancy there. Masters were required to be married, and journeyman were prohibited from being married, so normally a man simultaneously married and became a master, once he found a place.[240]

Many historians have argued that the powerful guilds became so entrenched and protectionist that they stifled innovation and retarded Germany's entry into the Industrial Revolution. In the well-documented worsted weaving industry in Württemberg's Black Forest region, they "controlled entry, output, employment, product selection, prices, and wages, and concertedly resisted competition and new techniques, resulting in the decline of worsted production after about 1800 and a late and difficult transition to factory production." After presenting additional examples of guild protectionism and conservatism, the historian concluded, "To an even greater extent than in other areas of Germany, therefore, industry in Württemberg was stagnating by 1800 partly because of the late survival of guild and merchant privileges."[241]

* * *

In 1835, the year that Johann Adam Mann died, the Badenese government conducted a census of the Hochfeld men's occupations and income for tax purposes. The tally showed that Hochfeld had one miller (*Müller*), three wagon builders (*Wagner*), two smithies (*Schmiede*), one butcher (*Metzger*), one baker (*Bäcker*), one innkeeper (*Wirte*), one peddler (*Krämer*), three carpenters (*Zimmerleute*), five shoemakers (*Schumacher*), 13 weavers (*Weber*), two tailors (*Schneider*), one bricklayer/stonemason (*Maurer*), one sackmaker (*Säckler*), one glassmaker (*Glaser*), one saddlemaker (*Sattler*), and two coopers (Küfer) including Johann Adam himself. These individuals were all subject to the rules of their rural guilds, which held jurisdiction over several villages in the area.[242]

In addition to the trade and craft occupations, many Hochfeld men held one or more positions under the authority of the village council, which were previously discussed in Chapter Five. Hochfeld lacked some specialized craftsmen; for these, the villagers traveled elsewhere, just as residents of other villages came to Hochfeld if their village lacked a craft that Hochfeld had. Some examples of these other crafts were locksmiths (*Schlösser*), cutlers (*Messerschmieden*), gunsmiths (*Büchsenmacher*), ropemakers (*Seiler*), barber-surgeons (*Chirurgus*), and potters (*Töpfer*).[243]

Hochfeld's ordinances required the villagers to buy only from Hochfeld craftsmen as long as one was represented in town. Nevertheless, few of the local craftsmen could earn all their living from their guild occupations. Most men also farmed some land. In the nineteenth century, construction work had begun to eclipse the crafts as an important source of income, and even some of the Hochfeld craftsmen spent part of the year on the road, working on road, bridge, and other building projects. After he became a journeyman cooper, Jacob Mann periodically joined construction crews when he was between employers as a cooper.

The income of local craftsmen had deteriorated in the late seventeenth and the eighteenth century as a result of increased competition. Even though the village council and the craft guilds attempted to prevent an increase in the number of craft masters, they were unable to withstand the intense pressure to grant more licenses. Across the Grand Duchy of Baden, the number of master tailors in Baden grew by 17 percent between 1810 and 1844; the number of master carpenters grew by 36 percent, master masons by 68 percent, and master cabinetmakers by 86 percent during the same period.[244]

Figure 23. Village butcher.

In 1835 Württemberg already contained nearly one master craftworker for every fourteen residents, a ratio far too high to permit a decent standard of living to masters, most of whom had little or no working capital. Baden reached the same point a decade later. The ranks of the masters there swelled by more than 20 percent during the 1830s and 1840s, approximately twice the growth rate of the general population. By 1844 Baden had one master for every thirteen people. Nine in ten masters had no working capital at all, and that proportion rose still higher in the most populous trades . . . Marginal producers, such as the nominal masters, lived at the edge of calamity . . . [245]

Of all the men in Hochfeld, the miller was the richest in the village as well as one of its most important Richter. In addition to operating his mill, Kilian Lipp was one of the three largest holders of farming land in the village. Because they represented such a good source of income, the mills in many villages were owned by the local lord, who severely punished any villager caught grinding his own grain. The lords who owned mills leased them out or hired millers, who seldom achieved the status or wealth of the men who had been able to purchase or construct a mill on their own.

In Hochfeld, the Steinweg family did not own the mill. During the economic dislocations after the Thirty Years' War, an ancestor of Kilian's had taken advantage of the Freiherr's labor and cash shortages and struck a deal with the lord. This ancestor agreed to construct a new mill at his own expense in exchange for the right to own and run it himself. The mill had remained in the family ever since. Hochfeld's miller was a well-respected leader of the community, but this was not the case in all villages. Because it was so easy for millers to rob their customers by siphoning off part of their grain, the occupation of miller was sometimes considered dishonorable.[246]

The Hochfeld innkeeper was almost as wealthy as the miller. While he owned little land, he had other assets that were just as valuable: the largest building in the community, a substantial stable, and significant numbers of horses, cows, and oxen. He was also the largest employer of servants and other staff in the village. Due to the constant flow of travelers through his doors, he was the most knowledgeable man in the village concerning village news and worldly affairs. The Hochfeld innkeeper was from a Wimpfen family, and he had only purchased the local inn about fifteen years earlier. The prior innkeeper had been a drunkard who allowed the inn to fall into disrepair. As the inn declined and the quality of food and drink deteriorated, respectable villagers stopped going there. The village council finally took away the former innkeeper's license to operate. The current innkeeper, whose father was himself a wealthy innkeeper in Wimpfen, had renovated the Hochfeld building, married the daughter of a Hochfeld Richter, and reestablished the inn's good reputation. He cemented the good will and regular patronage of the village leaders by reserving the best table, next to the fire, for their sole use. Middling villagers used other tables, while the day laborers and other marginal individuals were directed to the table near the kitchen.[247]

The Hochfeld farmers who held the most land came next in the tax listing; they are discussed later in this chapter. Had Hochfeld been large enough to have one or more substantial merchants, they would have been included in the top village earners. However, the village had no such merchants, only the Jewish peddler, and he was near the bottom of the scale in terms of wealth and status. Therefore, craftsmen whose trade required considerable skill, such as the butcher and the wagon maker, comprised the next tier of income level and social prestige. Next came the crafts that required fewer skills, yielded less income, and commanded less respect, such as the tailors and the smiths. The lowest craft on the income and prestige scale was weaving. After the craftsmen came the day laborers and the servants, then finally the herders—cattle herding considered slightly more prestigious than shepherding or hog-keeping.

The village pastor was not part of the village occupational ranking because he was an outsider whose social group was primarily comprised of other pastor families in the area. In addition to running his parish, the pastor supervised the village school teacher and monitored the moral conduct of his parishioners, a responsibility he discharged as late as the nineteenth century. Pastors were educated in one of the divinity schools such as the University of Tübingen, where they established a network of peers. Some pastors remained in one village for their entire working lives, but others moved from church to church. They tended to find their wives among the daughters of other pastors, and their sons often followed their father into the profession. A pastor's economic status was based on the wealth of his parish. In villages like Hochfeld, some of the pastor's income came from tithes, but another important part of came from the harvest. Village pastors were often granted a parcel of land as a condition of their appointments, so they were as dependent on agricultural conditions as their parishioners. By the seventeenth century, few pastors were impoverished, and in cities, pastors' income was on a par with the city councilors or high-level municipal advisors.[248]

Until the Badenese educational reforms of the nineteenth century, Hochfeld's schoolteacher enjoyed little status and less income, as was the case all over southwest Germany. He worked under the supervision of the pastor, since his primary job was to give the children religious training. A large part of his income derived from his collateral duties. He usually served as the church sacristan; as such, his responsibilities included church building maintenance, acting as assistant to the pastor, and serving as the village scribe at court and other village meetings. In addition, he frequently served as choirmaster and organist. It is not surprising, therefore, that the musical skills of candidates for the position were often valued more highly than their academic knowledge or teaching experience.

Hochfeld provided its schoolmaster a dwelling with a small garden, but the dwelling also served as the village school. He also received a small monthly payment from the parents of each child, so that his income dropped when parents pulled their children out of school during the planting and harvesting seasons. To keep the schoolmaster from starving, the Freiherr provided him an adequate allotment of wood and the villagers gave him a loaf of bread whenever he helped to conduct a burial, baptism, or wedding.[249]

Prior to the nineteenth century, the Hochfeld schoolmaster was typically a community member with little education himself who received his appointment from the village Gericht. The schoolmaster who served Hochfeld in 1817, however, was a well-educated man. He had completed his pastoral training, but had not yet obtained a church of his own. He suffered daily humiliations under the supervision of Pastor Pringsauff, who ordered him about in public and assigned him numerous menial tasks. Even though Baden had passed a series of educational reforms in 1803 to improve the quality of schooling and the skills and income of the schoolmaster, pastors were able to maintain their firm control over schools and schoolmasters until as late as the 1860s.[250]

By the middle of the nineteenth century, teaching salaries had improved enough, even in villages, that teachers were able to forego the many collateral duties that had previously been necessary in order to survive. Usually the only supplementary duty they still performed was as the village secretary during council meetings. As of 1857, the average teaching salary in Baden was 250 florin, while urban salaries were much higher. This meant that the typical village teacher now earned slightly more than an unskilled laborer, but less than a full-time craftsman. However, this level of income was at least a living wage, and his low salary was balanced by the fact that his job tenure was generally secure. Perhaps as important as his improved salary was the schoolteacher's improved status and standing in the community.[251]

As previously discussed, the occupations of miller and innkeeper, while lucrative, had a taint of dishonor in some locales because of some individuals' shoddy or dishonest practices. There were other occupations that were dishonorable in every village and territory. These included executioners, skinners, grave-diggers, latrine-cleaners, and brothel-keepers. Others that were often considered dishonorable were bathhouse operator, barber-surgeons, actors, night watchmen, and bailiffs. In some locations, the low-status occupations of linen weaving and shepherding also fell into this category.[252]

Hochfeld had never had a resident executioner because the Freiherr von Steinweg had chosen to erect his gallows outside one of his other villages. While an executioner's primary duty was to perform beheadings, hangings, and corporal punishments, he had additional duties in some locales, including supervising prostitutes, driving lepers out of town, and cleaning out latrines. Hochfeld did have a skinner or *Knacker*, who performed a variety of dishonorable but necessary duties. He cleaned the village's latrines, he destroyed wild or distempered dogs, and he buried the corpses of suicides. His primary responsibility was to dispose of animal carcasses which were considered unfit for human consumption. This could not be done at the village slaughterhouse because it would pollute the villager's meat, so the skinner lived on the edge of the village, where he rendered the carcasses in his yard. The Hochfeld skinner owned no property of his own; his yard and house belonged to the Freiherr. Hochfeld had never granted Bürger status to their skinners, but on the other hand, their skinners were also exempt from many local taxes and fees. While executioners were sometimes wealthy, the skinner families were seldom as well-off. Hochfeld's skinner was from a skinner family in Württemberg, and he had held his Hochfeld post for 12 years. His wife was also from a skinner family. Their two sons assisted their father in his work.[253]

One of the questionable occupations was bathhouse keeper. The reason the occupation had such an unsavory reputation is that many bathhouses also offered lascivious massages, or even sex. Community bathhouses, which were common in villages during the middle ages, gradually disappeared beginning in the seventeenth century. Before it faded away, the occupation of bathhouse keeper fell under guild regulations. Villages typically supported their bathhouses through an annual distribution of grain to their operators, who were often relatively well-off members of the community. Not only did villagers frequent the bathhouse for bathing, but they visited the bathhouse operator for minor medical treatment. The last Hochfeld bathhouse keeper was trained to perform minor surgical procedures, set fractures, bleed patients, and treat kidney stones and hernias. Hochfeld's bathhouse was destroyed during the Thirty Years' War, and was never rebuilt.[254]

*   *   *

The 1835 tax listing of Hochfeld men by occupation listed 16 men who were full-time farmers or *Bauern* (singular is *Bauer*). Full-time farming was most village men's highest ambition, although few men had enough land for farming to be their sole occupation. Of the five wealthiest villagers in Hochfeld, three including the Schultheiss were farmers. Earlier, at the beginning of the eighteenth century, Hochfeld's craftsmen had been just as likely to be village leaders as the farmers. But by the end of the eighteenth century, it was the wealthy farmers who held most of the village offices and possessed most of the power.[255]

> The dualism of agriculture and petty commodity production gave way to a tripartite structure composed of relatively wealthy landowners, locally resident craftsmen (whose collective and individual wealth had for the most part been eroded), and a mobile group of workers available for seasonal opportunities in agriculture and construction. This last group grew throughout the nineteenth century, absorbing most of the 70 percent increase in population to 1870. By then, there were 220 households [in the village of Neckarhausen], and the average amount of land available for each of them had fallen by two-thirds, to around 6 acres. By the end of the eighteenth century, local village power was firmly in the hands of the landed agricultural producers.[256]

The typical Bürger in a southwest German village did not farm the same amount of land his entire adult life. Instead, his parents began to dole out parcels as he matured and as the parents gradually retired. A young man would start with a very small parcel, then buy, lease, or be ceded more from the elder generation. Then, once a Bürger's children were ready to set up their own families, he would gradually begin the process of turning over parts of his land holdings to the next generation. The typical life pattern was that as a young husband, a Bürger would supplement his income with his family trade—for example, carpenter, mason, or shoemaker. If he was lucky, eventually he could cease working in trades and crafts as he acquired more land. One or two of his sons, meanwhile, would by then be ready to take over the family trade.[257]

One can identify those fortunate individuals who were able to farm full-time by looking at their family records in the church book or *Kirchenbuch*, because most men were consistently listed by occupation or by their village office. Over time, their designation would change with their circumstances. For example, a man who was listed as a *Bürger und Schuhmacher* on the baptismal records for his first children was almost certainly earning part of his income by farming, but he was principally known at that point as a shoemaker. Later, if he were elected to the village council, he would begin to be listed as a *Bürger und Gericht*. A man who was listed as a *Bürger und Bauer* was probably lucky enough to farm full-time.[258]

A family patriarch turned over his land gradually to his children—not only to accommodate his own gradual retirement, but also to exercise continuing control over the next generation. Sonya Salamon studied the persistence of this practice among German immigrants to America; she observed that "[c]ross-culturally, the elderly in agrarian societies play a sort of game in which personal resources are gradually dealt out to assure continued respect, sociability, and obligation on the part of the children."[259]

A detailed study of a village in Württemberg documented the same practice:

> Everything had to be balanced by the commitment to 'equalizing' all the children, at least in the end. This always meant setting up each of them with meager resources at the beginning, which kept the younger generation dependent . . . in many ways. Daughters were offered a bit more to counter the pull of their households into the orbit of their husbands' families. Everyone understood that property was laden with obligation, and any child who forgot that would receive a stern lecture from the Schultheiss or pastor . . . [P]arents dribbled out resources over a very long period of time, keeping tight reins on their children. Those who did not show the right degree of filial piety and respect or looked too longingly at the parents' land would be brought up sharply. Care was always exercised on the part of the senior generation to maintain authority and independence as long as they could.[260]

Hochfeld farmers followed the system of three-course crop rotation that European farmers had employed since the Middle Ages. The village left one-third of its field strips fallow each year. The village livestock was turned loose in the fallow field so that their manure would help to restore the land's fertility. The following year, the villagers planted winter-sown crops such as wheat and rye on the rested fields. On the third part of their land, they planted spring-sown crops such as barley and oats. They also planted nitrogen-fixing legumes, such as beans and peas. Farmers knew that these legumes improved the soil, although they did not understand why until the agricultural research advances of the late nineteenth century.[261]

Crop yields in Germany up to the end of the eighteenth century were abysmal; one estimate put the average seed-yield ratio across Germany at 1:4.5, while another put it at 1:5. This means that eighteenth-century farmers could expect to reap a yield between 4 and 5 times greater than the amount they sowed. One scientist has estimated that a family of five with an average-size holding could feed itself and 1.4 other persons if they achieved a seed-yield ratio of 1:4. But if the seed-yield ratio dropped to 1:3 as it could in a bad year, the family would barely be able to feed itself. Such a low average ratio meant that that the village farmers could generally feed the village during most of the eighteenth century, but have little if anything left to support a market economy.

By the end of the century, the burgeoning population made it increasingly difficult for farmers following traditional farming practices to feed their villages. Farmers developed marginal land, such as marsh or steep hillsides, to increase the supply of arable land, but it was not enough. Southwest German farmers, formerly suspicious of any innovations, were forced to experiment with new methods and processes. They substituted oxen for horses, tried out new crops in the three-course rotation, and intensified the use of stall feeding. The most productive change was stall feeding, which increased the farmers' supply of manure and allowed it to be applied exactly where they needed it. The better-fertilized fields immediately yielded better results; seed-yield ratios increased in southern Germany to 1:15 for rye, 1:7 for wheat, 1:8 for barley, and 1:9 for oats.[262]

Grains such as oats, barley, and spelt were the most common crops grown in southwest Germany, but they were not the only crops. Three Hochfeld farmers grew wine grapes on the hilly slopes overlooking the Neckar River. Many farmers grew fruit trees, such as apples and cherries; the fruit was dried and then consumed during the winter months. Vegetables other than turnips were seldom grown before the nineteenth century, and played a marginal role in farming and nutrition. By the early nineteenth century, market crops played a greater role in the Hochfeld area: hemp, chicory, and even tobacco. The flax needed for the growing weaving industry, however, was not grown in the Kraichgau, but was imported from further north.[263]

One crop that grew in importance in the eighteenth and nineteenth centuries was the potato. Potatoes had been introduced to Germany in the late sixteenth century, but most farmers refused to plant it; it was considered unfit for human consumption. It was not until the famine of the early 1770s that the potato became an important crop—and even then, some areas of southwest Germany such as Swabia continued to use it solely as animal feed.

Men were responsible for plowing and planting the fields, but women took over some of the tasks that arose or increased in importance with the innovations of the late eighteenth and early ninteenth century. The increased cultivation of root crops—potatoes, beets, and turnips—fell primarily to the women. They started the plants in their gardens, then moved them to the fields. They used poking sticks to plant potatoes in the furrows between the plowed rows, and they were responsible for the labor-intensive maintenance of the root crops—using hand hoes to weed and aerate the plants. Women shared this work with their children and any servants. They also hauled the fodder to feed the animals, which were now kept in stalls. All over the hills around Hochfeld, women could be seen each day, cutting the clover and alfalfa and carrying it down to the village in large kerchiefs on top of their heads.[264]

Figure 24. A woman cuts fodder.

Between 1860 and 1880, perhaps driven partly by the reduced population pressure, German farmers turned increasingly to the market as a result of several factors. First, the vast out-migration of Germans to the East and the Americas during the 1840s and 1850s had reduced the number of mouths to be fed. Second, under-employed villagers had begun to move into the cities to take up work in the nascent industrial sector. The city dwellers and construction workers could not grow their own food, so farmers benefited from increased prices for their harvests. "Although most farmers continued to produce much of their own food, concern had shifted to the supply of urban consumers. With the cash they received for their product, the German farmers acquired a taste for factory-made goods and other physical evidences of a higher standard of living."[265]

*   *   *

Side by side with the centuries-old practices of subsistence farming, change-resistant village power structures, guild rules, and village-based economies, a quiet revolution was gradually taking place. Historians and economists call this revolution proto-industrialization, and it formed the bridge between the traditional agrarian culture and a modern, industrialized society. Its first traces can be detected as early as the late sixteenth century, but its acme was the eighteenth and early nineteenth centuries. Proto-industrialization, or the rise of cottage industries, was made possible by the growing class of land-poor or landless peasants, urgently seeking a solution to their under-employment. Entrepreneurs from the cities' merchant class had attempted to introduce innovations into the crafts that would increase the supply of products, reduce costs, and transition to a broad, market-based economy. However, the guilds in the cities had a great deal invested in the *status quo*, one in which they controlled their members' output, the quality of their work, and the prices they charged in order to equalize the income of their members. When they refused to cooperate with the entrepreneurs, these capitalists simply bypassed them. They developed a network of workers from the under-employed out in the countryside.[266]

There were no modern factories during this early period. Workers remained in their own homes, in villages across Germany, and the new merchant entrepreneurs took the work to them. Proto-industrialization was a "putting out" system in which the merchants provided their laborers raw materials and then paid them at piece-work rates for their finished products. Rural workers in different areas of Germany specialized in various products, including yarn or thread, lace, ropes, hosiery, gloves, straw-plaiting, glass, and metal products such as nails, but the most important products in the Hochfeld area and much of southwest Germany were textiles—from wool, cotton, and especially flax. Despite their power, weaving guilds found that they were unable to prevent the proliferation of unlicensed weavers because these families operated outside the village economy. In Baden, the number of master linen weavers increased by 51 percent between 1810 and 1844, but the number of non-master linen weavers and helpers increased by 92 percent. As of 1844, more than 99 percent of the linen weavers lacked any working capital of their own; they were totally dependent on the merchant capitalists.[267]

Proto-industrialization had a radical impact on the lifestyle of the poor rural working families in southwest Germany, to say nothing of village culture. The average age at which couples married dropped because they no longer had to wait until they had enough land, money, or a craft license. The village council lost some of its control over young adults because couples no longer needed their approval to form a family. Where traditionally a man had chosen a wife based on family recommendations, compatibility of backgrounds, and a woman's relative respectability and honor, now a poor man was as likely to marry a woman for her craft skills and income potential. Their family's future survival would be based as much on her economic activity as his.

Family size increased for couples engaged in proto-industrial work. In a family whose primary income came from agriculture, every child was another mouth to feed, who contributed little to the family's coffers. In proto-industrial families, however, every child was another worker — in fact, the more children, the higher the family income. The children also stayed with their birth families later than their counterparts in agricultural families because they made more when they could work together as a group.

The life of the proto-industrial family was a drudgery. For long hours every day, each member of the family worked at the looms or other tools.

> In bad times the longest working day does not suffice; the weavers who have between two and four dependent children fall heavily into debt and must regularly resort to poor relief. Only when two or three children sit at the loom can debts be repaid and savings made. If the brothers and sisters remain within the family and conduct an orderly economy, this offers a period when savings are possible . . . With the birth of children, the parents become poor; with their maturation, they become rich, and with their marriage [the parents] fall back into misery.[268]

Figure 25. Girl at loom.

One branch of the Mann family in Hochfeld had become weavers. One of Johann Adam's sisters became a full-time weaver in 1810 along with her husband and children. Johann Adam and his first wife had seriously considered turning to weaving during the winter of 1814. His harvest had been poor that year, he had not yet been granted his cooper's license, and his wife was expecting their fifth child. But when the little girl was born, he looked at her tiny hands and sweet face and decided that he could not condemn her to a life at the linen loom. He wanted her to enjoy at least a short period of childhood before she assumed work responsibilities. Two years later, the little girl died along with her mother and most of her siblings. Until the day he died, Johann Adam would revisit his 1814 decision and wonder whether he could have saved his family if they had accepted the weaving life.

The Village Year

Christmas Eve dawned cold but clear in 1836. Johann Jacob Mann was back in Hochfeld for the holiday season. His father had been dead almost two years, and Jacob continued to spend most of his time out of the village, working as a journeyman cooper for a series of masters. He was still trying to save enough money to settle back in Hochfeld, marry his sweetheart, and establish his own cooperage.

Jacob was attending *Heiligabend* or Christmas Eve services in Hochfeld's Evangelisch church, where his parents had been married and he had been baptized. While he had never had much use for religion, he had always loved the Christmas Eve service. The church, filled with the sight and smell of evergreen boughs, took him back to his earliest memories as a small boy. He remembered sitting snugly between his parents in the church, dark and mysterious but for the multitude of glowing candles. This year as always, the schoolmaster was leading the older village boys in singing. The congregation joined the choir as each heart gladdened with the sound of the familiar and well-beloved German hymns.[269]

The church season of Advent—the season to prepare for the coming of the Christ child—began on the first Sunday after November 26; Advent also marked the beginning of the Christian year. The liturgical calendar, of course, was established by the Catholic Church. However, when the Evangelisch territorial princes and lords established their own state churches, they adopted the familiar liturgical cycle—although with many variations across the German Protestant lands. The Evangelisch churches downplayed the Catholic veneration of the saints, but they adapted and incorporated many of the festivities and customs which had always taken place on the saints' days. Well into the twentieth century, both Catholic and Evangelisch villages organized their year around the liturgical calendar.

The first Sunday of Advent was called *Grüner Sonntag* or Green Sunday. The Hochfeld villagers greeted the approach of the Christmas season by placing one evergreen bough on the altar of their church. The village custom was to add more greens and berries to the church decorations on each of the four Sundays of Advent, culminating with a final round of decoration and the lighting of candles throughout the church on Christmas Eve. At Christmas, the Freiherr von Steinweg granted the villagers a brief period of latitude in harvesting branches from his forests. Few villagers could afford to purchase and set up trees in their own houses, but all of them decorated their homes with a bough or two of evergreen. In the square in front of the church, the village men set up a large tree and decorated it with nuts, berries, and moss. After the Heiligabend service, the villagers gathered around the tree to watch the men place lighted candles on its boughs as the villagers enjoyed roasted chestnuts and *Glugwein*, warm spiced wine.[270]

The first documented use of evergreen trees to celebrate Christmas in Germany dated back to Alsace in the 1700s, but the practice of using evergreen boughs extended back to pagan times. Evergreen trees, which remained green and alive during the bleak winters, symbolized villagers' hopes for surviving the winter season and ushering in the new life of spring once more. Some early Evangelisch writers gave Martin Luther himself the credit for incorporating the formerly pagan Christmas tree into Christian worship. Whether or not Luther was actually responsible, it is undisputed that a sixteenth-century Alsatian pastor decided to incorporate the use of evergreens at Christmas in order to co-opt villagers' ancient superstitions. The tree that symbolized life therefore became the symbol of the man of life, Christ himself.

Hochfeld's children did not have to wait to receive gifts from a magical visitor on Christmas night. On December 5, called *Nikolausabend* or St. Nicholas's Eve, the children could barely sleep; they knew that St. Nicholas would arrive during the night and leave them gifts. Even the poorest families struggled to insure that their children would at least find a few nuts or an apple waiting for them the next day. Johann Adam Mann, Jacob's father, had woodworking skills and tools because he had trained as a cooper. Each year beginning in October, after the children had gone to sleep, he labored by the kitchen fire to make each of his children a small toy for *Nikolaustag* from his scraps of wood. Jacob still had the top that his father had made for him when he was five years old.

The last day of the Christmas season, January 6, was *Dreikönigstag* or Three Kings' Day, commemorating the day when the three kings arrived in Bethlehem to worship the Christ child and to bring him their gifts. In Hochfeld, the village boys, led by one with a star-topped pole, paraded through the streets singing carols and chalking the letters C, M, and B for Kings Caspar, Melchoir, and Balthasar above the doorway of the houses and stables. The superstition was that buildings marked by the kings' initials would be protected from lightning in the coming year.[271]

The chalking was just one of many superstitions associated with the Christmas season. In Swabian villages, south of Hochfeld, villagers decorated their fruit trees with leftovers from the Christmas meal: apples were hung, pastries were balanced between branches, nutshells were buried at the trees' bases, and the remains of Christmas drinks were sprinkled on the roots; in some villages, the trees were also decorated with garlands of straw. The villagers believed that this would insure a bounteous fruit harvest in the coming season. In the days leading up to Christmas, housewives scrubbed down their homes in order to purge them of any evil spirits, after which they spiritually cleansed the house with holy water and incense. Some villages had a custom of keeping hearth fires burning continuously throughout the Christmas season, extinguishing the fires only on Three Kings' Day; they then sprinkled the ash on their fields and gardens. Also on Three Kings' Day, villagers removed all of the season's decorations from their homes and consumed any remaining holiday foods. They believed that eradicating all signs of Christmas on the last day of the season would prevent misfortune in the coming year.[272]

The mixing of paganism and Christianity that characterized the German Christmas season affected the villagers throughout all the seasons of the village year. Dependent for their mostly marginal existence on the vagaries of weather and on the health of themselves, their crops, and their animals, the villagers dared not risk disaster by giving up the time-honored beliefs and customs handed down from their pre-Christian ancestors. The superstitions were all that the pagan ancestors had had at their disposal to attempt to control the mysterious forces of nature—or at least to avert the most catastrophic events. Conservative as always, the Early Modern Germans saw no reason to change their practices just because of Christianity; in fact, they saw no conflict between their old beliefs and their Christian faith. If their better-educated pastors objected to certain customs as sacrilege, the villagers simply went underground and continued the old practices.[273]

> Countrywomen might give way to resignation, to bitterness, to rage, but rarely to defeat. They found ways to explain, to justify, and to give value to their lives. Peasant women took comfort from their faith. They believed that they could influence the uncontrollable, even make sense of and bring order to the often brutal and capricious life of the countryside by spells and prayers, by ancient explanations and rituals. Countrywomen and men made no clear distinctions between material and spiritual reality, between the natural and the supernatural, the living and the dead, the real and the imaginary. This was a world of 'wishing' as countrywomen described it in their folktales. This was a world in which ghosts might appear at the fireside for wine once a year, a dog could turn into a raven, the croaking of a frog foretold the future, and a blue bead would keep away 'the evil eye.' Well into the twentieth century, peasant women and men continued to value and attempted to influence this world of the spirits. Thus they perpetuated age-old beliefs and customs in the modern countryside and in the towns and cities to which they migrated.

This world of older beliefs and customs did not conflict with the comforts of more formal religion. The shrines of Christian saints were built over older places of worship, and the Christian holy days came to coincide with those honoring other goddesses and gods and with days honoring the natural phenomena of the agricultural year, like the solstices. Formal religion gave countrywomen comfort in other ways. It explained and justified the harshness of life, honored their activities, and offered rewards in the future. Divine displeasure could explain a plague of caterpillars or an earthquake. A divine plan could make their place in the village world seem essential and honorable.[274]

*   *   *

Epiphany was the church season that lasted from Dreikönigstag until Lent. It coincided with the coldest, wettest, and darkest days in the Hochfeld year. Families spent most of their time huddled around the kitchen hearth, which was usually their only source of heat and light. They burned dung or peat, which they had dug during the autumn months and set aside to dry. Like the animals hibernating out in the woods to pass the winter season, the villagers went to bed early on the dark days, huddled under their quilts for warmth. Men spent this period on indoor work such as repairing equipment or perhaps constructing a bench or table for the house. Women, even those not from full-time weaving families, began to process the wool or flax from the last season; they carded, spun, wove, and sewed clothes and household linens.[275]

In the brief years before most children hired out as servants or began an apprenticeship, their pastimes once their chores were done were not much different than those of today's children. In the winter, they had snowball fights, they made snowmen, and they sledded or ice skated. Around the fire at night, their parents told them many of the same fairy tales that children still listen to today, such as *"Rumpelstilzchen," "Hänsel und Gretel," "Sneewittchen"* (Snow White), and *"Aschenputtel"* (Cinderella). Or the parents and elder siblings teased the younger children with riddles and tongue-twisters, like this one:

> *Blaukraut bleibt Blaukraut[†]*
> *und Brautkleid bleibt Brautkleid.*
>
> (Red cabbage is always red cabbage,
> And a bride's dress is always a bride's dress.)

The childrens' toys, though usually few in number, might include rattles, dolls, wagons, balls, tops, hoops, and stilts. In the summer, the children could be found playing ball, hide and seek, musical chairs, and freeze. They caught and tamed birds and small animals, jumped rope, played marbles,

---

[†] Red cabbage is referred to as "blue" (*blau*) in southern Germany because cooked red cabbage turns a purplish color if cooked without wine or vinegar.

and even flew kites. And as we have seen, they played a major part in village festivals, such as Three Kings' Day.[276]

During the weeks between Christmas and Lent, the young women in many villages gathered together in the evenings at one of their homes to spin, sew, and knit. These gatherings were known by a variety of names in

Figure 26. Children and their sled.

different areas of Germany: *Spinnstube, Lichtstube, Kaiserloß*, and *Vorsizt* to list just a few. It was a rare opportunity for the young women to enjoy conversation, gossiping, laughing, and singing as they worked. In some villages, primarily those with a high concentration of weaving families, the young men held their own separate *Spinnstuben*. The participants in the Spinnstuben gathered at a designated house after the evening meal and worked together until about 9 o'clock. Often, the village's young men would drop by a female Spinnstube around 9 o'clock to socialize with the young women for an hour or so, after which the participants all returned to their homes. On the final Spinnstube gathering of each year, participants often enjoyed a party with beer, sausages, and cakes.

These gatherings made many village elders nervous because of the threat they represented to the traditional ways. If young men and women were coming together to socialize, they feared the participants' parents would lose their influence over marriage decisions. As well, they feared that the gatherings provided an opportunity for participants to engage in sexual liaisons. Many villages tried to bann these gatherings, with little success, so they simply coopted them; they designated one set of parents who would host and supervise the gatherings in their home, in return for a small payment. Not just the village authorities were concerned about this institution; the church and the German territories also attempted to control, regulate, or abolish the gatherings. Nevertheless, the institution was so important to the young generation, and provided such a rare opportunity for informal social get-togethers of singles, that the Spinnstuben survived in some villages well into the twentieth century.[277]

*　　*　　*

Figure 27. Spring plowing begins.

Forty days after Christmas Day came *Lichtmess*, known in English as Candlemas, which fell on February 2. The full German name for the day was Mariä Lichtmess, and it commemorated the fortieth day after Jesus' birth, when his mother was churched and could again enter the synagogue. On Lichtmess, all the villagers took bunches of candles to the church to be blessed—the women tapers, the men heavy utility pillars. The candles would be used throughout the year—to mark celebrations, to protect the house during bad storms, and to mark the births of babies and the passing of the dead.[278]

As weather permitted, all the adults with land began their plowing after Lichtmess, the women leading the oxen while the men guided the plows. Traditionally, the villagers considered that Lichtmess marked the day when families could again eat by daylight rather than in the dark. It marked the point when families should still have half of the livestock fodder that they had put aside for their animals to get them through the winter. And it ushered in the frightening period when their' food supplies were at their lowest levels of the year. Housewives all watched their remaining stores with trepidation, planning how they would stretch the food to last until spring, when the garden's first plants could be harvested.[279]

Villagers believed that the weather on Lichtmess was a harbinger of the remaining length of the winter. One of their sayings was, "*Ist's zu Lichtmess mild und rein, wird's ein langer Winter sein.*" ("If Candlemas is mild and pure, Winter will be long for sure.") The villagers used hedgehogs to predict how many more weeks of winter weather they could expect. When the first wave of German immigrants arrived in Pennsylvania in the eighteenth century, there were no hedgehogs for them to use on Lichtmess, so they turned to the American native, the groundhog.[280]

Lichtmess was also considered the end of the working year for servants, laborers, and other hirelings including Jacob Mann. It was the day that they collected the last portion of their promised annual salary, and were free to find another employer. Jacob had spent the last year working for a cooper in Wimpfen, but he had decided to leave that master's workshop; Jacob found him unreasonably stingy and mean in his treatment of his employees. However, Jacob wanted to find a position near enough to Hochfeld so that he could come back occasionally to see his sweetheart, Maria Sophia Schramm. He was able to find a new position in the prosperous and growing city of Heilbronn, about 19 kilometers south of Hochfeld, and the city where he had completed his apprenticeship.[281]

*   *   *

The next celebration of the liturgical calendar was *Fastnacht*. It was named for the night before Lent (*die Fastzeit* or Fasting Time) began. The first day of *Fastzeit* was *Aschermittwoch* or Ash Wednesday. Following the Protestant Reformation, the *Fastnacht or Karneval* celebrations that took place in the week leading up to *Aschermittwoch* died away in the Evangelisch villages, although parades and celebrations once again became widespread across Germany in the Twentieth Century. However, in the Catholic Swabian villages south of Hochfeld, the week before Lent began was a time of riotous celebrations during the Early Modern period. The superstition and pagan symbolism, which marked the transition from winter to spring, played out in all its heathen splendor.[282]

Processions, masking, costuming, raucous dancing banish the spirits of winter so that the awakening, life-giving forces of spring may emerge unhindered. In some Swabian districts stuffed 'messengers of winter,' are banished by 'messengers of summer,' or an effigy of winter is dragged through the village on a sled and deposited beyond the communal boundary. Carnival is also a time for asserting popular concepts of justice in role reversal, mock trials, the ridiculing of authority—and for gluttony: eating and drinking to excess signify a plentiful harvest. Though Carnival ended on Ash Wednesday, in many districts the celebration of fertility was carried forward to the first Sunday in Lent. On *Funken* Sunday villagers ignite hilltop pyres of scrap wood laboriously assembled by youths during the week of Carnival. Young couples dance around the fire or jump across the embers. In Leutkirch, Wangen, Blaubeuren, and elsewhere, villagers burned straw effigies of witches to symbolize the destruction of winter. Flaming discs and barrels are hurled into the air or sent rolling down hillsides as sun symbols in order to enhance fertility in the fields and among humans. Youths bearing torches run across fields sown with winter crops, encouraging the seeds to germinate, or around the village boundary to dispel the forces opposing life.[283]

After the Fastzeit season came *Ostern* or Easter. Ostern, the most important day in the Christian year, was celebrated just as joyously in Evangelisch villages as in Catholic ones. Easter was the day on which Christ was resurrected from the dead. The relationship between Easter's celebrations and symbolism and that of the villagers' early pagan ancestors was unmistakable. Easter is a movable feast day; it always falls on the first Sunday, after the first full moon, after the vernal equinox — the springtime date on which the hours of light and dark are equal. So the rising of Christ is celebrated in concert with the rebirth of nature. The long "death" of winter is over, and the world is reawakening. In Hochfeld, the housewives scrubbed down their houses in preparation for Easter Sunday, and they decorated their church and homes with candles, the first sprouts from the fields, flowering bulbs, budding branches of willow, and tufts of fresh new-mown grass. After the Easter Sunday service, the villagers all gathered around an enormous bonfire where they exchanged decorated eggs with their neighbors; there was a good-natured competition between the women concerning whose eggs were the most beautiful. In good years, the better-off families feasted on lamb, the sacrificial symbol of Christ crucified; but irrespective of family wealth, all the women tried to insure that their Easter meals were special.[284]

Festivals and customs relating to fertility continued from Easter to June 24 — St. John's Day or *Sommerjohanni*, also known as Midsummer's Day. On May 1, villages across Baden, Württemberg, and Bavaria celebrated the day around a May Tree or *Maibaum*. The young men in the village erected a tree trunk — in some cases, an actual tree — in the center of the village. They first hauled the selected tree trunk through the streets of the villages, boisterously singing, as the villagers followed along behind. They made sure that their path to the village square passed by the homes of all the prettiest young maidens in the town as a particular compliment to their beauty. After they gathered their crowd and honored their favorite girls, they moved on to the village square where they spent the late afternoon erecting the enormous and hard-to-handle trunk. While the villagers, beers in hand, watched in amusement, the young men then shinnied back up the pole to attach a series of cloth streamers — a contest in bravado and masculinity, ironic since the first *Maibäumer* in pagan times were fertility phallic symbols. In many villages, including Hochfeld, the day ended with an evening dance around the pole.[285]

*   *   *

On Midsummer Eve and Midsummer Day, an Early Modern spectator standing on any hillock in Württemberg or Baden would have seen bonfires in every direction: in village squares, at crossroads, on the hilltops themselves. Villagers gathered around the fires, wearing decorations of live mugwort and vervain, which they threw into the fire before leaving it. Likewise, the spectator would hear, carried on the wind, the cheerful sound of pots clanging, drums banging, bells ringing, voices shouting—every type of noise the villagers could devise in order to drive out the witches and spirits that they believed gathered in strength on Midsummer's Eve. Down in the villages, our spectator would see women once again decorating their homes with greens and drying the medicinal plants which they had collected on Midsummer's Eve. The women braved the dangers of gathering evil spirits to gather their plants because they believed that any plants gathered on Midsummer's Eve had magical powers to heal.[286]

To the early pagans who created the custom of Midsummer bonfires, the flames were both fertility rituals and symbols of purification. Their Early Modern descendants remained dedicated to the bonfire tradition, even if they were not specifically aware of their original symbolism. Writes one Early Modern historian, "People dance around them, jump over them, stare into them (to improve vision). Animals are driven through the embers. Invalid children are carried across them. The fields bathed in their glow become more fertile as do the fields where the smoke descends."[287]

In June 1837, Johann Jacob Mann came back to Hochfeld to visit his sweetheart and to participate in one of the village's best-loved Midsummer traditions. Every year, every household contributed a portion of straw. On Midsummer's Night after the sun set , the village's male inhabitants gathered at the top of the ridge that overlooked the Neckar River while the women clustered below them, near the river banks. The men sheathed an enormous wheel with the straw they had each brought to the gathering, using the remainder to make torches. From each side of the wheel, long wooden axles extended. When the wheel was ready, the Schultheiss used a torch to light the straw-covered wheel. Two young men, one on each side, grabbed the axles and began to guide it down the path to the river, followed by the cheering men and their torches. By the light of the wheel and the torches, the girls and women could track the progress of the wheel as it descended down the slope. From the other side of the river, cheering inhabitants from the village of Gundelsheim were also enjoying the annual spectacle.

The goal was to reach the river and extinguish the flaming wheel before the straw could burn out on its own. It was a long and difficult route down the river bank, and many years the two chosen young men were unable to maneuver the wheel fast enough. If the two succeeded, they earned bragging rights for the next year and several rounds of drinks at the tavern; if they failed, they could expect to be taunted all year long. In 1837, they made it all the way to the water, accompanied by cheers from both sides of the river. Their accomplishment meant that the village could collect a wagon-load of white wine from the area vineyards. More importantly, superstition dictated that the villagers could expect a bounteous harvest season.[288]

While Jacob was back in Hochfeld for St. John's Day, he and Maria Sophia had the first serious argument of their long relationship. Jacob had turned 25 earlier that year, and Maria Sophia was about to have her 23rd birthday. She felt as if she had been waiting forever for Jacob to ask her father for her hand in marriage. She pointed out that Jacob already had the 2 morgen of land that he had inherited from his mother, as well as the promise of the Schultheiss to give him his father's cooperage license when he was ready to return to Hochfeld. Many couples started with less, she reminded him. But Jacob argued that the only way they could establish a home before he had saved more money was to rent a cottage. His stepmother might live for another thirty years in the home that he would eventually inherit along with his half-brother. The farming land and the cooperage income would be adequate for the two of them to live, but they would be unable to save money for their own house. With each new baby, their survival would become more difficult.[289]

As it turned out, Jacob learned that another young man had been courting Maria Sophia. Johann Stephan Lipp, the son of Hochfeld's miller, had begun spending time with her during the winter Spinnstuben. When Jacob confronted Maria Sophia, she protested that she could never consider Stephan as a husband because she had promised her heart to Jacob. But Jacob was certain that Maria Sophia's father *could* consider Stephan's suit. As the son of one of the richest men in town, Stephan was a prestigious match.

In truth, Jacob was beginning to look at his life's plan with a skeptical eye. He was a handsome man, with his father's blue eyes and his mother's fine blond hair. He still loved Maria Sophia as much as he had when he was 18, but he could not help but notice that women were attracted to him. Also, Jacob was no longer certain that he really wanted to come back to Hochfeld to live. He found that he enjoyed the bustle of Heilbronn.

Heilbronn was one of the first German cities to industrialize. Beginning with the establishment of a large paper mill in the 1820s, so many factories had been established in Heilbronn that by 1836, it was referred to as the Swabish Liverpool. Jacob liked the city's energy and prosperity, and he rather liked the fact that most people were strangers to one another. He was not sure he wanted to give up this new freedom for the straitjacket of village life, where everyone knew him and all his business. Jacob's father, despite his financial worries, had been content with his lot; he had worked hard, but accepted what came. In contrast, Jacob's canny stepmother had always been on the lookout for ways to stretch her money, find new ways to bring in a few *pfennige*, and negotiate the best prices for what she sold and bought.

Jacob suspected that he was more like her than his father when it came to money. In Heilbronn, Jacob sensed the financial possibilities of a larger world, and he wondered how long before a life as a village cooper would stultify him.[290]

*   *   *

All the festivals and celebrations in the village year came only after day after day of unending labor. During the growing season, villagers were out of bed between 4 and 5 o'clock in the morning to tend to the animals. Their first meal was around 9 o'clock, their second in the late afternoon. Otherwise, they were working. The men completed sowing the fields by the end of March, and by the beginning of April, both men and women began the back-breaking tasks of hoeing, weeding, and mulching the field strips and the garden. Women climbed the hill to the fields each day to gather fodder for their animals and to spread the manure gathered from the stalls. During the spring season, they had litters to care for, born to any cows, goats, sheep, pigs, or poultry the family owned. After the baby cows and goats were weaned, the women used the mothers' milk to make cheese and butter. Most of the butter, cheese, and eggs were sold to produce the money to pay rent, taxes and fees. If that income was inadequate, the women might also hire themselves out as servants or laundresses. Likewise, it became increasingly common by the mid-nineteenth century for the village men to hire out in the building trades, at work sites outside the village; if so, all of the field work fell to the women in their absence. Besides all this agricultural work, women still had to care for the children, nurse any babies, and cook each day as well as clean and do laundry each week.[291]

Figure 28. A woman tends her baby in the fields.

When it came time to harvest, it normally fell to the men and their sickles or two-handed sythes to reap the grain. Women came behind them to bind and stack the sheaves, after which the cattle might be turned loose in the harvested fields to eat the stubble. The women also harvested any flax and hemp the family had grown, which they could use to make cloth and ropes, and they finished harvesting root vegetables and cabbages in the garden. They gathered nuts and fruit, preserving them by drying.

When the weather turned cool enough to prevent quick spoilage, usually in November, the family slaughtered one or more of their pigs and cows, if

they were fortunate enough to have any. If the family was too poor to afford
feed for their livestock over the winter, they would sell most or all of their
animals in the fall and purchase new ones in the spring. But for those
animals that they did slaughter, the women would insure that nothing went
to waste. The meat was smoked and hung from the rafters, away from
rodents, or packed in salt in barrels. The blood went into sausage along with
some of the grain. The lard was saved for winter cooking, when it would add
the all-important fat content to the diet. Pig carcasses were boiled to render
their hair, for brushes or a plaster ingredient, and pig feet were boiled for
their gelatin. Families with no animals to slaughter, or those which could not
afford to eat meat, could look forward to winter meals of bread, gruel, any
gathered nuts and fruit, and root vegetables—which included potatoes by
the late eighteenth century.[292]

Jacob had promised Maria Sophia that he would return to see her on the
first Sunday in October, when the village celebrated *Erntedankfest*,
Thanksgiving Day, with a special church service and village festival. But he
was unable to leave Heilbronn because his master had fallen behind in filling
orders for barrels for the year's beer and wine harvests. A week later, he
received a letter from her. Maria Sophia's father had accepted a proposal of
marriage from Johann Stephan Lipp on Maria Sophia's behalf. She was to be
married on Advent Sunday.

*   *   *

The last Sunday before Advent, also the final Sunday in the liturgical
year, was called *Totensonntag*. On this day, Evangelisch villages
commemorated all those villagers who had died during the previous year.[293]
Jacob Mann returned to Hochfeld for one last time just before *Totensonntag*.
He was leaving Hochfeld for good, and he wanted to be out of the village
before Maria Sophia married Stephan Lipp. Jacob had decided to emigrate to
America, where he could make a new start in a new land. While he liked
living and working in the city of Heilbronn, he recognized that he was
unlikely to be granted citizenship there, and even less likely to receive his
master's license there because he would then compete against the established
masters such as his own employer. His other option was to take a job in one
of Heilbronn's factories—but he wanted to be his own boss.

Jacob had made a friend in Heilbronn, Martin Nolting, with whom he
planned to make the journey. Martin, who was even more restless and every
bit as ambitious as Jacob, had been urging him to emigrate for months.
Martin, a carpenter, was from Löhne, a Westphalian village in Prussia.
Martin's restlessness had led him far south to Heilbronn during his
journeyman Wanderjahr, but now he was eager to travel much farther. Many
Löhne villagers, including his sister and brother-in-law, had already
emigrated to St. Louis, and their enthusiastic letters from America had

spurred many people from the area to follow those already settled in Missouri.

Jacob made his last trip back to Hochfeld for three reasons: First, he needed to sell his 2 morgen of farm land to raise cash for his journey and reestablishment. Second, he wanted to obtain a *Taufschein* or certificate of baptism from Pastor Pringsauff, so that Jacob had proof of his legitimate birth, in case he needed it in America. And finally, he wanted to see his sweetheart one last time. Through a friend, Jacob had arranged to meet Maria Sophia at the edge of woodland outside Hochfeld, where they had so often met secretly over the years. Maria Sophia, looking nervous and a little scared, was waiting for him as he walked up the hill toward their meeting spot. They met awkwardly, not touching, both waiting for the other to begin the conversation. Finally, Maria Sophia told him that she could not wait any longer to get married. She would never forget her feelings for him, but she wanted her own home and children. And then he told her of his plans to emigrate. He asked her to come with him; if she truly loved him, they could start anew and take their chances together in a new land. Certainly there was risk, but there was also the possibility of a better life than they could ever achieve in Hochfeld.

Jacob watched the emotions play across Maria Sophia's face: first shock, then indecision as she considered his offer, and then finally, resignation and embarrassment. Jacob knew her well enough to imagine her internal deliberation. She loved him—but not enough to give up her family, her home, and all that was familiar for the uncertainties of a strange, far-away land. She weighed the risk and the danger against her love. But her decision was never truly in question. As the daughter-in-law and eventually the wife of Hochfeld's miller, she would enjoy material comfort and status. She valued security and familiarity, while Jacob was willing—even eager—to risk everything on a new and better future. Jacob saw all this, wished her well, turned heel, and walked back down the hill while she stood there watching him.[294]

Jacob signed papers to sell his land on the day before *Totensonntag*. He had one last task in Hochfeld before he left his village forever. He wanted to visit his parents' graves one last time. He found many other villagers already in the cemetery, mostly women, weeding and tidying the graves of their family members in preparation for *Totensonntag*, and he joined them in tending the graves of his mother, father, and siblings. Jacob sincerely doubted that he would ever return to Hochfeld, so this was likely the last time he would ever visit his family's graves. He knew that by the time he died in America, no trace of his parents would remain in Hochfeld. Land was simply too precious in German villages to permit the maintenance of permanent graves. Instead, graves were leased, typically for about 25 years. If the family failed to renew the lease at the end of this time, the grave was rented to a new family, and the new body was buried on top of the remains of the old one. Jacob was his mother's only descendant, and he would not be in Hochfeld to renew the lease on her grave. He knew that his stepmother would tend the grave of Jacob's father, weeding it and planting new flowers on it each year that she lived. Perhaps the future wife of Jacob's half-brother would take over this task after Jacob's stepmother died. But he doubted that his half-brother would spend the money to renew the lease when it came due.[295]

The following week, Jacob and Martin took seats on a freight wagon, headed west out of Heilbronn — the first leg of their journey to America.

12

Emigration

At the relatively early period of German migration to America when Jacob and Martin began their journey, the majority of southern Germans headed northward on the Rhine, either by boat or by roads that paralleled the river, and then embarked from Rotterdam. However, this was not an option for the two young men, because they were leaving their homelands illegally. If they had applied to their governments for official permission to leave—in Jacob's case, from Baden, and in Martin's case, from Prussia—they ran the risk of being refused because both were subject to possible military conscription. Even if their homelands had granted their applications, they would still have been subject to the payment of stiff exit taxes. Jacob had an additional financial entanglement: He was still technically in bondage to the Freiherr von Steinweg. The forced labor of the Fron had been converted in 1833 to an annual cash payment of 95 gulden, but liquidation of the bondage itself cost over 1,000 gulden. Jacob had sold his Hochfeld land for a tidy sum, but he needed to keep all that money to pay for his crossing and his overland travel once he reached America. So the two young men left without formal permission, *bei Nacht und Nebel* or under the cover of night and fog.[296]

The two men headed westward toward the French border, sometimes paying for wagon passage, sometimes walking. It was not uncommon for emigrants who could afford to do so to travel with several boxes and trunks—household goods, tools, and other personal possessions with which to start their new lives.[297] But Jacob and Martin traveled with no more than they could carry, just a change of clothes and a few personal items. Jacob also brought with him three favorite cooperage tools that he could not bear to leave behind-- a compass, a drawknife, and a head shave, which was a specialized plane he used to straighten his barrels' head boards.

The reason that the two could not travel down the Rhine was that the river journey would oblige them to pass through more than 30 checkpoints; not only would they have to pay tolls at each one, they also ran the risk that they would be imprisoned and returned to Baden and Prussia because they lacked the necessary approval and passage documents. A Rhine River trip would have been particularly risky for Martin, since the men would have had to pass through Prussian checkpoints. They had heard that once they crossed into France, authorities were casual about travelers' documentation. The other reason for leaving through France is that the port of Le Havre was the principal route from Germany to New Orleans. Martin had a sister and brother-in-law who lived upriver in St. Louis.[298]

In the 1830s and 1840s, New Orleans became one of the most important ports in America for the export of cheap southern cotton to European mills. Growers in Louisiana, Mississippi, Tennnessee, Arkansas, and Missouri could use the Mississippi River and its tributaries to ship their crops easily to European-bound ships waiting in New Orleans. Although England was the primary importer of cotton, Alsatian mills also bought significant quantities of raw cotton, which is why the New Orleans-Le Havre route had become so important. Shipping companies were delighted that the growing number of emigrants allowed them to fill their ships with paying customers for the return trip to New Orleans.[299]

Figure 29. Advertisement for Atlantic crossings out of Le Havre, 1850s.

When Jacob and Martin reached Karlsruhe in western Baden, the two men met a group of emigrants from a village near Stuttgart. They warned the two men that just a few months earlier, French authorities had imposed a new requirement on emigrants seeking to cross France to reach the harbor of Le Havre. Alarmed at the growing number of penniless Swiss and German emigrants who ended up stranded in Le Havre without passage money, the authorities now required all potential emigrants to present valid tickets as well as their passports when they entered France.[300]

Jacob and Martin purchased their tickets and crossed the Rhine just south of Karlsruhe. The tickets cost them about 30 taler—a significant sum, but less than the profit Jacob had made from selling his Hochfeld land a few weeks before. Once across the Rhine, they bid farewell to the emigrant group from Stuttgart. With a number of small children in the party as well as considerable baggage, that group had purchased wagon passage directly to Le Havre while Jacob and Martin headed west on foot.[301]

In Strasbourg, they passed a cold, bleak, and lonely Christmas. Strasbourg had been part of the Holy Roman Empire, and German culture still flourished there despite French rule. Watching the residents enjoying familiar Christmas customs, Jacob experienced sadness, homesickness, and doubt about his decision to leave his village, family, and friends. But he had sold his land, his sweetheart was now someone else's wife, and he had become an illegal runaway, subject to imprisonment if he returned to Baden. There was nothing to do but continue the journey.

By mid-January, the two men had reached a village called Aulnois-en-Perthois, about 85 kilometers east of the city of Nancy. Jacob had developed a limp, and both of them were suffering from coughs, the result of weeks of tramping through snow and frozen mud. There was no inn in the village, but the men could not go on, so they paid a farmer to let them sleep in his shed. By morning, Martin was feverish, burning up and barely coherent. He could not walk, but neither could they stay in the shed. Martin found a teamster on the road who was on his way to Saint-Dizier, about 15 kilometers to the west, and who agreed to give the two travelers a ride. Once in Saint-Dizier, they moved into an inn where Martin could recuperate while Jacob worried about their dwindling money supply. A week later, Martin was well enough again to travel, but not to walk. Saint-Dizier is located where the Marne River becomes navigable, so reluctantly, the men decided to pay for boat passage down the Marne to Paris. It would be better to arrive at their destination a little poorer than to die on the road.

Four days later, the two were in Paris. The Karlsruhe agent who had sold them their tickets to America had told them to contact his company's local agent as soon as they reached the city; he could arrange transportation for them down the Seine River to Le Havre. The agent's office was a bustling, noisy place, where emigrants were dispatched efficiently to temporary lodgings, Le Havre boat tickets in hand. It was a vast relief to Jacob and Martin to have the Paris agent's help after having struggled across eastern France on their own.

The next morning they boarded a barge on the Seine for the relatively short trip to the French coast. Disembarking on the quay in Le Havre, they found themselves surrounded by dozens of German-speaking emigrants, primarily from Baden, Württemberg, Bavaria, and Switzerland. The emigrants spoke such a wide variety of dialects that they understood one another only with difficulty. Even though he found some of his fellow travelers' accents almost incomprehensible, Jacob was delighted to be back among German speakers after spending weeks in the French-speaking countryside. There were also, of course, many French emigrants assembled on the quay as well as a few scattered groups of Norwegians. Jacob's 59 fellow passengers on the Atlantic crossing would turn out to be equally divided between Germans and Frenchmen. All told in 1838, 4,122 emigrants sailed from Le Havre to North America, 65 percent of whom were German — a number that was dwarfed by the tide of German emigrants who would make the crossing in the 1840s and 1850s.

Figure 30. Port of Le Havre, 1840s.

Just a few years before Jacob sailed, he likely would have spent weeks in Le Havre, waiting for a berth on a ship. However, logistics became more organized after the French imposed the requirement that emigrants purchase tickets before entering their country. By 1838, partly pushed by profit and partly by governments that were alarmed at reports of stranded or ill-treated passengers, shipping companies and their agents were well on their way to organizing efficient systems for recruiting emigrants across the European lands, facilitating their journeys to port cities, and transporting them to the New World. Jacob had to wait only a few days in Le Havre before boarding the ship *Russell*, a 350-ton 3-mast square rigger, on 30 January 1838.

Jacob and Martin had received some valuable advice from the Stuttgart emigrant group they met in Karlsruhe before they had purchased their tickets. The men had warned them not to purchase passage tickets from any agent until the agent had specified in writing what their ticket included. Until 1855, few emigrant ships provided food as part of the passage price, only water. Even if the agent promised that their meals would be included, the men recommended that Jacob and Martin buy additional provisions for the trip. If they could afford it, they should buy hams, eggs, beer, coffee, lemons, dried fruit, potatoes, and hard tack to last them for 10 weeks; to be safe, they should plan for 12 weeks. They would need to buy their cooking utensils, pots, and a bucket as well as bed linen. Passengers were allowed to have cook fires on deck in good weather, or small protected fires below in bad. The men would have to cook their own meals or pay someone else to do it for them.

The Le Havre merchants made tidy profits off emigrants, who had no choice but to pay the merchants' asking prices. Jacob and Martin bought the best food they could afford—potatoes, sausage, hard tack, and lemons to prevent scurvy. They also bought one pot to share; they would make do with the knives and the bedding they had carried with them since Heilbronn.[302]

There were 60 passengers on Jacob's ship, less than half of its passenger capacity, but that did not mean they were less crowded than they might have been with a full complement of emigrants; half of the ship's holds were filled with French furniture, household items, and other manufactured goods destined for the planters of Louisiana. The *Russell* had been designed to haul goods, not people, so the passenger cabins were nothing more than cargo holds about 6 feet high, retrofitted with two levels of wooden bunks. The *Russell* could accommodate up to two deck levels of passengers and a third and lowest level for cargo. On Jacob's crossing, however, all passenger compartments were located one level below the main deck, with cargo occupying the other two levels.

There were separate cabins for families, single women, and single men. The wooden bunks that lined each passenger cabin were wide enough to accommodate six persons each. Children under five shared their parents' bunk space, while children between five and fourteen received only one-half a bunk space each. The bunks had straw mattresses, but the passengers had to provide their own pillows and bedding. Not surprisingly, passengers who began the journey without lice or fleas were sure to have them by the time they reached their destination.[303]

When weather permitted, the passengers were allowed up on deck where they could stretch their legs and breathe fresh air. But the winter weather during the crossing was stormy and the seas were rough, so most days the passengers were confined to their decks. The ship had ventilation pipes to the passenger cabins, which were the only source of fresh air and light. In stormy seas, the pipes were closed to prevent the ship from taking on water. Most of the passengers were seasick, at least during the first part of the journey. The 60 passengers shared one toilet, so many sick passengers kept buckets nearby.

Soon the already stale and unpleasant air in the cabins became truly fetid, and those who were not seasick became ill from the stench. Jacob recovered from an initial bout of seasickness and volunteered to help the ship carpenter in order to get out of the foul cabin, but Martin was too sick to leave his bunk for the majority of the crossing.[304]

Transporting passengers was profitable business, but the ship captains hated the work. Some of them referred to emigrant ships as floating coffins, and residents in port cities said that they could tell which ships had carried emigrants by their nauseating smell. Rats, mice, and vermin were impossible to eradicate, but most captains did all they could to manage their ships' sanitation because of the dangers of epidemic diseases.

Figure 31. German emigrants en route.

On Jacob's ship, Master Robbins assigned all passengers rotational cleaning duties: twice weekly, passengers took turns airing out the mattresses on deck and washing down all surfaces in the cabins with vinegar and water. They emptied and cleaned out the slop buckets twice daily. When the weather permitted, all passengers were required to change and wash their clothes, hanging them to dry on lines stretched across the main deck. Passengers were required to keep food stocks covered and secure from rodents. Even with these preventative measures, five of the *Russell's* 60 passengers died of dysentery or typhoid on the long journey.[305]

Despite the physical discomforts of the crossing, Jacob rather enjoyed the adventure of the voyage once he had recovered from his initial seasickness. However, by the time the ship sailed into Havana harbor to take on fresh water for the three-week run into New Orleans, he was ready for the voyage to end.

On 12 April 1838, 73 days after leaving Le Havre, the *Russell* at last sailed into the New Orleans harbor. The weather was an unseasonably warm and humid 85 degrees Farenheit. Immigrants who had begun their journey in their thickest and warmest clothing to protect themselves from the cold, wet European winter were now sweltering; indeed, three women fainted while in line to disembark. As he waited his turn to walk down the gangway, Jacob looked down on a French-Spanish colonial town with its colorful two-story houses and wrought-iron balconies, so different from his German village. He heard French, English, Spanish, and African languages in addition to German. Jacob watched as a group of chained, wailing slaves were unloaded from a North Carolina ship and led to the slave market a few blocks away. No matter where he looked, he saw, heard, and smelled nothing that was like his homeland. At that moment, Jacob understood more clearly than at any time since leaving Heilbronn that his old life was gone forever.

*   *   *

Jacob had chosen to emigrate to seek better opportunities and because he was disappointed in love. But there were many reasons why millions of Germans and Swiss decided to come to North America. Like Jacob, millions were seeking greater economic opportunities. Others were evading military conscription. Some were seeking greater personal freedom, particularly after the Revolution of 1848, in which students and intellectuals fought unsuccessfully for a representative parliament, freedom of the press, self-organization of the universities, and better working and living conditions for the poor. The primary motivation for the first substantial group of German immigrants, however, was religious freedom.

Although they were not the first Germans to settle in North America, a group of 13 families from Krefeld in the Rhineland formed the first permanent German settlement in Pennsylvania in 1683. They were Mennonites, and they were seeking the religious toleration that William Penn had promised to any immigrant who settled in his Pennsylvania lands. Religious freedom continued to be the primary motivation for the approximately 300 Germans who immigrated to Pennsylvania through 1709. The bulk of this first generation of Germans traveled down the Rhine to Rotterdam, where their ships sailed for England. British law required that any ship sailing to a British colony must embark from a British port, which included London, Liverpool, or Irish ports such as Belfast.

The trickle of German settlers widened to a steady stream following the publication of a pamphlet in 1709, widely disseminated in the Rhine Valley, which promised immigrants free passage and assistance in settling in New York. The pamphlet circulated just as Germany was experiencing another disastrous agricultural year. Thousands of Germans descended on Rotterdam, seeking passage to England and on to America, so many that English officials could not handle the volume. Authorities sent many applicants home, but eventually did transport 2,400 in 10 ships to New York.

Many would-be immigrants lacked the funds to pay for their passage to America. But because the immigrant business was so profitable for shippers, they devised the redemptioner system under which they would transport emigrants under labor contracts. Upon their arrival, the immigrants were sold as indentured servants for a fixed number of years—typically five to seven, although for minor children the indenture often lasted until they were 21. Around the end of the eighteenth century, about half of new immigrants in Philadelphia were redemptioners.[306]

Economic opportunity became and remained the primary motivation for the majority of emigrants after the first, brief period in which religion predominated. Between 1714 and 1775, more than 80,000 Swiss and German immigrants relocated to North America. In 1751, there was such a high concentration of Germans in the Philadelphia area that Benjamin Franklin worried the area might become a permanent German enclave. By 1760, there were sizeable German-speaking communities in southeastern Pennsylvania, New York's Hudson River Valley, New Jersey, western Maryland, Virginia's Shenandoah Valley, coastal South Carolina, and the piedmont region of North Carolina. By 1790, when the United States conducted its first census, approximately one-twelfth of Americans were native Germans and Swiss or were descended from them.[307]

Canada also received its share of German immigrants, beginning in the late seventeenth century. By 1760, about 200 German families were living along the St. Lawrence River. One of the oldest German settlements in Canada was Lunenburg, founded in Nova Scotia between 1750 and 1753. Land grants in the 1760s in Nova Scotia's Annapolis Valley resulted in the immigration of another 1,000 Germans.

The next wave occurred during the American Revolution, when Germans loyal to the British crown fled northward beginning in 1776. They were joined by German Hessian troops, mercenaries engaged to fight the American colonists, many of whom were billeted in Quebec communities. So many chose to stay after the Revolution that German males comprised 3-4 percent of the Canadian male population by 1786. Mennonites also came to Canada from Pennsylvania as a result of the Revolution; their Waterloo County settlements in Ontario attracted another 50,000 immigrants from Germany. The co-founder of Toronto, then the city of York, was a land developer from Germany named William Berczy who cleared the land and built the first buildings along Yonge Street. In the west, Germans moved into British Columbia with the gold rushes of the 1850s.

German immigration continued at a slow but steady rate in the United States through the 1820s, when an average of less than 600 arrived in the United States each year. During the 1830s, however, the number increased to over 12,000 each year. During the early 1840s, the number grew to over 20,000 per year, and by the end of that decade, almost 60,000 arrived yearly. During the early 1850s, the average annual rate was greater than 130,000. Overall, nine out of ten European immigrants who arrived during the 1850s were Germans or Swiss. They continued to immigrate after 1860, but never again in the numbers seen between 1840 and 1855.[308]

Partible inheritance was a primary reason why emigrants from southwest Germany comprised a significant percentage of the total emigrant population. With the population increases of the eighteenth and nineteenth centuries, larger families were attempting to survive on ever smaller parcels of land. Many families had bridged the economic gap by turning to cottage industry, in particular weaving. When Germany finally began to industrialize and to build large mills and factories in the mid-nineteenth century, these families lost their livelihoods. Some German villages were so desperate to deal with their resulting welfare cases that they paid the passage costs for their poorest residents to emigrate, reasoning that a one-time expenditure for their tickets was a better bargain than a permanent requirement to support them from the village's charity funds.[309]

By the 1850s, one German pastor noted that "the name of America has now become as familiar to every peasant and laborer, yea to every child in the street, as that of the nearest neighboring country, whilst to thousands and hundreds of thousands, it is a goal of their warmest wishes and boldest hopes." The millions of friends and neighbors sent a steady stream of letters back to their villages to tell them about the wonders of their new homes. Certainly there were some who found their new lives a bitter failure; but for every disappointed writer, there were a dozen who could not say enough about how pleased they were in their new homeland.[310]

Mid-nineteenth-century Germans had a wide variety of ports from which to embark for their trip to North America. The Swiss and the south Germans continued to favor Le Havre, but north Germans were more likely to leave from Bremen, Bremerhaven, or Hamburg. Construction of German rail lines allowed would-be emigrants to make a much faster and easier trip to the coast than Jacob and Martin had experienced in the 1830s. Genealogists whose ancestors left from Hamburg are fortunate that the voluminous and detailed police records on all emigrants have been microfilmed and preserved. Unfortunately for those genealogists whose ancestors left from Bremen, those passage records have been destroyed.

The German word for emigrant is *Auswanderer*, and the term *Auswanderung* refers to the overall exodus of citizens. Over the many decades of the Auswanderung, German governments in Baden, Württemberg, and elsewhere demonstrated bewilderment, consternation, relief, and disapproval, in no particular order, concerning the monumental exodus of such a significant segment of its population. On the one hand, the Auswanderung helped to resolve the problem of feeding the excess population. But on the other, it was an obvious and embarrassing testimony to the governments' inability to take care of their own citizens, so much so that the Duke of Württemberg ordered all emigrant records to be destroyed at the beginning of the nineteenth century.

Periodically, governments would issue pamphlets or reports to discourage emigration, painting a gloomy picture of the risks and uncertain rewards of leaving. But when villagers weighed the negative reports against the letters from friends and relatives and the optimistic pamphlets published by shippers' agents, they inevitably dismissed the government reports as self-serving propaganda.[311]

In a village culture where the highest goal of most adult men was to have enough land to farm full-time, it would be hard to underestimate the impact of a letter such as the one a young immigrant in Heartland, Illinois, sent home to his mother in Germany in the 1850s:

> You need not fear about the land. It is not likely in this country that the land [will] be taken away. The government wants that we shall stay and improve the land. They fear that we will become rich and move to another place. It is not so, however . . . I now have one hundred acres of land by a paper and it is all mine. Some of it is still full of water but we are working fast to get the ditches in . . . When I am plowing I can shut my eyes and smell the dear land under me and say it is mine, mine, all mine. No one can take it away. I am king, as you said.[312]

*   *   *

The long journey from Heilbronn to New Orleans had exhausted almost all Jacob's and Martin's funds; they had no money to pay for a cabin on a steamboat to St. Louis. But talking with their fellow travelers, they learned that they could travel by steamboat at one-fifth the cost of a cabin passenger by purchasing deck passage. This meant that they would be living and sleeping on the open deck for the approximately two weeks it would take for them to travel the 1,200 miles up the Mississippi River to their destination. They would also have to buy their own food before embarking, and prepare it on a common deck stove, just as they had on the journey across the Atlantic. However, the most important feature of deck passage to Jacob was the cost: only about five dollars. He and Martin would have lots of company on deck; three times more passengers purchased deck tickets than those who purchased cabin accommodation. Jacob reluctantly sold one of his three cooper's tools, his drawknife, in order to pay for his share of food for the trip.[313]

They booked passage on a relatively small boat, the 63-ton *Frontier*, which was built early in the 1830s, principally to work the upper Mississippi River basin. It was a fast boat; in fact, it was famed for having achieved the fastest passage time between St. Louis and Galena, Illinois, in 1836. Jacob and Martin shared the boat with 22 other passengers, of whom 6 shared the two cabins and the rest were on deck. It was springtime on the Mississippi, and although the deck passengers spent several days in wet clothes due to rain, on the whole the temperature was temperate. In general, the deck passengers were a happy lot; their travels were almost over, and they had survived an arduous journey.[314]

The *Frontier* made several stops on the way to St. Louis to pick up or drop off mail, passengers, or cargo: Natchez, Vicksburg, Memphis, and Cairo, where the Ohio joined the Mississippi. In the scattered small cities, Jacob glimpsed ornate homes and small but prosperous-looking ports. Outside of the cities, he saw the occasional plantation with its stately house, outbuildings, and fields being worked by Black slaves. For the most part, however, he saw nothing but trees. America seemed to him an almost empty land, filled with riches for the taking by an ambitious young man who was willing to work hard.

Finally, Jacob's journey was over. As the *Frontier* approached the cobblestone levee, St. Louis appeared to him as a veritable forest of riverboat steamstacks. There were almost 100 boats moored along the levee that day — a relatively low-traffic day along a riverfront that often accommodated 150 boats at once. The first steamboat had docked at St. Louis in 1817, inaugurating a period of growth and prosperity. St. Louis was the gateway to the west, from which traders and settlers provisioned themselves and headed into the wilderness. It was also the last significant city on the Mississippi River below the Des Moines Rapids and Rock Island Rapids, which prevented northbound river passage of the larger boats, so that the city became the principal port in the interior West. By 1838, the commercial district east of Fourth Street featured banks, saloons, hotels, dozens of stores, and the new St. Louis Theater, which opened the previous year.[315]

In 1838, the City of St. Louis boasted more than 15,000 inhabitants. The first German immigrants had arrived in the mid-1830s; by the time that Jacob arrived just a few years later, the number of Germans had swelled to 6,000 — more than one-third the city's population.

Figure 32. St. Louis levee, late 1800s.

Germans were settling all over eastern Missouri, not just in the City. Martin's sister Anne Elisabetha lived with her husband Hermann in a small enclave of German farming families in northern St. Louis County. They had arrived in 1835, and already they owned their own farm. They had worked hard and done well, but they had also suffered. Anne Elisabetha had lost two toddlers to typhoid fever, and was suffering from depression and homesickness. Despite her husband's economic success, she was desperately unhappy, and longed to return to Germany. Her brother's arrival was a blessing from home that helped her begin to adjust to and accept her new life. Soon she was expecting another child, her first to be born in America.[316]

The two men received a warm welcome in the little German village, which the locals were beginning to call Black Jack. Martin moved in with his sister's family and helped Hermann to extend his arable acres, while Jacob went to work for a neighboring farmer, Heinrich Wedekind. Within a year, Martin was engaged to another young woman from his home village, Henriette Jacobsmeier, whose family had immigrated with Hermann, Anne Elisabetha, and a small group of other Westphalian villagers. With Hermann to guarantee his mortgage, Martin bought a small nearby farm.[317]

Martin had achieved his goal of owning his own land, and he was surrounded by friends and family. His immigration jouurney had more than satisfied his wanderlust; now he was ready to put down roots. Jacob, however, was not. The Black Jack residents had been friendly and helpful, but their little settlement had begun to remind him of Hochfeld — in sum, life under the constant microscope of the neighbors. He missed the anonymity of Heilbronn, and he had decided that he was not interested in becoming a full-time farmer. After a year in Black Jack, Jacob bid Martin farewell, deposited his savings in a local bank, and headed back to the City of St. Louis.

*   *   *

Jacob was far from alone in deciding to move to the city. The first generation of German-Americans was more likely to live in a city than either their former countrymen in Germany or their new countrymen in the United States. In 1850, almost 30 percent of German immigrants but only 8 percent of the total population was located in one of the country's eight largest cities. Many German immigrants moved directly to the cities, while others moved into a city after brief stays on a farm or small town. By 1860, German-born residents comprised 15.4 percent of the population in Baltimore, 22.5 percent in Buffalo, 20.4 percent in Chicago, 27.2 in Cincinnati, 31.4 percent in St. Louis, and 35.3 in Milwaukee. Germans comprised only 14.8 percent of the New York City population — but the sheer number of Germans in that city represented the third largest concentration of Germans in the world, after Berlin and Vienna.[318]

Whether the immigrants moved to the cities or stayed in the country, they tended to form exclusive German communities in the country and German neighborhoods in the city. The founding residents of villages like Black Jack were typically from the same area or even the same German village, because beginning with the first waves of immigrants, Germans tended to come in groups. Individuals traveling on their own usually settled near relatives or neighbors who had already immigrated. As German villages established satellite outposts in North America, letters sent back home encouraged even more former neighbors to relocate to the golden land.[319]

Immigration permitted ambitious German men to attain all their dearest ambitions. By leaving Germany, they shrugged off the last vestige of serfdom, the hated Fron requirement. No longer held in thrall by the Bürger system, which until the mid-nineteenth century limited them to citizenship in a single village or city, they were free to move wherever they wished. More land than they had ever dared to dream of in Germany was theirs in exchange for hard work. Their living conditions might be Spartan the first few years, but with luck, they could expect within a few years to build a house for their families that dwarfed those of their former German villages' richest men. No longer would their children and grandchildren watch their prospects wither with each generational division of family assets; instead, a man could help his sons acquire their own land, and he could expect that his daughters would find good German husbands nearby with farms of their own. The entire extended family could become prosperous together.[320]

The transition for German women was not nearly as smooth as for their menfolk. In leaving their German village, they lost forever some of the most cherished aspects of their lives. They bid farewell, usually forever, to their parents and other relatives. No longer would they meet their friends and neighbors on the street whenever they walked to the shops, no longer would they enjoy the comfort of spinning or sewing with the other women on long winter nights. In America, they were often isolated on farms some miles outside the German hamlets. They fought the wilting heat, the dirt and insects, the wild animals, and the dark silent nights. They longed for familiar foods and their former kitchen stoves. Most of all, they worried about unfamiliar illnesses that struck themselves and their families, and they feared being alone in their hours of childbirth.

Contemplating her imminent departure from Germany, one woman wrote to her brother,

> When I now think of our departure from here, . . . I have to say that since the New Year all courage has left me. But the decision will have to be made soon. I almost tremble when I think of it . . . Most of what was so dear and valuable to me in the house must be sold. I will have to leave the beloved home of our parents to strangers, perhaps never to step into it again . . . Will I ever be able to live through all this? I think of this often recently. I am so terribly frightened, and I cannot tell [my husband]. But I do not waver for a moment.[321]

In extreme cases, some families' hopes of a better life in North America were doomed for a variety of reasons including bad luck, inadequate starting capital, illness, and lack of skills. Some immigrants gave up and returned to Germany, where they became landless paupers in their own former villages because they had sold or forfitted any former property in order to leave. Others, lacking the funds, remained trapped over in North America. A German-language weekly newspaper published in St. Louis ran an article in 1836, which described some of these unfortunates: " . . . the ragged children and the dirty females whom one sees here in the streets and in front of the warehouses, where they [paw] through the trash for worthless, disgusting things, where they attempt to steal what they cannot find on the streets or gain by begging."[322]

Despite some challenges and setbacks, the German community in North America prospered and grew. By 1900, a "German belt" of German immigrants and their descendants extended across the center of the United States in an area bounded east

Figure 33. A family enjoys a German beer hall in Hoboken, NJ. Harper's Magazine, October 1878.

and west by Ohio and Nebraska, north and south by Wisconsin and Missouri. Sizable populations also existed in several Northeast cities including Hoboken, Baltimore, and New York. Germans owned 40 percent of all farms in the United States. Germans and their descendants continued to speak German, not simply at home but in their churches, schools, and stores. They read local German-language newspapers. They formed thousands of social organizations or *Vereine*—musical, theatrical, charitable, athletic, and political. They attended German-language concerts and lectures, and they relaxed on Sunday in German beer and wine gardens.[323]

Their German world survived until World War I, when their insular lives attracted the distrust of other Americans. When the United States declared war on Germany in 1917,

> . . . [n]o German-American was beyond suspicion; speaking German was enough to call one's loyalty into question. Hysteria degenerated into all sorts of absurd campaigns to stamp out everything German. Bach and Beethoven were taken off concert programs, streets and stores were renamed, even sauerkraut was turned into "liberty cabbage."[324]

To prove their loyalty to the United States, the communities began to conduct school classes only in English. They disbanded many of their organizations, and German newspapers ceased to publish. The German churches were slower in converting to English, but as more of their younger members grew up speaking English rather than German, even they made the change. By the onset of World War II a generation later, the golden era of German culture in North America was over.

*   *   *

When Jacob Mann moved to St. Louis City from Black Jack, he found a boarding house run by a German widow just south of the city's commercial

center. The boarding house was in the Frenchtown area, where newly built homes punctuated an area still mostly covered with fields and farms. The earliest inhabitants had been French, and the area had been surveyed by a Frenchman named Antoine Soulard. After his widow donated land at the

Figure 34. Photo of the Soulard market, ca. 1900; some of Soulard's characteristic brick rowhouses can be seen in the background.

corner of Seventh Street and Soulard Street (today's Lafayette Street) to build a public market, the growing neighborhood began to be called Soulard.

The neighborhood's blocks were divided into narrow European-style lots on which the growing population of Germans built red brick rowhouses. German schools, churches, stores, and other businesses quickly followed. Jacob advertised for cooperage work in a neighborhood newspaper, and he supported himself with construction jobs while he waited for his business to grow. Within a year, he was able to rent space in a shared warehouse where he worked almost full time as a cooper and occasional carpenter.

Jacob's lucky break occurred about five years later. A German from Hessen named Johann Adam Lemp had arrived in St. Louis in 1838, where he opened a grocery store. As a side business, he began to brew lager beer to meet the demand of the German community. By 1842, he had established the Western Brewing Company on South 2nd Street, where today the St. Louis

Arch is located. In 1845, Adam began excavating an underground limestone cave near the Mississippi to age his beer. To outfit the cavern, he needed 20 thirty-barrel oak casks plus dozens of new barrels for his sales. He hired Jacob and three other coopers to construct his casks and barrels.

From the start, Adam Lemp took a liking to Jacob, who was about 13 years his junior. Jacob reminded him of his favorite nephew back in Germany. Adam inspected Jacob's cask work and barrels carefully, and found they were neat, tight, and well constructed. Adam ended up offering Jacob an open-ended contract to produce all his barrels. Adam prospered, and became one of the City's leading brewers. He became Jacob's business mentor, and as his business exploded, so did Jacob's.[325]

To bolster his reputation as a respectable businessman, Jacob began to attend the South German Evangelical Church, later known as St. Marcus Church, founded in 1845 at the intersection of Fourth and Soulard streets. There he met his future wife, Dorothea Kappel, who with her parents and siblings had emigrated from Mecklenburg in 1842. They married in November 1846, exactly 9 years after Jacob left his German village. Dorothea was 25 and Jacob was 40. They used Jacob's savings from his first year in America to secure a mortgage on a tidy brick rowhouse in Soulard. Within a year, Dorothea was pregnant with their first son. She would bear him three sons and two daughters, all but one of whom lived to marry and have children of their own.

In 1851, Jacob's stepmother died in Hochfeld at age 57. As was her right under Hochfeld's inheritance laws and customs, she had continued to live in Jacob's father's half-house in the village for her entire life. Now that she was dead, Jacob's father's estate could finally be settled.

Jacob's elderly uncle had acted as Jacob's guardian since the death of Jacob's father. He and Jacob had exchanged a few letters over the years, so he knew his nephew was alive and well in St. Louis. He insisted that Jacob receive his legal share of the inheritance, even though he had fled Baden without permission. After a prolonged period of deliberation, the Badenese court finally agreed that Jacob was still one of his father's two legal heirs. After the half-house, furnishings, outbuilding, and farm equipment were sold, the proceeds were divided equally between Jacob and his half-brother, Johann Georg Mann, who still lived in Hochfeld. About a half-year later, a bank draft arrived for Jacob. Badenese authorities had subtracted the manumission fee Jacob should have paid for permission to emigrate, along with various other fees and taxes, but the remaining sum was nevertheless a respectable amount. With his inheritance, Jacob's mentor Adam Lemp allowed him to buy a small but significant interest in his brewery.[326]

Lemp's Western Brewery continued to grow and prosper, even after Adam's son William took over the company in the 1860s following his father's death. By the early 1870s, Lemp's was the largest brewery in St. Louis (Anheuser & Company ranked second), with a total production of

61,000 lager barrels per year. In addition to his minority interest in the brewery itself, Jacob continued to grow his barrel-making business, which supplied Lemp's as well as a significant number of the 29 other breweries in St. Louis. Jacob and his sons presided over their own empire of warehouses and manufacturing facilities for constructing and storing barrels. He had become a wealthy and important man.

For many years, the adult children of Jacob and Dorothea Mann urged them to move to a newer neighborhood north of the center city, nicknamed Germantown, where many upwardly mobile Germans had established a German-language community in large houses surrounded by gardens. The Soulard neighborhood had become increasingly industrial in character, and many Germans had moved out as new immigrant groups from eastern and southern Europe moved in. However, the couple stubbornly refused to leave the neighborhood where they had raised their children, attended church, and entertained their friends.

In 1881, Dorothea Mann died in the ornate brick townhouse that Jacob had built for her 25 years earlier. One year later, a lonely and retired Jacob died as well. Their children buried them at Bellefontaine Cemetery in Germantown, not far from the graves of Adam Lemp and his wife Louisa. Jacob was 76 years old. He had fathered five American children and 21 grandchildren.

Jacob lived his entire life in German culture, speaking German with his family, friends, and business associates. Yet the most he ever told his children about his life in his German village were a few happy anecdotes from his childhood. He never told them, nor did they ask, about his parents or his difficult early life in Hochfeld. He had left that life behind the day in 1837 that he began his walk towards the French border. But on his deathbed, the life accomplishment of which he was most proud was that he had given his wife and children a secure life in the land of opportunity. Through his own efforts, he had insured that the words of the Lord's Prayer that so haunted his own father—"Give us this day our daily bread"—had lost their fearful meaning, hopefully forever, for his American descendants.

Glossary

NOTE: The purpose of this glossary is to create a reference for the most frequently used German words in *Our Daily Bread*. A primary reference used to create this Glossary is Ernest Thode's *German-English Genealogical Dictionary* (Baltimore: Genealogical Publishing Co., Inc., 1992). Thode's dictionary is an excellent reference tool for genealogists who work with German records.

24ger. Short for *Vierundzwanziger*, the name given to the ruling council in some villages based on the 24 men who comprised the council. This name for the council was not uncommon in northern Baden and Württemberg, but it was by no means standard practice in all villages to name a ruling or advisory council based on the number of members. The actual number of council members varied from village to village.

Almosenpfleger. The administrator of church funds used to support the poor or those in temporary difficulty.

Amtmann or *Ammann.* An Amt is a jurisdiction or district, and the Amtmann is the magistrate or bailiff of that organizational entity. The exact definition of this individuals—his duties and his authority—varied from one location to another, as well as over time. Sometimes, for example, he was the head official in a village, while in other cases he represented the local lord or the government, e.g., that of Baden or Württemberg.

Anwalt or *Anwaldt.* While the exact definition of this term varies from village to village, this individual was an official who either worked for the local lord or who held a community office as deputy to the Schultheiss. By the 20th century, this official evolved into a lawyer.

Aufgebot. The banns which announced an impending marriage, and which were announced from the pulpit for the three weeks before the ceremony.

Auswanderer. Emigrant. The Auswanderung refers to the wave of emigration from Germany that occurred during the nineteenth century.

Bauer. Farmer. When used as an occupational descriptor in German parish records, it normally indicates an individual who holds enough property, either owned or leased, to make his living exclusively from farming. This is also the term used for peasant. As used in village documents such as parish registers, it is a neutral or even positive term, since the goal of most village men was to have enough land to farm full-time. However, the term when used by outsiders writing about "peasants" often has a negative connotation of backwardness and boorishness.

Bauernbefreiung. The lengthy process through which the peasants transitioned from their bondage to the lord and/or the land to freedom and emancipation.

Beisitzer. The term's modern definition is assessor or committee member. In Early Modern Germany, it could refer to an inhabitant without land and/or to an individual without citizenship rights or Bürgerrecht.

Blutverwandtschaft. Consanguinity or blood relationship, which exists when two persons share a common ancestor.

Bürger. While many authors limit use of the term Bürger or burgher to residents in early cities, the term actually refers to citizens of any city, town, or village. This status was typically purchased or inherited, and could not be transferred to another locality. Not all male residents held this status. Bürger status included the rights to vote and to hold office as well as the right to use common town assets such as the forest and pasturage.

Bürgermeister. Currently this term refers to the mayor of a town or village. Prior to the mid-nineteenth century, it often referred to the local official who was responsible for managing a town's financial and physical assets.

Bürgerrecht. The set of privileges that Bürger status conferred on an individual within a specific village or town.

Bürgerschaft. The collective citizens of a village, town, or city.

Dorfordnungen. The ordinances that governed all aspects of village life. The singular form of this word is *Dorfordnung.*

Eigenmann. Bondsman.

Einwohner. Literally, this refers to a male inhabitant. In some villages, it was used to designate legal residents of a village who were not Bürger.

Erblehenrecht. The right to pass on one's property to one's heirs.

Evangelisch. Evangelical; a term that includes both the Lutheran and Reformed churches of Germany.

Fastnacht. Shrove Tuesday. The word also refers to the carnivals celebrated in many towns and villages in the days leading up to Ash Wednesday and the beginning of Lent.

Florin. A gold coin, also known as a gulden.

Freiherr. Equivalent to an English baron. The plural is Freiherren. In general, the German Freiherren were absolute rulers, subject only to the oversight of the Emperor.

Fron, Fronen, Frondienst. Compulsory labor services owed to the lord by his peasants, e.g., working in his fields and pastures without pay and working on the lord's construction projects such as castles, roads, and bridges.

Gärtner. See *Kötter.*

Gemeinde. This collective noun has a number of meanings in English, including community, communality, municipality, township, borough, and commune. It is often used in the context of the citizens of a village or town making collective decisions.

Gemeinderechnung. An accounting or *Rechnung* of community expenditures and income.

Gericht. Usually defined as a local court, made up of the most respected village citizens or Bürger. However, its traditional function was broader than merely a local court that dealt with minor infractions. Prior to the nineteenth century, the Gericht also served as the village council in some locations. Following political reforms of the early and mid-nineteenth century, the responsibilities of the Gericht were divided into two separate entities. The Gericht became simply a first-level court and the Rat became the village or town council. Be aware, however, that terms and functions varied from location to location, and administrative reform occurred at different times in different regions and villages.

Gerichtsherrschaft. The legal authority of a territorial lord that permitted him to establish laws and issue legal decisions.

Gotteshausrecht. This was a lesser property right than *Ehrblehenrecht*, under which property was heritable. A tenant with a grant of *Gotteshausrecht* held a property for his life but had no right to pass on the property to heirs.

Grundherr, Grundherrschaft. Literally, "Ground Lord," translated as landlord or lord of the manor. Grundherrschaft was the system that predominated in the South and West of Germany. In general, peasants under this system lived on and worked family-sized holdings, paying rent and/or fees to the *Grundherr*.

Gült. Rent owed in grain.

Gutsherr, Gutsherrschaft. Generally, this pattern of land usage was found in eastern Germany. It was characterized by demesne farming, in which the lord did not rent parts of his land to tenants, thereby living off rent proceeds, but instead directly farmed his own land, using tenant labor.

Heilige Römische Reich Deutscher Nation. Holy Roman Empire of the German Nation.

Heiratsgut. An endowment given to adult children as they began their married life. It could include land, buildings, household goods, livestock, and implements. Assuming the bride's and groom's parents were still alive, the *Heiratsgut* was only a provisional endowment. The permanent division of parental assets occurred when the parents' estates were settled.

Herrschaft. Pertaining to the local lord, his property, and his rights.

Hof. An estate, manor, or farm; the plural is *Höfe*. The term also may refer to a small community within a larger village, composed of all the houses, farm buildings, and persons who work the associated land. In areas of partible inheritance, the land of a Hof was often divided among the village's cultivated fields rather than existing as one entity.

Homines proprii. A category of nonfree status, also called serfdom, under which the individuals and their descendants belonged to a lord from birth. Even if they had settled on the land of another lord, they continued to belong to their original lord. They owed their lord labor services and rent as well as various payments and fees, e.g., to purchase the right to take a spouse not owned by the lord.

Heuerling. See *Kötter*.

Inventarium or *Inventur*. A detailed inventory of an individual's assets and possessions, prepared upon marriage or following a death.

Kleiderordnungen. Literally, the term means "clothing regulations" or "dress codes." It was used in the early modern period to refer to sumptuary laws, which dictated what clothing articles or types could be worn by various classes of individuals. The sumptuary laws attempted to control excess expenditure and also to reinforce social rank by prohibiting the lower classes from imitating the dress of higher classes.

Köbler: Farmers who held small holdings, these individuals fell below the village elite with larger Höfe, but above the Kötter.

Kötter: These individuals were cottagers, who rented a place to stay and may have had a small garden, but who were wholly dependent on their wages to live. In some areas, many Kötter turned to linen weaving, an occupation in which the entire family could participate, in order to survive.

Küfer. Cooper, barrel maker.

Leibeigener, Leibeigene, Leibeigenschaft. Serf, serfs, serfdom. These individuals were bound to the land, subject to dues (or rent) in money or kind, services (Fronen) and tithes, and special dues to the Church. Depending on the laws governing the locality as well as the time period, these individuals might be as much the property of their lord as his animals and goods, while in other cases, the lord owned the serfs' labor and controlled their movement, but technically did not own the individuals themselves. This particular form of bondage had largely disappeared by the end of the eighteenth century.

Leibherr. A Leibherr is the lord of an unfree peasant, usually referred to as a serf but sometimes referred to by the somewhat less restrictive status of a subject or Untertan.

Morgen. Refers to the amount of land a man could plow in a morning. The morgen was in use in many locales in northern Baden and Württemberg, including the area profiled in this book.

Ortsherr. The generic term for the lord of a certain locality. While the local lord has other terms to describe his various relationships to the villagers, such as *Grundherr* (landlord) or *Leibherr* (lord of a serf), the Ortsherr is a general term with no such connotation of relationship.

Pfarrer. Priest or pastor.

Pfleger. Court-appointed guardian for a child who has lost a parent, a widow, or occasionally for an adult male who has been deemed incapable of handling his own affairs.

Pfennig. Penny, plural is pfennige.

Rathaus. Town hall.

Realteilung. The practice and procedures for "partible inheritance," in which all children share equally in the estates of their parents.

Reichstand. An imperial estate or territorial entity, such as Württemberg, which had a vote in the imperial diet or legislature. Plural is *Reichsstände.*

Richter. A member of the local court or Gericht.

Ritterschaft. The imperial knights.

Rufname. Literally, "called name." Of a child's two or three Christian names given in baptism, the Rufname was the one by which the child was known. Johann Jacob, for example, had the Rufname of Jacob.

Ruggericht. A session of the local court or Gericht.

Schultheiss. In the period before the early nineteenth century, the Schultheiss was the village head man or mayor. Typically, he was appointed by the local lord, although some villages were allowed to vote for their own leader.

Schutzverwandte. Village inhabitants who lived under the protection or *Schutz* of the local lord, who lacked Bürger status. *Schutzverwandte* owed the lord an annual payment, called the *Schutzgeld.* Jews were *Schutzverwandte,* as were Mennonites in some villages.

Seldner. See Kötter.

Straße or *Strasse.* Street or road.

Teilung. An inventory of assets and possessions, prepared following an individual's death.

Taglöhner or *Tageloehner.* Day laborer.

Unehrlich. Dishonorable. Also used to refer to illegitimate children.

Untertanen. Subjects of a lord.

Vetterleswirtschaft. Nepotism.

Vogt or *Vogtherr.* A steward or administrator of a secular or ecclesiastical lord.

Volkskunde. The study of everyday peasant life and culture, using a variety of sources such as historical archives and artifacts and a variety of disciplines such as ethnology and anthropology.

Vormünder. See *Pfleger.*

Waisengericht. Guardianship court.

Zehnt. A tithe or 10-percent tax on crops, animals, or other owned items, payable to the church or the overlord.

Notes

Chapter 1

1 See Koslofsky, *The Reformation of the Dead*, 96-100, concerning burial practices in early modern Germany.

2 The first through third verses of this hymn were written by Martin Luther in 1524.

3 Walker, *Germany and the Emigration, 1816-1885*, 10-11.

4 Sabean, *Property, Production, and Family in Neckarhausen*, 51.

5 Sieglerschmidt, in "Social and Economic Landscapes," 6-7 and 30, notes that most early modern Germans spent the majority of their lives undernourished, which increased their susceptibility to illness and infection. Their vulnerability was increased by their damp houses, inadequate fuel supplies, and quality or quantity of clothing. The result was an extremely short life expectancy.

6 A handy website for genealogists is Geogen Surname Mapping, which allows a user to query on a German surname to determine its frequency of usage, its relative distribution across the country, and its percentage distribution among the German states. See http://christoph.stoepel.net/geogen/en/Default.aspx. (web site address current as of 2010)

7 See, for example, Benecke, *Society and Politics in Germany*, 4, and Burke, *Popular Culture in Early Modern Europe*, xi.

8 Brittingham and de la Cruz, *Ancestry: 2000: Census 2000 Brief*, 2-4. Statistics on Canadians come from the Canadian Embassy in Germany and Statistics Canada.

9 Robisheaux, *Rural Society and the Search for Order in Early Modern Germany*, 4. Duggan, *Bishop and Chapter: The Governance of the Bishopric of Speyer to 1552*, 3. Blickle, "The Economic, Social and Political Background of the Twelve Articles of the Swabian Peasants of 1525," 72. Midelfort, *Witch Hunting in Southwestern Germany*, 8.

Chapter 2

10 Schubert, "Daily Life, Consumption, and Material Culture," 359-360. The description of the Mann house is taken directly from Schubert's narrative on peasant home interiors and furnishings.

11 Concerning the division of houses, see Sabean, *Property [in] Neckarhausen*, 266-267. Concerning houses and their furnishings, see Schubert, "Daily Life," 357-360. Anderson and Zinsser, *A History of Their Own*, 92-93. Jordan, *German Seed in Texas Soil*, 36. Robisheaux, *Rural Society*, 90. For a detailed discussion of Fachwerk construction, see Tishler, "Fachwerk Construction in the German Settlements of Wisconsin," 275-292.

12 These percentages match those of two nearby villages, Rappenau and Ittlingen, whose religious percentages as of 1825 were both 88 percent Evangelisch; both villages' percentages of Catholics, Jews, and Mennonites were similar. Neuwirth, *Geschichte der Stadt Bad Rappenau*, 173, and Neuwirth, *Geschichte der Gemeinde Ittlingen*, 255.

13 Rublack, *The Crimes of Women in Early Modern Germany*, 211: "What everyone did was visible — and audible. Houses were built close to each other and with thin walls: neighbours overheard every row. Through low windows and open workshop doors one could see how people worked."

[14] Warde, *Ecology, Economy and State Formation in Early Modern Germany*, 57-58. Of central Württemberg villages, he writes that the villagers' field strips were tiny and generally split into several small pieces in the various village fields. See also Barnum, *Market Centers and Hinterlands in Baden-Württemberg*, 1-4. Robisheaux, *Rural Society*, 23. Benz, "Population Change and the Economy,"46. Ashley, "Meitzen's Siedelung und Agrarwesen der Germanen," 144-145.

[15] The German letter ß or "eszett" can also be written as a double "s," as in *Strasse*. It is pronounced as a double s would be pronounced in English, while a single "s" in German is pronounced like the English z.

[16] This imaginary location is on the L588 road, just north of Heinsheim and across the Neckar River from Gundelsheim. Wimpfen is now referred to as Bad Wimpfen. Wimpfen was a free imperial city until 1803, when it became part of Hesse (in German, *Hessen*) as part of the Napoleonic consolidation of German territories and principalities. In 1945, the occupying Allied forces allocated Wimpfen to the new state or *Land* of Baden-Württemberg.

[17] The von Oberdorf and von Steinweg families are fictional. The von Steinweg family is modeled on an actual family in the area, the Freiherren (or barons) von Gemmingen. The von Gemmingen castle in Guttenberg was one of Barbarossa's defensive castles. The von Gemmingen family purchased the castle and several nearby villages from the von Weinsberg family in 1449. See Gemmingen-Guttenberg, *Life in Guttenberg Castle*.

[18] Crossley, *Peasants' War*, 14-16. Flenley, *Modern German History*, 7-8. Fogleman, *Hopeful Journeys*, 39-65. Burgert, *Eighteenth Century Emigrants from German-Speaking Lands to North America*, 3-4.

[19] Winder, *Germania: In Wayward Pursuit of the Germans and Their History*, 14.

[20] Quotation from Marius, *Martin Luther: The Christian Between God and Death*, 1. See also Hughes, *Early Modern Germany*, 2-12. Gooch, *Studies in German History*, 1. Wilson, *The Holy Roman Empire, 1495-1806*, 2-19. Benecke, *Society and Politics in Germany*, 6-7.

[21] Wilson, *The Holy Roman Empire*, 10-13; and Gardiner, *The Thirty Years' War*, 1-9.

[22] Wheatcroft, *The Habsburgs: Embodying Empire*, 1. Benecke, *Society and Politics in Germany*, 8-9. Flenley, *Modern German History*, 4-5.

[23] Wilson, *War, State and Society in Württemberg, 1677-1793*, 13. Flenley, *Modern German History*, 7-8.

[24] Kriedte, *Peasants, Landlords and Merchant Capitalists: Europe and the World Economy, 1500-1800*, 71 and 101. Hughes, *Early Modern Germany*, 11-13. Ergang, *The Myth of the All-Destructive Fury of the Thirty Years' War*, 8-9.

[25] Sieglerschmidt, "Social and Economic Landscapes,"30-31; and Kriedte, *Peasants, Landlords and Merchant Capitalists*, 101.

[26] Gagliardo, *From Pariah to Patriot. 1770-1840*, 6-7.

[27] Quotation is from Crossley, *Peasants' War*, 30. Concerning the German attitude towards peasants, see Gagliardo, *Pariah to Patriot*, 27-28, and Sreenivasan, *The Peasants of Ottobeuren*, 73-75.

[28] Walker, *German Home Towns*, 138. See also Benecke, *Society and Politics in Germany*, 16-18; and Ogilvie, *State Corporatism and Proto-Industry: The Württemberg Black Forest, 1580-1797*, 44-57.

[29] Prior to the nineteenth century, there was a bewildering variety of coins and coinage systems across Europe and within the German territories, which made monetary transactions across jurisdictional boundaries problematic. Among the coins

in circulation in Germany were various versions of *gulden* (*florin*), *pfund, heller, kreuzen, batzen, pfennig,* and *taler* (*thaler*). Even if two jurisdictions claimed to employ the same coinage system, there was no guarantee that two florins, for example, contained the same amount of precious metal. The coins, minted in different locations, were unlikely to weigh the same, even when new. Over time, the coins would have worn down at different rates. One or both might contain some base metal such as copper or nickel, used to extend the precious gold or silver. Finally, one or both might have been clipped or shaved along the edges; these shavings were saved and then eventually melted down. The practice of coin clipping is the reason that most modern coins have ridged edges, so that any clipping is obvious. The penalties for clipping coins in early modern Europe could be just as severe as for counterfeiting.

By the nineteenth century, monetary systems in the German lands were in the process of standardization. Both the Grand Duchy of Baden and the Kingdom of Württemberg had adopted the gulden as their official currency standards. The gulden had its roots in medieval Florence, from which derived the coin's other name, the florin. The gulden began as a golden coin, but was a silver coin by the nineteenth century. The gulden became the currency of Baden in 1754, although it was only issued as paper banknotes. Baden issued its first gulden coin in 1821. Each gulden was worth 60 kreuzer, which was a small coin imprinted with a cross. Each kreuzer was worth 4 pfennige (pennies) or 8 heller. In 1829, the taler, worth 100 kreuzer, became the currency of Baden. In 1857, Baden adopted the *Vereinsthaler* or "unified dollar," which was the first attempt to establish a single currency across German lands. Finally in 1873, the German Mark was introduced, worth 35 kreuzer. The evolution of money and coinage in Württemberg followed a similar path to that of Baden's.

One should keep in mind that prior to the nineteenth century, many if not most transactions between villagers and between villagers and their overlords took place using barter or in-kind payments, not currency.

[30] These hypothetical ordinances are representative of common restrictions promulgated in villages across Baden and Württemberg. For an excellent discussion of the privileges and limitations of Bürger status, see Walker, *German Home Towns,* 137-142. The hypothetical ordinances from Hochfeld were adapted from the ordinances in Fürfeld, a nearby Kraichgau village. See Schüßler et al., *Fürfeld,* 273, for the entry fees in 1763. Money equivalents are almost impossible to ascertain, but the estimate of 8 florin per sheep was based on the sale of a sheep in a Neckar valley village somewhat earlier, in 1729, for 6 florin.

[31] Lowenstein, "The Rural Community and the Urbanization of German Jewry," 219-221. The name Josua Hirsch belonged to a Jewish family head living in Ittlingen in 1851. Concerning the issue of distrust of strangers and the concern that they were not subject to village authorities, see Schindler, *Rebellion, Community and Custom in Early Modern Germany,* 242-243; and Frank, "Satan's Service or Authorities' Agent? Publicans in Eighteenth-Century Germany," 33.

[32] Two villages of about the same size near fictitious Hochfeld each supported only two barrel makers during the same time period; Ittlingen's list of trade workers dates to 1807, and Fürfeld's to 1830. A village farther to the south in Württemberg, Neckarhausen, also supported two barrel makers as of 1790. Neuwirth, *Ittlingen,* 299. Schüßler *et al., Fürfeld,* 363. Sabean, *Property [in] Neckarhausen,* 461.

Chapter 3

[33] In a historical example of the drive to consolidate, the von Gemmingen family purchased several villages from the von Weinsberg family beginning in 1449: Guttenberg, Kälbertshausen, Hüffenhardt, Siegelsbach, and Mühlbach (today, Neckarmühlbach). In 1476, they added Bonfeld and Eschenaw (today, Treschlinken); and in 1516, Ehrstädt and Steinsfurt. In 1593, they added Fürfeld. Their final purchases were Talheim and Wollenberg in 1717. Konnerth, ed., *1200 Jahre Wollenberg: Ein Heimatbuch*, 62; and Schüßler *et al.*, *Fürfeld*, 109-110. Concerning the mortality rate of the Black Death, see Gottfried, *The Black Death: Natural and Human Disaster in Medieval Europe*, 68-69. Kelly, *The Great Mortality: An Intimate History of the Black Death, the Most Devastating Plague of all Time*, 260-261. Scott and Duncan, *The Return of the Black Death*, 30-31.

[34] Württemberg did not become a duchy until 1495. When the fictional baron von Steinweg purchased Hochfeld in 1449, the County of Württemberg was still split among the descendants of Conrad von Beutelsbach, the first to call himself the Count of Württemberg, which was the name of his castle. In 1482, the County was reunited under Eberhard V, who then became Eberhard I when his County became a duchy.

[35] For example, nearby in Ittlingen, various branches of the von Gemmingen family as well as the von Kochendorf family shared ownership of the village through the 18th century. Neuwirth, *Bad Rappenau*, 80-81 and 89-90. In neighboring Fürfeld and Guttenberg, two branches of the von Gemmingen families continue to live in their ancestral castles in the early 21st century, and still own some parcels of the land that their family controlled for centuries.

[36] Strauss, *Law, Resistance, and the State*, 56-57.

[37] Huebner, *A History of Germanic Private Law*, 208. This work has an extensive discussion of the "good old law," the Germanic concept of property, and the reception of Roman law. For another discussion of the dual ownership system, see Mayhew, *Rural Settlement and Farming in Germany*, 43. For a discussion of Grundherrschaft and Gutsherrschaft, see Wunder, "Agriculture and Agrarian Society," 75-76.

[38] Theibault, "Community and *Herrschaft* in the Seventeenth-Century German Village," 3-5. See also Robisheaux, *Rural Society*, 8-9.

[39] Blickle, *The Revolution of 1525*, 47-55.

[40] From a 22 Nov 2005 email, David Sabean to author: "During the Middle Ages the serfs of a manor in principle held land from the lord to which they were subject. They probably paid the tithe to him for the upkeep of the church and were subject to his courts. That is, of course, a model--but it broke up in the 13th, 14th, and 15th centuries. That meant that a villager could hold land from one lord, be the Leibeigene of another, and be subject to the court jurisdiction of yet another. Many of the late 15th century issues involved lords trying to bring the relationships back together." As Bak makes clear in "Serfs and Serfdom: Words and Things," 6-8, there is little agreement on the terminology of serfdom nor on the dates of its rise and fall. See also Wunder, "Serfdom in Later Medieval and Early Modern Germany, 257. Blickle, *The Revolution of 1525*, 29-30. Duby, *The Early Growth of the European Economy: Warriors and Peasants from the Seventh to the Twelfth Century*, 82-117, 128, 168-184.

[41] "It was more difficult to build territorial rule on serfdom than on landlordship. Serfs could not be sold. So lords found a solution by trading serfs, at first one man for one man, a woman for a woman, but then in groups of ten to twenty persons, and finally in exchanges involving more than a thousand serfs . . . This process of territorial formation played itself out essentially in the fifteenth century although there had been modest beginnings in the fourteenth century and a rearguard action that stretched down to the mid-sixteenth century . . . " Blickle, *The Revolution of 1525*, 48-49. Concerning the practice of using death duties as a method of land confiscation, see Wunder, "Serfdom," 255-256. Sreenivasan, *Peasants*, 47. Blickle, *Ibid.*, 69-70. Concerning the inheritability of servile status, Wunder in the above-referenced source noted that even children with one free parent generally inherited the other parent's unfree status, so the percentage of unfree peasants increased in each generation.

[42] Hughes, *Early Modern Germany*, 156-157. Gagliardo, *Pariah to Patriot: The Changing Image of the German Peasant*, 11. Danziger and Gillingham, *1215: The Year of Magna Carta*, 28.

[43] Villagers in Fürfeld, located a few kilometers west of fictional Hochfeld, were still providing unpaid labor services to the von Gemmingen family as late as 1834. Schüßler *et al.*, *Fürfeld*, 85. Based on an agreement reached in 1833, villagers in Wollenberg, a few kilometers to the northwest, were allowed to pay a fee of 95 gulden in lieu of their labor requirement. Konnerth, *Wollenberg*, 123.

[44] Adapted from the oaths required of villagers in Fürfeld. Schüßler *et al.*, *Fürfeld*, 133-134. Concerning the enforceability of the oaths, see Blickle, *The Revolution of 1525*, 55.

[45] Adapted and, in some cases, reordered, from the Dorfordnungen first imposed on the village of Fürfeld in the fifteenth century by the barons von Gemmingen. Schüßler *et al.*, *Fürfeld*, 112-132.

[46] The hypothetical Hochfeld Fron rates are based on those in the village of Ittlingen. Neuwirth, *Ittlingen*, 84 and 327. See also Ogilvie, *State Corporatism and Proto-Industry*, 41. Wunder, "Agriculture and Agrarian Society," 76. Pascel, *The Social Basis of the German Reformation: Martin Luther and his Times*, 11-12.

[47] Blickle, *The Revolution of 1525*, 41-42.

[48] Listing from Konnerth, *Wollenberg*, 123-126. See also Luckhaupt, *900 Jahre Hüffenhardt*, 119-121. The estimate of the overall burden is from Blickle, *The Revolution of 1525: The German Peasants' War From a New Perspective*, 79. See n. 15, p. 225 of this same source for a listing of the animals and footstuffs covered by the Small Tithe. Concerning the entry fee, see Sreenivasan, *Peasants*, 9-13 and 19-20. See also 3 sources under the footnotes to the same chapter concerning the use of the death tax as an instrument of peasant usurpation.

[49] Quotation taken from two separate passages from Robisheaux, *Rural Society*, 10 and 34.

[50] The term *morgen* referred to the amount of land a man could plow in a morning. The morgen was in use in many locales in northern Baden and Württemberg, including the area profiled in this book. A distinction was sometimes made between the morgen, used to measure fields and forest land, and the *tagwerk* ("day's work"), used to measure meadows and gardens.

Not all locales measured their land using a morgen; some used a standard called a *jochert* or *jauchert*. The name derived from the yoke-teams of oxen used to plow the fields, and it referred to the amount of land a man could plow in a day. This measurement was common in southern Württemberg, where a jauchert measured about .33 hectares; in Austria, .58 hectares; in Bavaria, .35 hectares, and in

Switzerland, .36 hectares. The size of the morgen also varied from one place to another. The measurement standard from the city of Speyer was common, but both Baden and Württemberg also had standards. No matter which standard was used, the basic unit of measure was called the *messrute* or measuring rod. Under the Speyer system, for example, the messrute was equivalent to 12 *schuhe*, or 3.3224 meters. A morgen calculated using the Speyer length would have equaled 37.58 square meters, or just under an acre. A morgen calculated using the Badenese-approved length would have been slightly less — just under .9 of an acre. It has been estimated that in a moderately successful harvest year, an average family of 4.71 persons could be supported on a minimum of 6.5 morgen of cultivated land, once rents and taxes had been paid and assuming that one-third of the land lay fallow each year.

[51] Based on the *Bonfelder Vertrag* of 6 July 1579 between the *Grafen* or counts von Öttingen and the villagers of Ittlingen. The agreement came about as a result of a village protest concerning the increased burden of lordly requirements and charges. The purpose of including this segment is to emphasize the reciprocal nature of the relationship between lord and village. Neuwirth, *Ittlingen*, 81-87. The requirement to plant three saplings for each tree taken comes from the Fürfeld Dortordnungen, Schüßler *et al., Fürfeld*, 119. The limited rights to hunt, referred to in the hypothetical *Allerheiligener Vertrag*, were taken from a sixteenth-century agreement between lords and villagers in the Upper Rhine. See Blickle, *The Revolution of 1525: The German Peasants' War From a New Perspective*, 175. Blickle also has an informative discussion on forest laws and the frequency of peasant demands to harvest wood, 74-76.

[52] Kaschuba, "Peasants and Others: The Historical Contours of Village Class Society," 243, writes about the "substantial redistribution" in village land holdings from the poorer to the richer families after 1849. The dates and financial details of the Frondienst and tenancy redemptions were adapted from Neuwirth, *Ittlingen*, 123 and 127. See also Luckhaupt, *900 Jahre Hüffenhardt*, 40-42. Concerning the abolishment of tithes, see Lee, *The Politics of Harmony: Civil Service, Liberalism, and Social Reform in Baden, 1800-1850*, 150-151.

Chapter 4

[53] Hillerbrand, *The World of the Reformation*, 6, wrote that few parish priests had studied at university before the Reformation, but he also concluded that most of them sincerely attempted to be good shepherds to their flocks. See also Schorn-Schütte, "Priest, Preacher, Pastor: Research on Clerical Office in Early Modern Europe," 1-39. Singman, *Daily Life in Medieval Europe*, 13. Burke, *Popular Culture*, 271. Concerning the widespread practice of priests' keeping concubines, see Forster, *The Counter-Reformation in the Villages: Religion and Reform in the Bishopric of Speyer, 1560-1720*, 21-27. More than half the priests in the Bishopric kept concubines, based on a series of church visitations in the 1580s. Until the Napoleonic period, the Bishopric of Speyer included most of the southern Palatinate, northern Baden, and part of Württemberg.

[54] Gemmingen-Guttenberg, *Life in Guttenberg Castle*, 24. Wolf von Gemmingen introduced Reformation-style worship in the village of Guttenberg in 1521. In *Counter-Reformation* (143 n.90), Forster writes, "The von Gemmingen family resisted even the slightest interference on the part of the bishop." See also Hughes, *Early Modern Germany, 1477-1806*, 30-31.

[55] In 1521, the von Gemmingen family installed a new pastor in the village church of Fürfeld, not far from Hochfeld's imagined site. Martin Germanus, considered to be the village's first Evangelisch pastor, had studied at the University of Heidelberg and later at Martin Luther's University of Wittenberg. Schüßler *et al.*, *Fürfeld*, 218.

[56] Pascel, *Social Basis*, 93, and Brendler, *Martin Luther: Theology and Revolution*, 70-73.

[57] Marius, *Martin Luther*, 72 and 138-139, and Beutel, "Luther's Life," 8-9.

[58] Marius, *Ibid.*, 132, and Brendler, *Martin Luther*, 100-104.

[59] Aland, *Martin Luther's 95 Theses*, 54-57, and Brendler, *Ibid*, 106-108.

[60] Marius, *Martin Luther*, 6 and 146; and Whitford, "Luther's Political Encounters," 179-182.

[61] Marius, *Ibid.*, xi. Hughes, *Early Modern Germany*, 28-38. Hillerbrand, *The World of the Reformation*, 28. Kolb, "Luther's Function in an Age of Confessionalization," 219-221.

[62] Hughes, *Ibid.*, 38.

[63] Marius, *Martin Luther*, 129; and Brendler, *Martin Luther*, 105-109.

[64] Marius, *Ibid*, 273-274; and Brendler, *Ibid.*, 190-191.

[65] Marius, *Ibid.*, 275-289; and Brendler, *Ibid.*, 192 and 203.

[66] Hillerbrand, *The World of the Reformation*, 31.

[67] Barzun, *From Dawn to Decadence: 500 Years of Western Cultural Life*, 10, and Hillerbrand, *Ibid.*, 28.

[68] McNeill, *The History and Character of Calvinism*, 44-47 and 210-212. Burke, *Popular Culture*, 216-218 and 226-229. Marius, *Martin Luther*, 49.

[69] The United Church of Christ website hosts a short on-line course about its early history. Refer to http://www.ucc.org/about-us/short-course/, accessed 12 July 2010.

[70] Goertz, *The Anabaptists*, 7 and 13-14, and Clasen, *Anabaptism: A Social History, 1525-1618*, 1-14 and 95-151.

[71] Goertz, *Ibid.*, 7. Clasen, *Ibid.*, 358-394. Fogleman, *Hopeful Journeys*, 5.

[72] Forster, *Counter-Reformation*, 5-9 and 58-60.

[73] Gawthrop, *Pietism and the Making of Eighteenth-Century Prussia*, 104-120.

[74] Guggenheim, "Meeting on the Road: Encounters between German Jews and Christians on the Margins of Society," 126-127. Haverkamp, "The Jewish Quarters in German Towns during the late Middle Ages," 14-18. Toch, "Aspects of Stratification of Early Modern German Jewry," 81-82. Daxelmüller, "Organizational Forms of Jewish Popular Culture since the Middle Ages," 14-15. Lowenstein, "The Rural Community and the Urbanization of German Jewry," 219-220.

[75] Trevor-Roper, *The Crisis of the Seventeenth Century*, 109. Hughes, *Early Modern Germany*, 75-76. Ozment, *The Burgermeister's Daughter*, 75. Guggenheim, "Meeting on the Road: Encounters between German Jews and Christians on the Margins of Society," 125-127. Jersch-Wenzel, "Jewish Economic Activity in Early Modern Times", 95. Daxelmüller, "Organizational Forms of Jewish Popular Culture since the Middle Ages," 29. For a discussion of Jews and crime, see Ulbright, "Criminality and Punishment of the Jews in the early modern period," 49-70.

[76] Jersch-Wenzel, *Ibid.*, 92-93.

[77] Richard Marius, *Martin Luther*, 471-472.

[78] Lortz, *The Reformation in Germany*, 45-46; and Clasen, *Anabaptism*, 376-380.

[79] Hillerbrand, *The World of the Reformation*, 97-102. Whitford, "Luther's Political Encounters," 187. Lortz, *The Reformation in Germany*, 59-63 and 73-74.

[80] Hillerbrand, *The World of the Reformation*, 107-108. Hughes, *Early Modern Germany*, 31-32. Lortz, *The Reformation in Germany*, 322-324. Pascel, *Social Basis*, 90-91.

[81] Forster, *Counter-Reformation*, 1-4.

[82] Schüßler *et al., Fürfeld*, 132. Residents in Fürfeld were forbidden to work on Sundays and festival days except when bad weather threatened the harvest or the hay was in danger of blight from rain.

Chapter 5

[83] Luther. *Sermons on the Most Interesting Doctrines of the Gospel*, 107.

[84] Ozment, *The Burgermeister's Daughter*, 77-78, wrote about how the knowledge of Christ's teaching, which peasants acquired during the Reformation, motivated them to reject their servile status. See also Midelfort's book review, "The Revolution of 1525? Recent Studies of the Peasants' War," 192-194; and Hillerbrand, *The World of the Reformation*, 50.

[85] The first local disturbance in the Peasants' War occurred the summer of 1524 in Stühlingen, near the Black Forest, and was an altercation between lord and peasant that was similar to the hypothetical incident in Hochfeld. In the historical event, the local countess required that her peasants pick berries and snail shells for her in the midst of harvest season. See Crossley, *Luther and the Peasants' War*, 33. The description of the practice of using peasants to aid the hunt came from Marius, *Martin Luther*, 417. The two-day Fron imposition for hunting came from the village ordinances in Schüßler *et al., Fürfeld*, 284-285.

[86] Geyer was a historical figure; see Blickle, *The Revolution of 1525*, xvii and 113-115.

[87] Hillerbrand, *The World of the Reformation*, 83; and Blickle, *Ibid.*, 5, xiv and 120-122.

[88] Crossley, *Peasants' War*, 27-29. Hughes, *Early Modern Germany*, 46-47. Wunder, "'Old Law' and 'Divine Law' in the German Peasant War," 54. Huebner, *Germanic Private Law*, 19 27 and 186 189.

[89] Crossley, *Peasants' War*, 31-32. Graus, "From Resistance to Revolt: The Late Medieval Peasant Wars in the Context of Social Crisis," 5-6. Sreenivasan, "The Social Origins of the Peasants' War of 1525 in Upper Swabia," 44-45. Midelfort's book review, "The Revolution of 1525," 190-191. Blickle, *The Revolution of 1525*, xiii-xiv and 87.

[90] Robisheaux, *Rural Society*, 49 and 53; and Hughes, *Early Modern Germany*, 46-47.

[91] Blickle, *The Revolution of 1525*, 195-201. Pascel, *Social Basis*, 133-135. Cohn, "The Peasants of Swabia," 10-11.

[92] Bax, *The Peasants War in Germany, 1525-1526*, 218-221; and Blickle, *Ibid.*, xiv.

[93] Quoted in Bax, *The Peasants War in Germany*, 164. See also Blickle, *Ibid.*, xxi-xxii.

[94] The incident in Heilbronn is historical, as is the quotation, although of course Hans Mann is fictional. See Burke, *Popular Culture*, 189. See also Marius, *Martin Luther*, 423-424; and Pascel, *Social Basis*, 142-143.

[95] Richard Marius, *Ibid.*, 424-427; and Crossley, *Peasants' War*, 52-55.

[96] Richard Marius, *Ibid.*, 430-431; and Crossley, *Ibid.*, 56-59.

[97] Some eminent historians have interpreted the Peasants' War as a struggle between a well-off village oligarchy and the peasants living on the edge of subsistence; see for example Sreenivasan, "Social Origins of the Peasants' War," 32. This view is not shared by the preeminent historian of the Peasants' War, Blickle, who framed the rebellion as a conflict between lord and peasant. Nevertheless, it is logical that the richer peasants with the most to lose would be motivated to negotiate a settlement of the conflict.

[98] According to Robisheaux, *Rural Society*, 66, many overlords eased restrictions on and signed agreements with their peasants following the Peasants' War in order to prevent another widespread rebellion.

[99] Bax, *The Peasants War in Germany*, 275-325 and 353-356. Marius, *Martin Luther*, 432. Robisheaux, *Rural Society*, 65-66. Pascel, *Social Basis*, 146. Hillerbrand, *The World of the Reformation.*, 83. Ozment, *A Mighty Fortress: A New History of the German People*, 76.

[100] Dülmen, in *Theater of Horror: Crime and Punishment in Early Modern Germany*, 92-93, discussed the relative infrequency of the most severe punishments such as quartering.

[101] Gawthrop, *Pietism*, 18-19. Schulze, "Peasant Resistance in Sixteenth- and Seventeenth-Century Germany in a European Context," 81-87. Hughes, *Early Modern Germany*, 50. Robisheaux, *Rural Society*, 65-69. Blickle, *The Revolution of 1525*, 172-176.

[102] As of 1573, the nearby village of Fürfeld had four large *Höfe* and about eight middling Höfe; the rest of the families farmed strips in the common field. The largest *Hof* had 50½ morgen in fields, 7 morgen in meadowland, and a ½-morgen garden. Schüßler *et al.*, *Fürfeld*, 167-178.

[103] Ozment, *A Mighty Fortress*, 108-111.

[104] Robisheaux, *Rural Society*, 235; and Gardiner, *The Thirty Years' War, 1618-1648*, 21-82.

[105] Gardiner, *Ibid.*, 62-63.

[106] The term "swarm of locust" is from Gardiner, *Ibid.*, 63.

[107] Adapted from the journal of Stephan Meyer, pastor of Uteregg in Swabia, which covered the period 1623-1634. Quoted in Sreenivasan, *Peasants*, 282. See also Mortimer, "Individual Experience and Perception of the Thirty Years War in Eyewitness Personal Accounts," 147-149.

[108] Ergang, *Myth*, 20. Ergang noted that despite the severe devastation wrought in parts of Germany, in most cases peasants who had fled to the safety of city walls eventually returned to rebuild their villages.

[109] Robisheaux, *Rural Society*, 79.

[110] Schüßler *et al.*, *Fürfeld*. In Fürfeld, a nearby village to hypothetical Hochfeld, there were 48 families in 1617, 29 in 1628, 6 in 1642, and 9 in 1648; the population did not return to pre-war levels until the mid-eighteenth century. There was not a single cow left in Fürfeld in 1648, and only 3 horses (see pp. 192-195). As in Hochfeld, almost all of Fürfeld's residents who were born between 1634 and 1650 were born in Wimpfen. A summary of the destruction in Fürfeld in the years 1622 and 1634 can be found on pp. 256-257. Wimpfen itself dropped from 400 families to 37 (see p. 255). For a discussion concerning the common practice of burying money, and the extortion and murder practiced by soldiers to unearth these caches, see Mortimer, "Individual Experience and Perception of the Thirty Years War," 150-155.

[111] Gardiner, *The Thirty Years' War*, 213-220; and Hughes, *Early Modern Germany*, 94-97.

[112] Stier and von Hippel, "War, Economy, and Society," 235. Hughes, *Early Modern Germany*, 106-109. Ergang, *Myth*, 4-27. Mortimer, "Individual Experience and Perception of the Thirty Years War," 142. Flenley, *Modern German History*, 23.

[113] Sreenivasan, *Peasants*, 312-314, documented the fact that the peasant families who were richer and more powerful *before* the Thirty Years' War frequently resumed their former status *after* it. See also Schubert, "Daily Life," 350-353. Concerning the arrival of Mennonite families in the Kraichgau and the Palatinate following the Thirty Years' War, see Schüßler *et al.*, *Fürfeld*, 175 and 186-187).

Chapter 6

[114] The list of duties is taken from those in a Württemberg village in Sabean, *Property [in] Neckarhausen*, 67.

[115] Modeled after Ittlingen, whose early Rathaus burned during the Thirty Years' War and was replaced after 1648. Neuwirth, *Ittlingen*, 226-227.

[116] This *Gemeinderechnung* is loosely based on the 1749 community accounting for the village of Wollenberg. Konnerth, *Wollenberg*, 164.

[117] Theibault, "Community and *Herrschaft*," 6, and Wunder, "Serfdom," 261. Concerning the fifteenth-century intrusion by Grundherren into community affairs, see chapter 2 of this book and Blickle, *The Revolution of 1525*, 71-72. Blum, who was writing about village self-government across Europe, placed the final disintegration of self-government as beginning in some locales by the eighteenth century and lasting in others through the twentieth. Blum is referring here to the evolution of modern governmental administration by political states rather than the personalized power balance between community and local lord. Blum, "The Internal Structure and Polity of the European Village Community from the Fifteenth to the Nineteenth Century," 541.

[118] Blum, *Ibid.*, 556.

[119] Blum, *Ibid.*, 541-543; and Blickle, *The Revolution of 1525*, 82.

[120] Blum, *Ibid.*, 544-547; and Warde, *Ecology, Economy and State Formation*.

[121] Walker, *German Home Towns*, 133-134.

[122] Walker, *Ibid.*, 137-142. Sabean, *Property [in] Neckarhausen*, 61. Blum, "Internal Structure and Polity," 549-551. Benecke, *Society and Politics in Germany*, 16-19.

[123] The percentage of households holding wealth was based on the percentage found in the Württemberg village of Kornwestheim, just south of Ludwigsburg, where by 1628, "30.6 percent of the population, owned 76.5 percent of all the property in the village." An assumption was made that family size averaged 4.5, so that for the 627 inhabitants in Hochfeld in 1817, there would have been approximately 139 heads of household; 30.9 percent of those households would have equaled 43. The Kornwestheim data are from Blum, "Internal Structure and Polity," 572. The Hochfeld hypothetical elite of six households was based on data from Bächlingen, about 70 kilometers east of Hochfeld, where six families controlled 54 percent of the land. This is also similar to the number of elite households in the Kraichgau village of Fürfeld, where in 1573, there were four large farm holdings, eight middling holdings, and the rest of the households held strips scattered among the village fields. Robisheaux, *Rural Society*, 87-88; and Schüßler *et al.*, *Fürfeld*, 167-178. See also Sreenivasan, *Peasants*, 150-151, which discusses village poverty rates and poor relief. Sabean's *Property [in] Neckarhausen*, 454-469, discusses the distribution of village wealth in Neckarhausen, where in 1710, the lowest 50 percent of residents held 16.5 percent of village wealth, while the top 10 percent held 28.6 percent; by 1870, given the pressure of population growth, those statistics were 13.8 percent for the lowest 50 percent and 32.5 for the highest 10 percent.

[124] The percentage of Bürger children who became landless is from Sreenivasan, *Peasants*, 193. See also Sabean, "German Agrarian Institutions at the Beginning of the Sixteenth Century: Upper Swabia as an Example" 83. Robisheaux, *Rural Society*, 84. Sreenivasan, "Social Origins of the Peasants' War," 31-32. Schlumbohm, "From

Peasant Society to Class Society: Some Aspects of Family and Class in a Northwest German Protoindustrial parish, 17th-19th Centuries," 193, discussed the downward mobility caused by increasing populations.

[125] Blum, "Internal Structure and Polity," 573-576; and Sabean, *Power in the Blood: Popular Culture and Village Discourse in Early Modern Germany*, 165.

[126] Information on the *Vetter-Gericht* or *Vetterlesgericht* is from Sabean, *Kinship in Neckarhausen, 1700-1870*, 37-57. Information on the Badenese governmental reforms of community councils is from Lee, *The Politics of Harmony*, 112. The Hochfeld Bürgermeister from 1893 is, of course, fictional. However, in two actual villages near hypothetical Hochfeld, some family names of village leaders from the early modern period were still appearing in the twentieth century: In Fürfeld, Johann Michael Betz was Schultheiss in 1843, Christian Dietrich Betz was Schultheiss from 1858-1866, and Christian Jakob Betz held the same office from 1894-1904. In Hüffenhardt, the same family names that appeared on lists of the Gericht members and other offices, including Schneider, Dallmus, Sigmann, and Widmann were still appearing as late as the 1980s, when Ernst-Georg Schneider II was a member of the Gemeinderat. Following in the footsteps of their ancestors, Karl Schneider, Philipp Ludwig Dallmus, and Gustav Sigmann, served as Bürgermeister in the nineteenth century, and Ernst B. Widmann served from 1945-1954.

[127] Walker, *German Home Towns*, 56-57. For a discussion of the relationship between rich and poor farmers, see also Sreenivasan, *Peasants*, 42-49.

[128] It was not uncommon for a village to have so many administrative posts. In one documented listing, Wildberg in southern Württemberg, with a population of 1,328, had 95 such posts in 1717, held by one-fifth of the male heads of household. Nearby Gültlingen, with a population of 860, had 51 posts; this ratio has been used to set the number of hypothetical posts in Hochfeld. Ogilvie, *State Corporatism and Proto-Industry*, 59-60. The description of the night watchman post is from Neuwirth, *Ittlingen*, 209-210.

[129] From the description of the Feldrichter in Ittlingen. Neuwirth, *Ibid.*, 210-212.

[130] From the description of the Schultheiss in Ittlingen. Neuwirth, *Ibid.*, 202-208.

[131] Vann, *The Making of a State: Württemberg, 1593-1793*, 39-40, provides a concise summary of the duties of a typical *Gericht*. See also Wegert, *Popular Culture, Crime, and Social Control in 18th-Century Württemberg*, 37-38, and Sabean, *Property [in] Neckarhausen*, 66-67.

[132] From the description of the Amtmann for the von Gemmingen family. Schüßler *et al., Fürfeld*, 277.

[133] Lee, *The Politics of Harmony*, 17-19.

[134] Hughes, *Early Modern Germany*, 180-189. For a discussion of the impact of mediatization on territories in southwest Germany under the Napoleonic Confederation of the Rhine, see Schmitt, "A Closer Look at the Confederation of the Rhine," 9-39. Concerning the mediatized lords in Baden, see Lee, *Ibid.*, 21 and 27. It is likely that some of the Grundherren to which Lee refers in this statistic were already subject to the Grand Duke; Lee does not differentiate between new and existing Badenese lords.

[135] Lee, *Ibid.*, 25.

[136] Lee, *Ibid.*, 48-56.

[137] Lee, *Ibid.*, 34.

[138] Lee, *Ibid.*, 140-145. See also Walker, *German Home Towns*, 326-322.

[139] Walker, *Ibid.*, 205-206.

[140] The Hochfeld election experience is based on the 1844 election in Ittlingen, in which the local Freiherr convinced the district administrator to confirm his own rent collector as Bürgermeister over the two other candidates; the winner in the popular vote, who admitted to political activity, was coerced to withdraw his name from the election. Neuwirth, *Ittlingen*, 216-217.

Chapter 7

[141] The Ruggericht was a common institution in early modern Germany. Hochfeld's Ruggericht has been based on that in Fürfeld, an actual village a view kilometers to the west of hypothetical Hochfeld. Most of the court cases were taken from an 1836 Ruggericht session in Fürfeld. Schüßler *et al.*, *Fürfeld*, 163-166.

[142] Wegert, *Popular Culture*, 25-26; and Rublack, *Crimes of Women*, 46.

[143] Sabean, *Kinship in Neckarhausen*, 31.

[144] Sreenivasan, *Peasants*, 67, writes about the pastoral families as outsiders to the village, and also the pastors' supervision of the schoolmasters.

[145] Hull, *Sexuality, State, and Civil Society*, 381.

[146] In a 1795 case from the village of Wollenberg, near fictional Hochfeld, a woman bore an illegitimate child. She had left her husband many years before, and she had lived alone with her two children. After her illegitimate child was born, the local lord assessed a fine of 10 gulden. She pleaded for mercy, telling the court that she was poor and unlucky. The lord acknowledged her adversity but refused to waive the fine. He also ordered that she be placed in a public place in the village for two hours in the *Geige*, which was a large wooden device that locked about the neck of a convicted person; its purpose was to add to the shame the individual experienced as a result of his or her transgression. Konnerth, *Wollenberg*, 182. According to Isabel Hull (*Sexuality, State, and Civil Society*, 59), the Ruggerichte in Baden and Württemberg "very occasionally . . . decided cases of sexual misbehavior, [but] generally they focused on economic and other police matters."

[147] Dülmen, *Theatre of Horror*, 46-49.

[148] Evans, *Rituals of Retribution: Capital Punishhment in Germany, 1600-1987*, 53-54.

[149] Stuart, *Defiled Trades and Social Outcasts: Honor and Ritual Pollution in Early Modern Germany*, 2-5 and 69-70. Evans, *Rituals of Retribution: Capital Punishment in Germany, 1600-1987*, 53-55. Dülmen, *Theatre of Horror*, 46. Merback, *The Thief, the Cross and the Wheel: Pain and the Spectacle of Punishment in Medieval and Renaissance Europe*, 130-134.

[150] Evans, *Ibid.*, 54-55. Rublack, *Crimes of Women*, 33-35. Roper, *The Holy Household: Women and Morals in Reformation Augsburg*, 37-38.

[151] Thompson, "Rough Music," 514-515. See also Spierenburg, "Social Control and History: An Introduction," 10-14; and Ulinka Rublack, *Ibid.*, 149-152 and 204.

[152] Stuart, *Defiled Trades and Social Outcasts*, 131. Wunder, *He Is the Sun, She Is the Moon: Women in Early Modern Germany*, 190. Dülmen, *Theatre of Horror*, 53. For a discussion on a failed 1798 attempt in Baden to reform punishment systems relating to sexual crimes, see Hull, *Sexuality, State and Civil Society*, 130-133.

[153] Roodenburg and Spierenburg, eds., *Social Control in Europe*; and Evans, *Rituals of Retribution*, 53-55.

[154] 1487 was the the year that the Freiherr von Gemmingen received the Blutbann for his cluster of Kraichgau villages. Schüßler *et al.*, *Fürfeld*, 104. Concerning the polluting nature of the gallows, see Stuart, *Defiled Trades and Social Outcasts*, 123-128.

[155] Wegert, *Popular Culture*, 23-26.

[156] Hull, *Sexuality, State, and Civil Society*, 57, notes that local ordinances varied widely from village to village, relying heavily on common law, and often in contradiction of the supposed statewide ordinances.

[157] Merback, *The Thief, the Cross and the Wheel*, 130. Wegert, *Popular Culture*, 94-95. Rublack, *Crimes of Women*, 54. Anderson and Zinsser, *A History of Their Own: Women in Europe From Prehistory to the Present*, 169-170. Danziger and Gillingham, *1215*, 184-188.

[158] Midelfort, *Witch Hunting*, entire volume. Brauner, *Fearless Wives and Frightened Shrews: The Construction of the Witch in Early Modern Germany*, vii-19. Trevor-Roper, *The Crisis of the Seventeenth Century*, 91-93. Wunder, *He Is the Sun, She Is the Moon: Women in Early Modern Germany*, 143-152. Anderson and Zinser, *Ibid.*, 167.

[159] This was an actual witchcraft case, which occurred in 1716 in Fürfeld. Schüßler *et al.*, *Fürfeld*, 311-323.

Chapter 8

[160] Benz, "Population Change and the Economy," 43, notes that widowers normally married again during the first year, while widows waited somewhat longer.

[161] Concerning the role of male guardians for unmarried women or widows, see Ozment, *The Burgermeister's Daughter*, 111; and Ozment, *Ancestors: The Loving Family in Old Europe*, 27-28.

[162] Ozment, *When Fathers Ruled: Family Life in Reformation Europe*, 61; see also Steven Ozment, *Flesh and Spirit: Private Life in Early Modern Germany*, 43.

[163] The computation of blood relationship using the Germanic system is complicated. Sabean, *Kinship in Neckarhausen*, 74-79, discusses relationship computations and includes diagrams on German consanguinity prohibitions.

[164] This fictional episode is modeled after a historical example from Ozment, *When Fathers Ruled*, 73-74; Ozment's example is, however, from the sixteenth century. The giving of a coin is from Robisheaux, *Rural Society*, 117, who was describing a custom from nearby Hohenlohe villages. A Kriegsvogt is "sometimes [called] a *Tutor*. He represents married women before a court and is court appointed. The representation, however, is of a peculiar kind. It is his job to read documents to the woman and to explain everything and elicit her will. He has no right to decide anything for her. In a sense, he is there to protect her property against her husband." From a 9 February 2008 email of Sabean to the author.

[165] Quotation from Roper, *The Holy Household: Women and Morals in Reformation Augsburg*, 134-135. See also Ozment, *Flesh and Spirit*, 42-44.

[166] Ozment, *When Fathers Ruled*, 37-38.

[167] Robisheaux, *Rural Society*, 116-117. Ozment, *When Fathers Ruled*, 73-74. Anderson and Zinsser, *A History of Their Own*, 123. Greyerz, "Confession as a Social and Economic Factor," 223.

[168] Sreenivasan *Peasants*, 245-246, describes how marriages were used to demonstrate family status in the village. See also Roper, *The Holy Household*, 153. Robisheaux, *Rural Society*, 117-119. Ozment, *Flesh and Spirit*, 43-46.

[169] Taken from the ordinances of the nearby village of Fürfeld. Schüßler *et al.*, *Fürfeld*, 125. See also Robisheaux, *Rural Society*, 117-118.

[170] Greenfield, *Sumptuary Law in Nürnberg: A Study in Paternal Government*. Hunt, *Governance of the Consuming Passions: A History of Sumptuary Law*. Hughes, *Early Modern Germany*, 77-78. Stuart, *Defiled Trades and Social Outcasts*, 29.

[171] Ozment, *The Burgermeister's Daughter*, 104.

[172] Benz, "Population Change and the Economy," 43, describes village blended families.

[173] Sreenivasan, *Peasants*, 148.

[174] Concerning the relative wealth of prospective spouses and the management of the marital fund, see Sabean, *Property [in] Neckarhausen*, 223-246. Concerning the Voraus, see Sreenivasan, *Peasants*, 244.

[175] Sabean, *Ibid.*, 198-201.

[176] The inheritance practices described for the hypothetical village of Hochfeld have been based on practices and ordinances from Württemberg. Since one aim of the author is to make research references accessible to North American readers who are interested in further research, it was necessary to use the outstanding books written by Sabean and Sreenivasan, both of whom studied Württemberg villages. There are no comparable English-language sources for any Badenese villages, nor any German-language sources readily available in U.S. and Canadian libraries.

[177] This pre-marriage inventory was known by several names: *Zubringensinventarium* or *Zubringensinventur*, *Zusammenbringensinven –tarium* or *-tur*, *Beibringensinven –tarium* or *-tur*, or simply *Inventarium allatorum*. Concerning the involvement of various parties and the roster of attendance, see Sabean, *Property [in] Neckarhausen*, 196-197.

[178] Sabean, *Ibid.*, 188-189.

[179] The organization and contents of the Inventur is from Sabean, *Property [in] Neckarhausen*, 194-195. See also Roeber, "The Origins and Transfer of German-American Concepts of Property and Inheritance," 128-136.

[180] Sabean, *Property [in] Neckarhausen*, 197.

[181] Sabean, *Ibid.*, 201, describes the rights and limitations on women concerning the disposition of their own property. See also 166-174 and 111-114 from the same source; Benz, "Population Change and the Economy," 49; and Ozment, *The Bürgermeister's Daughter*, 130-131.

[182] See map, Barbara Willenbacher, "Individualism and Traditionalism in Inheritance Law in Germany, France, England, and the United States," 214. See also Osmond, "Land, Peasant and Lord in German Agriculture since 1800," 75. Roeber, "The Origins and Transfer of German-American Concepts of Property and Inheritance," 127. Sabean, *Property [in] Neckarhausen*, 13. Fogleman, *Hopeful Journeys*, 186 n. 24. Robisheaux, *Rural Society*, 81.

[183] Roeber, "Origins and Transfer," 128.

[184] Sabean, *Property [in] Neckarhausen*, 18 and 207.

[185] Sreenivasan's *Peasants* analyzes a village in which population pressures led to this type of inheritance structure as early as the late sixteenth century. See also Schlumbohm, "From Peasant Society to Class Society," 187-189.

[186] Schlumbohm, *Ibid.*, 193.

[187] Benz, "Population Change and the Economy," 52.

[188] Walker, *German Home Towns*, 398-399.

[189] Data concerning illegitimacy are from Lee, "Bastardy and the Socioeconomic Structure of South Germany, 405. Lee directly links the rate of illegitimacy to the presence of restrictive marriage ordinances. See also Walker, *Germany and the Emigration*, 54-55; and Ogilvie, *State Corporatism and Proto-Industry*, 61-64.

190 Mack Walker, *Ibid.*, 398.

191 Sreenivasan, *Peasants*, 248. See also Wunder, *He Is the Sun*, 190-191; and Sabean, *Property [in] Neckarhausen*, 330-334.

192 Ozment, *The Burgermeister's Daughter*, 27-28, and 59-60. Ogilvie, *State Corporatism and Proto-Industry*, 47. Burghartz, "Ordering Discourse and Society: Moral Politics, Marriage, and Fornication during the Reformation and the Confessionalization Process in Germany and Switzerland," 87-91.

193 Jette Geisberg Bruns, quoted in *Hold Dear, As Always: Jette, a German Immigrant Life in Letters*, ed. Schroeder and Schulz-Geisberg, 47. Concerning the impact of partible inheritance on emigration, see Walker, *Germany and the Emigration*, 48; Roeber, "The Origins and Transfer," 761-763; and Kamphoefner *et al.*, eds., *News from the Land of Freedom: German Immigrants Write Home*, 2-3.

Chapter 9

194 Pine, "Women and the Family," 357. Karant-Nunn, "'Fragrant Wedding Roses': Lutheran Wedding Sermons and Gender Definition in Early Modern Germany," 29. Oakes and Hill, *Rural Costume: Its Origin and Development in Western Europe and the British Isles*, 75, 127, and 164. Sabean, *Property [in] Neckarhausen*, 209.

195 Ozment, *Ancestors*, 22-43.

196 Sreenivasan, *Peasants*, 57. Sabean, *Property [in] Neckarhausen*, 209-211. Ozment, *The Bürgermeister's Daughter*, 112.

197 Hendrix, "Masculinity and Patriarchy in Reformation Germany," 178-179; and Wunder, *He Is the Sun*, 38 and 172.

198 Abrams, "Whores, Whore-Chasers, and Swine: The Regulation of Sexuality and the Restoration of Order in the Nineteenth Century German Divorce Court," 268.

199 Ozment, *When Fathers Ruled*, 51. See also Wunder, *He Is the Sun, She Is the Moon*, 191

200 Phillips, *Untying the Knot: A Short History of Divorce*, 13-19. Ozment, *When Fathers Ruled*, 89-99.

201 Sabean, *Property [in] Neckarhausen*, 124-146, 163-182; and Abrams, "Whores, Whore-Chasers, and Swine," 267-280.

202 Wunder, *He Is the Sun*, 171.

203 Ozment, *Ancestors*, 109.

204 Quotation is from *Oeconomia ruralis et domestica* I, v, 3, quoted in Ozment, *When Fathers Ruled*, 50. See also Hendrix, "Masculinity and Patriarchy," 177.

205 According to the Württemberg census of 1857, 92 percent of families still owned or leased some kind of property. However, beginning in the seventeenth century, agriculture gradually became a smaller and smaller percentage of the family income as family plots shrank and other employment options became available. Cited in Sabean, *Property [in] Neckarhausen*, 38; see also 28-29, 62, 171, and 209.

206 Ozment, *When Fathers Ruled*, 8 and 132.

207 Wunder, *He is the Sun, She is the Moon*, 16.

208 Pine, "Women and the Family," 357; and Anderson and Zinsser, *A History of Their Own*, 88-99, 130.

209 Rublack, "Pregnancy, Childbirth and the Female Body in Early Modern Germany," 97-98; and Anderson and Zinsser, *Ibid.*, 105.

[210] Aikin, "Gendered Theologies of Childbirth in Early Modern Germany and the Devotional Handbook for Pregnant Women by Aemilie Juliane, Countess of Schwarzburg-Rudolstadt (1683)," 51-52. The text in German appears in endnote 36 of the paper.

[211] Rublack, "Pregnancy, Childbirth and the Female Body," 85.

[212] Gottlieb, *The Family in the Western World: From the Black Death to the Industrial Age*, 126-128.

[213] Rublack, "Pregnancy, Childbirth and the Female Body," 93-95.

[214] Coler, quoted in Ozment, *When Fathers Ruled*, 112-113.

[215] Ozment, *Ibid.*, 105-107.

[216] Sabean, *Kinship in Neckarhausen*, 23-26 and 147-157.

[217] Karent-Nunn, *The Reformation of Ritual: An Interpretation of Early Modern Germany*, 76.

[218] Banks, *Birth Chairs, Widwives, and Medicine*, 1-32 and photo, p. 48; Ozment, "The Family in Reformation Germany: The Bearing and Rearing of Children," 161-162.

[219] McIntosh, "Urban Demographic Stagnation in Early Modern Germany: A Simulation," 589-590, writes about the significant variations in infant mortality rates across Germany, and provides specific rates for various regions and cities

[220] Ozment, *When Fathers Ruled*, 116 and 162-166. See also Ozment, *Ancestors*, 18-20; and Sreenivasan, *Peasants*, 207.

[221] Anderson and Zinsser, *A History of Their Own*, 109. Rublack, "Pregnancy, Childbirth and the Female Body," 98-102 and 98-102. Ozment, "The Family in Reformation Germany," 163-165.

[222] Karent-Nunn, *The Reformation of Ritual*, 80-90.

[223] Anderson and Zinsser, *A History of Their Own*, 110-111, describe the folk treatments used by peasant wives in the early modern period.

[224] Melton, *Absolutism and the Eighteenth-Century Origins of Compulsory Schooling in Prussia and Austria*, xiii-5.

[225] Gawthrop and Strauss, "Protestantism and Literacy in Early Modern Germany," 31-55. Maynes, *Schooling for the People: Comparative Local Studies of Schooling History in France and Germany, 1750-1850*, 4. Melton, *Ibid.*, 8.

[226] Melton, *Ibid.*, 11-13; and Friedrichs, "Whose House of Learning? Some Thoughts on German Schools in Post-Reformation Germany," 372-375.

[227] Maynes, *Schooling for the People*, 46-47, 78-82, and 181-184. Maynes writes that almost every child in Baden spent some time in school by the middle of the nineteenth century, and that literacy was by then commonplace. Concerning the ownership of Bibles and hymnals, see Greyerz, "Confession as a Social and Economic Factor," 330. See also Gawthrop and Strauss, "Protestantism and Literacy in Early Modern Germany," 53-54.

[228] The training fee amount and its wage equivalent was taken from the Württemberg village of Ottobeuren; see Sreenivasan, *Peasants*, 215-216. Concerning attainment of master status, see Burgert, *Eighteenth Century Emigrants*, 17. See also Sabean, *Property [in] Neckarhausen*, who writes of the difficulty craftsmen from outside Neckarhausen's territory faced to establish themselves there, 218.

[229] Sabean, *Ibid.*, 97, discusses the fact that at least 60 percent of families in central Europe lacked enough land to feed themselves by the eighteenth century, forcing both men and wome to spend substantial blocks of time away from the home village seeking employment. Concerning the practice of working a decade or more to earn marriage money, see Ozment, *The Bürgermeister's Daughter*, 8.

[230] Kriedte, *Peasants, Landlords and Merchant Capitalists*, 1, notes that it was rare for three or more generations to live together; the basic unit of production was a married couple with their children. See also Sabean, *Ibid.*, 346-348; and Sreenivasan, *Peasants*, 233-236.

[231] Roeber, "The Origins and Transfer," 135. Robisheaux, *Rural Society*, 82-83. Sreenivasan, *Ibid.*, 238-239.

[232] Sabean, *Property [in] Neckarhausen*, 152; and Ozment, *Ancestors*, 75-76. Ozment describes the end of schooling and the beginning of apprenticeships or other training.

[233] Sabean, *Power in the Blood*, 130: writes that while widows and widowers had close to absolute control over joint marriage property, their financial actions were monitored closely by guardians and other family members in order to protect the children's interests.

[234] Roeber, "The Origins and Transfer," 136; he notes that funds provided for job training or emigration expenses were subsequently taken into consideration in property inventories.

Chapter 10

[235] Walker, *German Home Towns*, 76-107.

[236] Sreenivasan, *Peasants*, 333.

[237] Ogilvie, *State Corporatism and Proto-Industry*, 73-75.

[238] Walker, *German Home Towns*, 81.

[239] Hull, *Sexuality, State, and Civil Society*, 42-43. Boes, "'Dishonourable' youth, guilds, and the changed world view of sex, illegitimacy, and women in late-sixteenth-century Gerrmany," 345-372. Roper, *The Holy Household*, 71.

[240] Ogilvie, "Guilds, Efficiency, and Social Capital: Evidence from German Proto-industry," 293-310. Benz, "Population Change and the Economy," 47. Walker, *German Home Towns*, 84-87.

[241] Ogilvie, "The Beginnings of Industrialization," 289 and 290. See also Epstein, "Craft Guilds, Apprenticeship, and Technological Change in Preindustrial Europe," 684.

[242] This list was taken from the guild-covered occupations in the nearby village of Ittlingen in 1803. Neuwirth, *Ittlingen*, 299. One occupation, that of baker, was added to the Ittlingen list.

[243] The additional crafts were taken from a list from Walker, *German Home Towns*, 99. The list was drawn up in the 1780s in a nearby city, Fulda, which is now part of Hessen just north of the Hochfeld area.

[244] See Table 6, "Growth of Principal Handicrafts in Baden, 1810-1844," in Levine, *The Spirit of 1848: German Immigrants, Labor Conflict, and the Coming of the Civil War*, 30.

[245] Levine, *Ibid.*, 33-34.

[246] Robisheaux, *Rural Society*, 90, writes that of the wealthiest 15 villagers in Langenburg, near fictitious Hochfeld, four were millers. Concerning the dishonorable status of millers, the reference was taken from a village book for Hüffenhardt, near fictitious Hochfeld. Luckhaupt, *900 Jahre Hüffenhardt*, 117.

[247] Frank, "Publicans," 28-29, documents that tables in the village tavern were informally "reserved" based on social standing, with the best table set aside for the wealthiest farmers, down to the last table for beggars, gypsies, and the poorest laborers.

[248] Schorn-Schütte, "Priest, Preacher, Pastor: Research on Clerical Office in Early Modern Europe," 12-14 and 20-23.

[249] Burgert, *Eighteenth Century Emigrants*, 14-15. Maynes, *Schooling for the People*, 36-37 and 63-67. Melton, *Absolutism*, 13-15.

[250] Wegert, *Popular Culture*, 37-38: "Arrogant, strutting pastors tyrannized schoolmasters . . . Until the closing decades of the [18th] century schoolmasters in Württemberg were still often artisans with no paedagogical skills who were elected by village notables." See also Maynes, *Schooling for the People*, 59.

[251] Maynes, *Ibid.*, 65-68.

[252] Stuart, *Defiled Trades and Social Outcasts*, 2. Roper, *The Holy Household: Women and Morals in Reformation Augsburg*, 36-38. Walker, *German Home Towns*, 102-107.

[253] Stuart, *Ibid.*, 69-93.

[254] Schüßler *et al.*, *Fürfeld*, 304: The bathhouse in the Kraichgau village of Fürfeld was destroyed during the Thirty Years' War. Concerning the medical services offered by a village bathhouse keeper during the seventeenth century, see Sreenivasan, *Peasants*, 200-201. Concerning the unsavory reputation of bathhouses, see Ariès and Duby, Georges, eds., *A History of Private Life*, Vol. 2, *Revelations of the Medieval World*, 602-603; and Luckhaupt, *900 Jahre Hüffenhardt*, 117.

[255] An 1830 tax listing for the nearby village of Fürfeld, which was one-third larger than fictitious Hochfeld, listed 24 Bauern. Schüßler *et al.*, *Fürfeld*, 363.

[256] Sabean, *Property [in] Neckarhausen*, 65.

[257] Catt, "Farmers and Factory Workers: Rural Society in Imperial Germany: the Example of Maudach," 138-139.

[258] Sabean, *Property [in] Neckarhausen*, 62.

[259] Salamon, *Prairie Patrimony: Family, Farming, and Community in the Midwest*, 160.

[260] Sabean, *Property [in] Neckarhausen*, 255-256.

[261] Mai, *Deutsche Geschichte*, 23-26. Warde, *Ecology, Economy and State Formation*, 56-57. Sreenivasan, *Peasants*, 123-124. Danziger and Gillingham, *1215*, 21-22.

[262] Gagliardo, *Pariah to Patriot*, 8-9. Blanning, *The French Revolution in Germany: Occupation and Resistance in the Rhineland, 1792-1802*, 26-27. Schubert, "Daily Life," 373. Sieglerschmidt, "Social and Economic Landscapes," 18-20. Hughes, *Early Modern Germany*, 14-15. Robisheaux, *Rural Society*, 25-27. Sabean, *Property [in] Neckarhausen*, 21-22.

[263] Sieglerschmidt, *Ibid.*, 16-17.

[264] Sabean, *Property [in] Neckarhausen*, 148-151.

[265] Jordan, *German Seed in Texas Soil*, 37.

[266] Medick, "The Proto-Industrial Family Economy: the Structural Function of Household and Family During the Transition from Peasant Society to Industrial Capitalism," 296-297. Mendels, "Proto-Industrialization: The First Phase of the Industrialization Process," 241-243. Ogilvie, *State Corporatism and Proto-Industry*, 71-31. Sabean, "German Agrarian Institutions," 85.

[267] Ogilvie, *State Corporatism and Proto-Industry*, 1-2. Levine, *The Spirit of 1848*, 30-33. Sreenivasan, *Peasants*, 335.

[268] Medick, "The Proto-Industrial Family Economy," 301-306; and Kriedte, *Peasants, Landlords and Merchant Capitalists*, 64-65.

Chapter 11

[269] During Jacob's earliest years, the hymns would not have included "Silent Night," which was written in Austria in 1818.

[270] The Hochfeld customs described here are imaginary, but based on information from Alexander Tille, "German Christmas and the Christmas-Tree," 166-182. The Hochfeld villagers used boughs rather than today's Advent wreath to decorate their homes and churches. The use of an Advent wreath, which consists of an evergreen wreath decorated with four candles for the four Sundays in Advent, was not documented until 1839 in Hamburg.

[271] Wegert, *Popular Culture*, 49-50. Wegert states that the male villagers themselves chalked the kings' initials, using chalk blessed by the pastor. In some villages, however, this was a child's ritual.

[272] *Ibid.*

[273] Scribner, "Cosmic Order and Daily Life," 17-33.

[274] Anderson and Zinsser, *A History of Their Own*, 90-91. See also Wegert, *Popular Culture*, 44, who notes that 18th century German Christianity contained many elements of the primitive pagan practices.

[275] Anderson and Zinsser, *A History of Their Own*, 99-102.

[276] Ozment, *Ancestors*, 71-73; and Ozment, *When Fathers Ruled*, 153.

[277] Medick, "Village Spinning Bees: Sexual Culture and Free Time Among Rural Youth in Early Modern Germany," 317-331.

[278] Wegert, *Popular Culture*, 50; and "Darstellung des Herrn,": http://de.wikipedia.org/wiki/Darstellung_des_Herrn, accessed 26 Jul 2010.

[279] Anderson and Zinsser, *A History of Their Own*, 98-104. "Darstellung des Herrn," *Ibid.*

[280] http://german.about.com/library/blbraeuche_feb.htm; see the article entitled "German Customs in February, "accessed 26 Jul 2010.

[281] "Darstellung des Herrn"; see web address above, Note 276.

[282] "Karneval, Fastnacht und Fasching," http://de.wikipedia.org/wiki/Fastnacht; accessed 26 Jul 2010.

[283] Wegert, *Popular Culture*, 51.

[284] Blind, "May-Chafer and Spring Songs in Germany," 189.

[285] "Maibaum," http://de.wikipedia.org/wiki/Maibaum; accessed 27 Jul 2010.

[286] Frazer, *The Golden Bough: A Study in Magic and Religion*, writes about the bonfires of St. John's day. On-line at http://www.gutenberg.org/dirs/etext03/bough11h.htm; accessed 26 Jul 2010.

[287] Wegert, *Popular Culture*, 52.

[288] Adapted from a village in the Moselle River valley, taken from Jacob Grimm, *Teutonic Mythology*, Vol. II. Another version can be found in Frazer, *The Golden Bough: A Study in Magic and Religion*.

[289] Roper, *The Holy Household*, 137, writing about sixteenth century Augsburg, notes the extreme difficulty that journeymen experienced in attempting to be certified as master craftsmen.

[290] http://de.wikipedia.org/wiki/Heilbronn#W.C3.BCrttembergische_Oberamtsstadt _ab_1802; this citation is an article entitled "Heilbronn," accessed 26 Jul 2010.

[291] Sabean, *Property [in] Neckarhausen*, 152-157. Anderson and Zinsser, *A History of Their Own*, 88-89 and 130. Mai, *Deutsche Geschichte*, 23-26.

[292] Schubert, "Daily Life," 363-366. Sabean, *Property [in] Neckarhausen*, 150-151. Anderson and Zinsser, *A History of Their Own*, 94-97.

[293] While Evangelisch villages emphasize Totensonntag, also called Ewigkeitssonntag, Catholic villages focus on Allerheiligen (All Saints Day, November 1), and Allerseelen (All Souls Day, November 2).

[294] Fogleman, *Hopeful Journeys*, 17, writes about the baptismal certificates that German pastors provided the emigrants.

[295] Jim Eggert's "Frequently Asked Questions List" for German genealogists, found at http://www.genealogy.net/faqs/sgg.html (accessed 26 Jul 2010), notes that German cemeteries are of limited use to genealogists because most gravesites are not permanent. Families lease plots for a set term, for example 25 years, after which the plot is leased to someone new and reused. For more information, refer to Eggert's questions. The practice of grave leasing continues to this day in most villages. Family members carefully tend their family members' graves, treating each as a tiny garden. They know they will be disgraced in the village if they allow a family grave to become neglected

Chapter 12

[296] Walker, *Germany and the Emigration*, 7. Burgert, *Eighteenth Century Emigrants*, 17. Fogleman, *Hopeful Journeys*, 20. Roeber, "The Origins and Transfer," 147. Hansen, *The Atlantic Migration, 1607-1860*, 5.

[297] See, for example, the manifest for the ship *Marengo*, arriving in New Orleans from Le Havre on 9 July 1938, which lists passengers' baggage as well as their names, occupations, and nationalities. Many of the ships on this route in the late 1830s listed passengers' on-board baggage. See also Wokeck, *Trade in Strangers: The Beginnings of Mass Migration to North America*, 118, who notes that emigrants with money traveled with considerable luggage including household goods.

[298] Wokeck, *Ibid.*, 121, documents the frequency of toll stations along the emigrant routes in Germany, compared to the relative ease for German travelers to journey across France. See also Hansen, *The Atlantic Migration*, 289.

[298] Walker, *German Home Towns*, 116

[299] Hansen, *The Atlantic Migration*, 290-291, documents the system developed to handle the growing number of emigrants in ports and on ships. He also notes the popularity of Le Havre for both the German and Swiss emigrants.

[300] The requirement to present a valid ticket before entering France was imposed in 1837.

[301] Wokeck, *Trade in Strangers*, 121, writes about the widespread use of agents, particularly popular among young single travelers. See also Kamephoefner, Helbich, and Sommer, eds., *News from the Land of Freedom*, 7-8: "The cost of passage was some 30 taler per adult. Compared to daily wages, these were no small sums; compared to the high price of land in Germany, they were insignificant." It is almost impossible to compute an accurate equivalent of money values, but according to a seventeenth-century narrative of German immigrants to Pennsylvania when passage cost 36 taler, 6 taler was then equivalent to 1 British pound (Albert Cook Myers, *Narratives of Early Pennsylvania, West New Jersey, and Delaware, 1630-1707*, 388). An on-line conversion

system of real-value-over-time between U.S. dollars and British pounds yields a dollar value of $109.50 in 2007 dollars for one 1830 pound sterling. At 6 taler to the pound, Jacob's passage cost about $657 in 2007 dollars. See http://www.measuringworth.com/exchange/, accessed 26 Jul 2010, for the conversion formula.

302 Burnett and Luebbering, *German Settlement in Missouri: New Land, Old Ways*, 14, write about the logistical challenge the adequate provision of food and water proved to be for passengers. See also Wokeck, *Trade in Strangers*, 115.

303 Wokeck, *Ibid.*, 129-131. Also, there are several informative pages on the immigrant transatlantic crossing on the Norway Heritage site. Concerning information on passenger accommodations, see "Steerage Passengers – Emigrants Between Decks," http://www.norwayheritage.com/steerage.htm; accessed 26 Jul 2010. The ship *Russell* did indeed make the Le Havre/New Orleans crossing with 60 passengers, arriving in New Orleans on 7 March 1838 — a few weeks earlier than Jacob's fictional crossing. The ship passengers were evenly divided between Germans and French. This was the first and only Le Havre/New Orleans crossing for the *Russell*; on 21 April 1835, it made the Liverpool/New York crossing, commanded by the same captain as on the 1838 crossing, and carrying a full complement of 143 primarily English and Irish immigrants. It is not known what cargo the *Russell* actually carried on its Le Havre/New Orleans run, nor how the cabins were actually set up. The cabins as described are a composite of several immigrant ships' configurations, principally those at the Norway Heritage web site listed earlier in this note.

304 See the brief description of a transatlantic crossing in Fogleman, *Hopeful Journeys*, 34. See also the informative article "Sanitary conditions on board – health and sickness," http://www.norwayheritage.com/health.htm, accessed 26 Jul 2010.

305 See Wokeck, *Trade in Strangers*, 132-135, for a description of sanitary arrangements on the ships. Although the death rate for this voyage is fictitious, it is based on fact. Per Burnett and Luebbering, *German Settlement in Missouri*, 16-17, sickness and infection on board the immigrant ships were epidemic.

306 Grubb, "Redemptioner Immigration to Pennsylvania: Evidence on Contract Choice and Profitability," 407-410; and Doherty, *Puritans, Pilgrims, and Merchants: Founders of the Northeastern Colonies*, 155.

307 Fogleman, *Hopeful Journeys*, 1-11.

308 Levine, *The Spirit of 1848*, 15.

309 Walker, *Germany and the Emigration*, 3. Burnett and Luebbering, *German Settlement in Missouri*, 4. Bruce Levine, *Ibid.*, 23. Concerning one example of a village that subsidized the passage costs for their poorest 30 families, see Natter, *Aspects of Palatine Emigration: Independent and Community Subsidized Emigration from Otterstadt, 1816-1852*. Concerning the impact of partible inheritance on the emigration rate, see Fenske, "International Migration: Germany in the Eighteenth Century," 339. Concerning the decline of weaving as a cottage industry, see Kamphoefner, *The Westfalians: From Germany to Missouri*, 19.

310 The unnamed pastor was quoted in Levine, *The Spirit of 1848*, 53.

311 Roeber, "The Origins and Transfer," 144-145, and "In German Ways? Problems and Potentials of Eighteenth-Century German Social and Emigration History," 761. Walker, *Germany and the Emigration*, 62-63, 75. Jordan, *German Seed in Texas Soil*, 41.

312 Salamon, *Prairie Patrimony*, 18-19, quoting from Faye E. Corner, "A non-mobile, Cooperative Type of Community: A Study of the Descendants of an East Frisian Group," 15-80.

[313] Hunter and Hunter, *Steamboats on the Western Rivers: an Economic and Technological History*, 420-426.

[314] The *Frontier* was an actual riverboat, and its speed record is historical. It is not known if the *Frontier* ever traveled as far south on the river as New Orleans. Based on a review of steamboats on the Louisville-New Orleans route, steamboats in the 1830s averaged 310 tons and carried an average of 124 passengers on their upstream trips. The *Frontier's* tonnage was only 20 percent of that average, so for purposes of this fictitious trip, it was assumed that it would carry about 20 percent of the average upstream passenger load. The ratio of cabin to deck passengers is from Hunter and Hunter, *Steamboats on the Western Rivers: an Economic and Technological History*. The average tonnage and passenger load data are from Haites and Mak, "Steamboating on the Mississippi, 1810-1860: A Purely Competitive Industry," 76.

[315] Concerning the volume of steamboat traffic, see the Wikipedia entry on St. Louis, http://en.wikipedia.org/wiki/St._Louis,_Missouri, accessed 26 Jul 2010. Concerning the rapids that impeded northward Mississippi River traffic above St. Louis through most of the nineteenth century, see the Wikipedia entry on the Des Moines Rapids, accessed 2 Jul 2008.

[316] See http://genealogyinstlouis.accessgenealogy.com/1840.htm, accessed 26 Jul 2010, concerning the 1840 population of the City. For St. Louis' German settlers, see http://stlouis.missouri.org/government/heritage/history/immigrant.htm, accessed 26 Jul 2010.

[317] The family names in this fictitious account are all early names in the real community called Black Jack. Some of the earliest residents were from Westfalian villages including Löhne and Biefeld, and from Hannover villages including Lödingsen. Black Jack, which is located about 12 miles from the St. Louis County Courthouse near the current intersection of Parker and Halls Ferry Roads, featured a clump of three large Black Jack oak trees, which became a meeting place for farmers traveling to market.

[318] Levine, *The Spirit of 1848*, 60; and Kamphoefner *et al.*, eds., News from the Land of Freedom, 12.

[319] Fogleman, *Hopeful Journeys*, 149. Burnett and Luebbering, *German Settlement in Missouri*, 1-7. Kamphoefner, *The Westfalians*, 77. Jordan, *German Seed in Texas Soil*, 41-47. Roeber, "The Origins and Transfer," 765-766.

[320] For a fascinating discussion of the persistence of German farming practices and culture into the twentieth century, see Salamon, *Prairie Patrimony*.

[321] Jette Geisberg Bruns, quoted in *Hold Dear, As Always: Jette, a German Immigrant Life in Letters*, 47-48.

[322] The newspaper was *Der Anzeiger des Westens*, 29 April 1836, quoted in Pickle, "Stereotypes and Reality: Nineteenth Century German Women in Missouri," 293.

[323] Statistics from Kamphoefner *et al.*, eds., *News from the Land of Freedom*, 12-16, from which the phrase "German belt" was taken. Narratives on the flowering of German culture in North America can be found in Levine, *The Spirit of 1848*, 59-60, 81-84; and Burnett and Luebbering, *German Settlement in Missouri*, 83-84 and 103-107.

[324] Kamphoefner *et al.*, eds., *News from the Land of Freedom*, 24-25

[325] Adam Lemp was an actual brewer, known as the father of modern brewing in St. Louis.

[326] Roeber, "The Origins and Transfer," 765: "Germans in America understood their legal rights to property in the villages from which they came and for years after their departure continued to send powers of attorney with returning relatives or friends

for use in converting inherited property into cash for transfer to America. Even poor people who had absconded without paying manumission dues were bold enough to try this. More astonishing still, they sometimes succeeded, after officials deducted the dues and penalties for illegal immigration." Jacob's purchase of a minority interest in the Lemp Brewery is of course fictitious; Adam Lemp's family members were its sole owners during this period.

Bibliography

Abrams, Lynn. "Whores, Whore-Chasers, and Swine: The Regulation of Sexuality and the Restoration of Order in the Nineteenth Century German Divorce Court," *Journal of Family History* 21 (July 1996): 267-280.

Aikin, Judith Popovich. "Gendered Theologies of Childbirth in Early Modern Germany and the Devotional Handbook for Pregnant Women by Aemilie Juliane, Countess of Schwarzburg-Rudolstadt (1683)," *Journal of Women's History* 15 (Summer 2003): 40-67.

Aland, Kurt, ed. *Martin Luther's 95 Theses.* St. Louis: Concordia Publishing House, 1965.

Anderson, Bonnie S. and Judith P. Zinsser. *A History of Their Own: Women in Europe From Prehistory to the Present*, Vol. I. New York: Harper & Row, 1988.

Ariès, Philippe and Georges Duby, eds. *A History of Private Life*, Vol. 2, *Revelations of the Medieval World*. Cambridge: The Belknap Press of Harvard University Press, 1988.

Ashley, W.J. "Meitzen's Siedelung und Agrarwesen der Germanen," *Political Science Quarterly* 13 (March 1898): 143-155.

Bak, Janos. "'The Peasant War in Germany' by Friedrich Engels — 125 Years After," Janos Bak, ed., *The German Peasant War of 1525*. London: Frank Cass and Company Ltd., 1976, 89-98.

_____. "Serfs and Serfdom: Words and Things," *Review* 4 (Summer 1980): 3-18.

Banks, Amanda Carson. *Birth Chairs, Widwives, and Medicine*. Jackson: University Press of Mississippi, 1999.

Barnum, H. Gardiner. *Market Centers and Hinterlands in Baden-Württemberg*. Chicago: The University of Chicago, 1966.

Barzun, Jacques. *From Dawn to Decadence: 500 Years of Western Cultural Life, 1500 to the Present*. New York: HarperCollins, 2000.

Baten, Jörg. "Anthropometrics, Consumption, and Leisure: The Standard of Living," in Sheilagh Ogilvie and Richard Overy, *Germany: A New Social and Economic History*, Vol. III. London: Hodder Arnold, 2003, 383-422.

Bax, E. Belfort. *The Peasants War in Germany, 1525-1526*. New York: Augustus M. Kelley, 1968 (reprint of the 1899 edition).

Behringer, Wolfgang. "Weather, Hunger and Fear: Origins of the European Witch-Hunts in Climate, Society and Mentality," *German History* 13 (1995): 1-27.

Benecke, Gerhard. *Society and Politics in Germany, 1500-1750*. London: Routledge & Kegan Paul, 1974.

Benz, Ernest. "Population Change and the Economy," in Sheilagh Ogilvie and Bob Scribner, eds., *Germany: A New Social and Economic History*, Vol. II. London: Arnold, 1996, 39-62.

Beutel, Albrecht. "Luther's Life," in Donald K. McKim, ed., *The Cambridge Companion to Martin Luther*. Cambridge: Cambridge University Press, 2003, 3-19.

Blanning, T.C.W. *The French Revolution in Germany: Occupation and Resistance in the Rhineland, 1792-1802*. Oxford: Clarendon Press, 1983.

Blickle, Peter. "The Economic, Social and Political Background of the Twelve Articles of the Swabian Peasants of 1525," in Janos Bak, ed., *The German Peasant War of 1525*. London: Frank Cass and Company Ltd., 1976, 63-75.

_____. *The Revolution of 1525: The German Peasants' War From a New Perspective*, trans. Thomas A Brady, Jr., and H.C. Erik Midelfort. Baltimore: The Johns Hopkins Press, 1981.

Blind, Karl. "May-Chafer and Spring Songs in Germany," *The Folk-Lore Journal* (Jun 1883): 187-190.

Blum, Jerome. "The Internal Structure and Polity of the European Village Community from the Fifteenth to the Nineteenth Century," *The Journal of Modern History* 43 (Dec. 1971): 541-576.

Boes, Maria R. "'Dishonourable' youth, guilds, and the changed world view of sex, illegitimacy, and women in late-sixteenth-century Gerrmany," *Continuity and Change* 18 (Dec 2003): 345-372.

Brendler, Gerhard. *Martin Luther: Theology and Revolution*. New York: Oxford University Press, 1991.

Breuilly, John. "Urbanization and Social Transformation, 1800-1914" in Sheilagh Ogilvie and Richard Overy, *Germany: A New Social and Economic History*, Vol. III. London: Hodder Arnold, 2003, 192-226.

Brittingham, Angela and Patricia G. de la Cruz. *Ancestry: 2000: Census 2000 Brief*, Publication C2KBR-35. Washington, D.C.: United States Census Bureau, June 2004.

Brauner, Sigrid. *Fearless Wives and Frightened Shrews: The Construction of the Witch in Early Modern Germany*. Amherst: University of Massachusetts Press, 1995.

Bruns, Jette Geisberg. *Hold Dear, As Always: Jette, a German Immigrant Life in Letters*, ed. Adolf E. Schroeder and Carla Schulz-Geisberg. Columbia: University of Missouri Press, 1988.

Burgert, Annette Kunselman. *Eighteenth Century Emigrants from German-Speaking Lands to North America*, Vol. I: The Northern Kraichgau. Breinigsville, PA: The Pennsylvania German Society, 1983.

Burke, Peter. *Popular Culture in Early Modern Europe*. Aldershot, Hampshire: Ashgate Publishing Ltd., 1994.

Burghartz, Susanna. "Ordering Discourse and Society: Moral Politics, Marriage, and Fornication during the Reformation and the Confessionalization Process in Germany and Switzerland," in Herman Roodenburg and Pieter Spierenburg, eds., *Social Control in Europe*, Vol. 1, 1500-1800. Columbus: The Ohio State University Press, 2004, 78-98.

Burnett, Robyn and Ken Luebbering. *German Settlement in Missouri: New Land, Old Ways*. Columbia: University of Missouri Press, 1996.

Carsten, F.L. *Princes and Parliaments in Germany: From the Fifteenth to the Eighteenth Century*. Oxford: Oxford University Press, 1959.

Catt, Cathleen S. "Farmers and Factory Workers: Rural Society in Imperial Germany: the Example of Maudach," in Richard J. Evans and W.R. Lee, eds., *The German Peasantry: Conflict and Community in Rural Society from the Eighteenth to the Twentieth Centuries*. New York: St. Martin's Press, 1986, 129-157.

Clasen, Claus-Peter. *Anabaptism: A Social History, 1525 1618*. Ithaca: Cornell University Press, 1972.

Cohn, Henry J. "The Peasants of Swabia, 1525," in Janos Bak, ed., *The German Peasant War of 1525*. London: Frank Cass and Company Ltd., 1976, 10-28.

Craig, John E. Book Review of John G. Gagliardo's *From Pariah to Patriot: The Changing Image of the German Peasant, 1770-1840*. *Central European History* 6 (1973): 278-282.

Crossley, Robert N. *Luther and the Peasants' War: Luther's Actions and Reactions*. New York: Exposition Press, 1974.

Danziger, Danny and John Gillingham. *1215: The Year of Magna Carta*. New York: Touchstone, 2003.

Dawson, William Harbutt. *German Life in Town and Country*. London: George Newnes, Ltd., 1901.

Daxelmüller, Christoph. "Organizational Forms of Jewish Popular Culture since the Middle Ages," in R. Po-Chia Hsia and Hartmut Lehman, eds., *In and Out of the Ghetto: Jewish-Gentile Relations in Late Medieval and Early Modern Germany*. Washington, D.C.: The German Historical Institute, 1995, 29-48.

Doherty, Kieran. *Puritans, Pilgrims, and Merchants: Founders of the Northeastern Colonies*. Minneapolis: Oliver Press, 1999.

Dorson, Richard Mercer. *Folklore and Folklife: An Introduction*. Chicago: University of Chicago Press, 1972.

Duby, Georges. *The Early Growth of the European Economy: Warriors and Peasants from the Seventh to the Twelfth Century*, trans. Howard B. Clarke. Ithaca: Cornell University Press, 1974.

Duggan, Lawrence G. *Bishop and Chapter: The Governance of the Bishopric of Speyer to 1552*. New Brunswick, NJ: Rutgers University Press, 1978.

Dülmen, Richard van. *Theater of Horror: Crime and Punishment in Early Modern Germany*, transl. Elisabeth Neu. Cambridge, UK: Polity Press, 1990.

Eaker, Lorena S. "The Germans in North Carolina," *The Palatine Immigrant* 6 (1980): 3-34.

Eire, Carlos M.N. *War Against the Idols: The Reformation of Worship from Erasmus to Calvin*. Cambridge: Cambridge University Press, 1986.

Epstein, S.R. "Craft Guilds, Apprenticeship, and Technological Change in Preindustrial Europe," *The Journal of Economic History* 58 (3) (Sept 1998): 684-713.

Ergang, Robert. *The Myth of the All-Destructive Fury of the Thirty Years' War*. Pocono Pines, PA: The Craftsmen, 1956.

Estes, James M. "Johannes Brenz and the Institutionalization of the Reformation in Württemberg," *Central European History* 6 (1973): 44-59.

Evans, Richard J. *Rituals of Retribution: Capital Punishment in Germany, 1600-1987*. Oxford: Oxford University Press, 1966.

Fenske, Hans. "International Migration: Germany in the Eighteenth Century," *Central European History* 13 (1980): 332-347.

Flenley, Ralph. *Modern German History*, 4th ed. London: J.M. Dent & Sons Ltd., 1968.

Fogleman, Aaron Spencer. *Hopeful Journeys: German Immigration, Settlement, and Political Culture in Colonial America, 1717-1775*. Philadelphia: University of Pennsylvania Press, 1996.

Forster, Marc R. *The Counter-Reformation in the Villages: Religion and Reform in the Bishopric of Speyer, 1560-1720*. Ithaca: Cornell University Press, 1992.

Frank, Michael. "Satan's Service or Authorities' Agent? Publicans in Eighteenth-Century Germany," in Beat Kümin and B. Ann Tlusty, eds., *The World of the Tavern: Public Houses in Early Modern Europe*. Aldershot, England: Ashgate Publishing Limited, 2002, 12-43.

Frazer, Sir James George. *The Golden Bough: A Study in Magic and Religion*, abridged edition. New York: The Macmillan Company, 1923.

Friedeburg, Robert von. "The Making of Popular Cultures of Social Control: A Comparison of Essex (England) and Hesse-Cassel (Germany) during the Reformation," in Herman Roodenburg and Pieter Spierenburg, eds., *Social Control in Europe*, Vol. 1, 1500-1800. Columbus: The Ohio State University Press, 2004, 247-266.

Friedrichs, Christopher R. "Whose House of Learning? Some Thoughts on German Schools in Post-Reformation Germany," *History of Education Quarterly* 22 (Fall 1982): 371-377.

Frommer, Helmut and Hermann Bizer. *1950: Ein schwäbisches Dorf*. Tübingen: Silverburg-Verlag, 2005.

Gagliardo, John G. *From Pariah to Patriot: The Changing Image of the German Peasant, 1770-1840*. Lexington: University Press of Kentucky, 1969.

Gardiner, Samuel Rawson. *The Thirty Years' War, 1618-1648*. New York: Haskell House Publishers, Ltd., 1968. First published 1874.

Gawthrop, Richard and Gerald Strauss. "Protestantism and Literacy in Early Modern Germany," *Past and Present* 104 (August 1984): 31-55.

Gawthrop, Richard L. *Pietism and the Making of Eighteenth-Century Prussia*. Cambridge: Cambridge University Press, 1993.

Gemmingen-Guttenberg, Christoph von. *Life in Guttenberg Castle*, trans. David Syverson and Ehrengard von Gemmingen-Guttenberg. Haßmersheim-Neckarmühlback: Museum of Guttenberg Castle, 1999.

Goertz, Hans-Jürgen. *The Anabaptists*, trans. Trevor Johnson. London: Routledge, 1996.

Gooch, G.P. *Studies in German History*. London: Longmans, Green and Co., 1948.

Gottfried, Robert S. *The Black Death: Natural and Human Disaster in Medieval Europe*. New York: The Free Press, 1983.

Gottlieb, Beatrice. *The Family in the Western World: From the Black Death to the Industrial Age*. New York: Oxford University Press, 1993.

Graus, František. "From Resistance to Revolt: The Late Medieval Peasant Wars in the Context of Social Crisis," in Janos Bak, ed., *The German Peasant War of 1525*. London: Frank Cass and Company Ltd., 1976, 1-9.

Greenfield, Kent Roberts. *Sumptuary Law in Nürnberg: A Study in Paternal Government*. Baltimore: The Johns Hopkins Press, 1918.

Greyerz, Kaspar von. "Confession as a Social and Economic Factor," in Sheilagh Ogilvie and Bob Scribner, eds., *Germany: A New Social and Economic History*. London: Arnold, 1996, 309-349.

Grimm, Jacob. *Teutonic Mythology*, Vol. II. Mineola, NY: Dover Publications, 2004 (a reprint of the original 1883 volume).

Grubb, Farley. "Redemptioner Immigration to Pennsylvania: Evidence on Contract Choice and Profitability," *The Journal of Economic History* 46 (June 1986): 407-418.

Guggenheim, Yacov. "Meeting on the Road: Encounters between German Jews and Christians on the Margins of Society," in R. Po-Chia Hsia and Hartmut Lehman, eds., *In and Out of the Ghetto: Jewish-Gentile Relations in Late Medieval and Early Modern Germany*. Washington, D.C.: The German Historical Institute, 1995, 125-136.

Guinnane, Timothy W. "Population and the Economy in Germany, 1800-1900," in Sheilagh Ogilvie and Bob Scribner, eds., *Germany: A New Social and Economic History*, Vol. III. London: Arnold, 2003, 35-70.

Haites, Erik F. and James Mak. "Steamboating on the Mississippi, 1810-1860: A Purely Competitive Industry," *The Business History Review* 45 (Spring 1971): 52-78.

Haverkamp, Alfred. "The Jewish Quarters in German Towns during the late Middle Ages," in R. Po-Chia Hsia and Hartmut Lehman, eds., *In and Out of the Ghetto: Jewish-Gentile Relations in Late Medieval and Early Modern Germany*. Washington, D.C.: The German Historical Institute, 1995, 13-28.

Heinrich, Christel. "Peasant Customs and Social Structure: Rural Marriage Festivals in the Magdeburg Region in the 1920s," in Richard J. Evans and W.R. Lee, eds., *The German Peasantry: Conflict and Community in Rural Society from the Eighteenth to the Twentieth Centuries*. New York: St. Martin's Press, 1986, 224-234.

Hendrix, Scott. "Masculinity and Patriarchy in Reformation Germany," *Journal of the History of Ideas* 56 (April 1995): 177-193.

Hillerbrand, Hans J. *The World of the Reformation*. New York: Charles Scribner's Sons, 1973.

Hippel, Wolfgang von. *Die Bauernbefreiung im Königreich Württemberg*. 2 vols. Boppard am Rhein: Harald Boldt Verlag, 1977.

Huebner, Rudolf. *A History of Germanic Private Law*, trans. Francis S. Philbrick. London: John Murray, 1918.

Hughes, Michael. *Law and Politics in Eighteenth Century Germany: The Imperial Aulic Council in the Reign of Charles VI*. Bury St. Edmunds: St. Edmundsbury Press, 1988.

_____. *Early Modern Germany, 1477-1806*. Philadelphia: University of Pennsylvania Press, 1992.

Hull, Isabel V. *Sexuality, State, and Civil Society in Germany, 1600-1815*. Ithaca and London: Cornell University Press, 1996.

Hunt, Alan. *Governance of the Consuming Passions: A History of Sumptuary Law*. New York: St. Martin's Press, 1996.

_____. *Governing Morals: A Social History of Moral Regulation*. Cambridge: Cambridge University Press, 1999.

Hunter, Louis C. and Beatrice Jones Hunter. *Steamboats on the Western Rivers: an Economic and Technological History*. New York: Dover Publications, 1993.

Ingram, Martin. "Charivari and Shame Punishments: Folk Justice and State Justice in Early Modern England," in Herman Roodenburg and Pieter Spierenburg, eds., *Social Control in Europe*, Vol. 1, 1500-1800. Columbus: The Ohio State University Press, 2004, 288-308.

Israel, Jonathan I. "Germany and its Jews: A Changing Relationship (1300-1800)," in R. Po-Chia Hsia and Hartmut Lehman, eds., *In and Out of the Ghetto: Jewish-Gentile Relations in Late Medieval and Early Modern Germany*. Washington, D.C.: The German Historical Institute, 1995, 295-304.

Jeggle, Utz. "The Rules of the Village: On the Cultural History of the Peasant World in the Last 150 Years," in Richard J. Evans and W.R. Lee, eds., *The German Peasantry: Conflict and Community in Rural Society from the Eighteenth to the Twentieth Centuries*. New York: St. Martin's Press, 1986, 265-289.

Jersch-Wenzel, Stefi. "Jewish Economic Activity in Early Modern Times," in R. Po-Chia Hsia and Hartmut Lehman, eds., *In and Out of the Ghetto: Jewish-Gentile Relations in Late Medieval and Early Modern Germany*. Washington, D.C.: The German Historical Institute, 1995, 91-101.

Jordan, Terry G. *German Seed in Texas Soil: Immigrant Farmers in Nineetenth-Century Texas*. Austin: University of Texas Press, 1966.

Jütte, Robert. "Poverty and Poor Relief," in Sheilagh Ogilvie and Bob Scribner, eds., *Germany: A New Social and Economic History*. London: Arnold, 1996, 377-404.

Kamphoefner, Walter D. *The Westfalians: From Germany to Missouri*. Princeton: Princeton University Press, 1987.

Kamphoefner, Walter D.; Helbich, Wolfgang; and Sommer, Ulrike, eds. *News from the Land of Freedom: German Immigrants Write Home*. Ithaca: Cornell University Press, 1991.

Karent-Nunn, Susan C. *The Reformation of Ritual: An Interpretation of Early Modern Germany*. London and New York: Routledge, 1997.

_____. "'Fragrant Wedding Roses': Lutheran Wedding Sermons and Gender Definition in Early Modern Germany," *German History* 17 (January 1999): 25-40.

Kaschuba, Wolfgang. "Peasants and Others: The Historical Contours of Village Class Society," in Richard J. Evans and W.R. Lee, eds., *The German Peasantry: Conflict and Community in Rural Society from the Eighteenth to the Twentieth Centuries*. New York: St. Martin's Press, 1986, 235-264.

Kelly, John. *The Great Mortality: An Intimate History of the Black Death, the Most Devastating Plague of all Time*. New York: HarperCollins, 2005.

Kolb, Robert. "Luther's Function in an Age of Confessionalization," in Donald K. McKim, ed., *The Cambridge Companion to Martin Luther*. Cambridge: Cambridge University Press, 2003, 209-226.

Konnerth, Michael, ed. *1200 Jahre Wollenberg: Ein Heimatbuch*. Bad Rappenau: Druckerei Stein GmbH, 1992.

Koslofsky, Craig M. *The Reformation of the Dead: Death and Ritual in Early Modern Germany, 1450-1700*. New York: St. Martin's Press, Inc., 2000.

Kramer, Karl-Sigismund. *Bauern und Bürger im nachmittelalterlichen Unterfranken: Eine Volkskunde auf Grund archivalischer Quellen*. Würzburg: Kommissionsverlag Ferdinand Schöningh, 1957.

Kriedte, Peter. *Peasants, Landlords and Merchant Capitalists: Europe and the World Economy, 1500-1800*. Leamington Spa, England: Berg Publishers Ltd., 1983.

_____. "Trade," in Sheilagh Ogilvie and Bob Scribner, eds., *Germany: A New Social and Economic History*. London: Arnold, 1996, 100-133.

Kümin, Beat and Ann B. Tlusty. "The World of the Tavern: An Introduction," in Beat Kümin and B. Ann Tlusty, eds., *The World of the Tavern: Public Houses in Early Modern Europe*. Aldershot, England: Ashgate Publishing Limited, 2002, 3-11.

Kümin, Beat. "Public Houses and their Patrons in Early Modern Europe," in Beat Kümin and B. Ann Tlusty, eds., *The World of the Tavern: Public Houses in Early Modern Europe*. Aldershot, England: Ashgate Publishing Limited, 2002, 44-62.

Laube, Adolph. "Precursors of the Peasant War: 'Bundschuh' and 'Armer Konnrad' — Popular Movements at the Eve of the Reformation," in Janos Bak, ed., *The German Peasant War of 1525*. London: Frank Cass and Company Ltd., 1976, 48-53.

Lee, Loyd E. *The Politics of Harmony: Civil Service, Liberalism, and Social Reform in Baden, 1800-1850*. Newark: University of Delaware Press, 1980.

Lee, W.R. "Bastardy and the Socioeconomic Structure of South Germany," *Journal of Interdisciplinary History* 7 (Winter 1977): 403-425.

Levine, Bruce. *The Spirit of 1848: German Immigrants, Labor Conflict, and the Coming of the Civil War*. Urbana: University of Illinois Press, 1992.

Liebel, H.P. "The Bourgeoisie in Southwestern Germany, 1500-1789: A Rising Class?," *International Review of Social History* 10 (1965): 283-344.

Long, Pamela O. *Technology, Society, and Culture in Late Medieval and Renaissance Europe, 1300-1600*. Washington, D.C.: American Historical Association, 2000.

Lortz, Joseph. *The Reformation in Germany*, Vol. 2. London: Darton, Longman & Todd: 1968.

Lowenstein, Steven M. "The Rural Community and the Urbanization of German Jewry," *Central European History* 13 (1880): 218-236.

Luckhaupt, Hans. *900 Jahre Hüffenhardt*. Hüffenhardt, Baden-Württemberg: Gemeinde Hüffenhardt, Druckerei Laub GmbH + Co., 1983.

Luther, Martin. *Sermons on the Most Interesting Doctrines of the Gospel*. London: James Duncan, 1830.

Mai, Manfred. *Deutsche Geschichte*. Weinheim: Beltz & Gelberg, 1999.

Marius, Richard. *Martin Luther: The Christian Between God and Death*. Cambridge: Harvard University Press, 1999.

Mayhew, Alan. *Rural Settlement and Farming in Germany*. London: B.T. Batsford Ltd., 1973.

Maynes, Mary J. *Schooling for the People: Comparative Local Studies of Schooling History in France and Germany, 1750-1850*. New York: Holmes & Meier, 1985.

McIntosh, Terence. "Urban Demographic Stagnation in Early Modern Germany: A Simulation," *Journal of Interdisciplinary History* 31 (Spring 2001): 581-612.

McNeill, John T. *The History and Character of Calvinism*. New York: Oxford University Press, 1967.

Medick, Hans. "The Proto-Industrial Family Economy: the Structural Function of Household and Family During the Transition from Peasant Society to Industrial Capitalism," *Social History* 3 (1-2, October 1976): 291-315.

_____. "Village Spinning Bees: Sexual Culture and Free Time Among Rural Youth in Early Modern Germany," in Hans Medick and David Warren Sabean, eds., *Interest and Emotion: Essays on the Study of Family and Kinship*. Cambridge: Cambridge University Press, 1984, 317-339.

Melton, James Van Horn. *Absolutism and the Eighteenth-Century Origins of Compulsory Schooling in Prussia and Austria*. Cambridge: Cambridge University Press, 1988.

Mendels, F.F. "Proto-Industrialization: The First Phase of the Industrialization Process," *Journal of Economic History* 32 (1): 241-261.

Merback, Mitchell B. *The Thief, the Cross and the Wheel: Pain and the Spectacle of Punishment in Medieval and Renaissance Europe*. London: Reaktion Books Ltd., 1999.

Midelfort, H.C. Erik. Book Review, "The Revolution of 1525? Recent Studies of the Peasants' War," *Central European History* 11 (1978): 189-206.

_____. *Witch Hunting in Southwestern Germany, 1562-1684: The Social and Intellectual Foundations*. Stanford: Stanford University Press, 1972.

Mörke, Olaf. "Social Structure," in Sheilagh Ogilvie and Bob Scribner, eds., *Germany: A New Social and Economic History*. London: Arnold, 1996, 134-163.

Myers, Albert Cook. *Narratives of Early Pennsylvania, West New Jersey, and Delaware, 1630-1707*. New York: C. Scribners' Sons, 1912.

Mortimer, Geoffrey. "Individual Experience and Perception of the Thirty Years War in Eyewitness Personal Accounts," *German History* 20 (1 May 2002): 141-160.

Natter, Wolfgang. *Aspects of Palatine emigration: independent and community subsidized emigration from Otterstadt, 1816-1852*. Lexington, KY: The author, 1980.

Neuwirth, Gustav. *Geschichte der Stadt Bad Rappenau*. Bad Rappenau: Druckerei H. Stein, 1978.

_____. *Geschichte der Gemeinde Ittlingen*. Karlsruhe: Harschdruck GmbH, 1981.

Oakes, Alma and Hill, Margot Hamilton. *Rural Costume: Its Origin and Development in Western Europe and the British Isles*. London: B.T. Batsford Ltd., 1970.

Ogilvie, Sheilagh. "The Beginnings of Industrialization," in Sheilagh Ogilvie and Bob Scribner, eds., *Germany: A New Social and Economic History*, Vol. II. London: Arnold, 1996, 263-308.

_____. *State Corporatism and Proto-Industry: The Württemberg Black Forest, 1580-1797*. Cambridge: Cambridge University Press, 1997.

_____. "Guilds, Efficiency, and Social Capital: Evidence from German Proto-industry." *Economic History Review* 57 (May 2004): 286-333.

Osmond, Jonathan. "Land, Peasant and Lord in German Agriculture since 1800," in Sheilagh Ogilvie and Richard Overy, *Germany: A New Social and Economic History*, Vol. III. London: Hodder Arnold, 2003, 71-105.

Ozment, Steven. "The Family in Reformation Germany: The Bearing and Rearing of Children," *Journal of Family History* 8 (1983): 159-176.

_____. *When Fathers Ruled: Family Life in Reformation Europe*. Cambridge: Harvard University Press, 1983.

_____. *The Burgermeister's Daughter: Scandal in a Sixteenth Century German Town*. New York: HarperCollins Books, 1st Perennial ed., 1997.

_____. *Flesh and Spirit: Private Life in Early Modern Germany*. New York: Viking, 1999.

_____. *Ancestors: The Loving Family in Old Europe*. Cambridge: Harvard University Press, 2001.

_____. *A Mighty Fortress: A New History of the German People*. New York: HarperCollins, 2004.

Pascel, Roy. *The Social Basis of the German Reformation: Martin Luther and his Times*. New York: Augustus M. Kelley, 1971 reprint.

Phillips, Roderick. *Untying the Knot: A Short History of Divorce*. Cambridge: Cambridge University Press, 1991.

Pickle, Linda S. "Stereotypes and Reality: Nineteenth Century German Women in Missouri," *Missouri Historical Review* 79 (1987): 291-312.

Pine, Lisa. "Women and the Family," in Sheilagh Ogilvie and Richard Overy, *Germany: A New Social and Economic History*, Vol. III. London: Hodder Arnold, 2003, 355-382.

Postan, M.M. "Feudalism and its Decline," in T.H. Aston *et al*, eds., *Social Relations and Ideas: Essays in Honour of R.H. Hilton*. Cambridge, 1983, 73-87.

Prak, Maarten. "Moral Order in the World of Work: Social Control and the Guilds in Europe," in Herman Roodenburg and Pieter Spierenburg, eds., *Social Control in Europe*, Vol. 1, 1500-1800. Columbus: The Ohio State University Press, 2004: 176-199.

Rabb, Theodore K. "Jews and Gentiles in the Holy Roman Empire — A Comment," in R. Po-Chia Hsia and Hartmut Lehman, eds., *In and Out of the Ghetto: Jewish-Gentile Relations in Late Medieval and Early Modern Germany*. Washington, D.C.: The German Historical Institute, 1995, 71-74.

Ries, Rotraud. "German Territorial Princes and the Jews," in R. Po-Chia Hsia and Hartmut Lehman, eds., *In and Out of the Ghetto: Jewish-Gentile Relations in Late Medieval and Early Modern Germany*. Washington, D.C.: The German Historical Institute, 1995, 215-245.

Robisheaux, Thomas R. *Rural Society and the Search for Order in Early Modern Germany*. Cambridge: Cambridge University Press, 1989.

Roeber, A.G. "The Origins and Transfer of German-American Concepts of Property and Inheritance," *Perspectives in American History* 3 (1986): 115-171.

_____. "In German Ways? Problems and Potentials of Eighteenth-Century German Social and Emigration History," *The William and Mary Quarterly*, Vol. 44, No. 4 (Oct 1987): 750-774.

Roodenburg, Herman. "Social Control Viewed from Below: New Perspectives," in Herman Roodenburg and Pieter Spierenburg, eds., *Social Control in Europe*, Vol. 1, 1500-1800. Columbus: The Ohio State University Press, 2004: 145-158.

Roper, Lyndal. *The Holy Household: Women and Morals in Reformation Augsburg*. Oxford: Clarendon Press, 1989.

Rublack, Ulinka. *The Crimes of Women in Early Modern Germany*. Oxford: Clarendon Press, 1999.

_____. "Pregnancy, Childbirth and the Female Body in Early Modern Germany," *Past and Present* 150 (1996): 84-110.

Sabean, David Warren. "German Agrarian Institutions at the Beginning of the Sixteenth Century: Upper Swabia as an Example," in Janos Bak, ed., *The German Peasant War of 1525*. London: Frank Cass and Company Ltd., 1976, 76-88.

_____. *Power in the Blood: Popular Culture and Village Discourse in Early Modern Germany*. Cambridge: Cambridge University Press, 1984.

_____. *Property, Production, and Family in Neckarhausen, 1700-1870*. Cambridge: Cambridge University Press, 1990.

_____. *Kinship in Neckarhausen, 1700-1870*. Cambridge: Cambridge University Press, 1998.

Salamon, Sonya. *Prairie Patrimony: Family, Farming, and Community in the Midwest.* Chapel Hill: The University of North Carolina Press, 1992.

Schindler, Norbert. *Rebellion, Community and Custom in Early Modern Germany,* trans. Pamela E. Selwyn. Cambridge: Cambridge University Press, 2002.

Schlumbohm, Jürgen. "From Peasant Society to Class Society: Some Aspects of Family and Class in a Northwest German Protoindustrial Parish, 17th-19th Centuries," *Journal of Family History* 17 (1992): 183-199.

Schmitt, Hans A. "A Closer Look at the Confederation of the Rhine," *German Studies Review* 6 (February 1983): 9-39.

Schorn-Schütte, Luise. "Priest, Preacher, Pastor: Research on Clerical Office in Early Modern Europe," *Central European History* 33 (2000): 1-39.

Schroeder, Adolf E. and Carla Schulz-Geisberg, eds. *Hold Dear, As Always: Jette, a German Immigrant Life in Letters.* Columbia: University of Missouri Press, 1988.

Schubert, Ernst. "Daily Life, Consumption, and Material Culture," in Sheilagh Ogilvie and Bob Scribner, eds., *Germany: A New Social and Economic History.* London: Arnold, 1996, 350-376.

Schulze, Winfried. "Peasant Resistance in Sixteenth- and Seventeenth-Century Germany in a European Context," in *Religion, Poltics and Social Protest: Three Studies on Early Modern Germany,* ed. Kaspar von Greyerz. London: The German Historical Institute, publisher George Allen & Unwin, 1984.

Schüßler, Anne; Schüßler, Helmut; and Hartmann, Hans-Heinz. *Fürfeld.* Bad Rappenau: Druckerei Odenwälder Buchen-Walldürn, 2001.

Scott, Susan and Christopher Duncan. *The Return of the Black Death: The World's Greatest Serial Killer.* Chichester, UK: John Wiley & Sons Ltd., 2004.

Scott, Tom. *Freiburg and the Breisgau: Town-Country Relations in the Age of Reformation and Peasants' War.* Oxford: Clarendon Press, 1986.

Scribner, R.W. *For the Sake of Simple Folk: Popular Propaganda for the German Reformation.* Cambridge: Cambridge University Press, 1981.

Scribner, R.W. "Cosmic Order and Daily Life, in K. von Greyerz, ed., *Religion and Society in Early Modern Europe, 1500-1800.* London: German Historical Institute, 1984, 17-33.

_____. *Popular Culture and Popular Movements in Reformation Germany.* London: The Hambledon Press, 1987.

Sheehan, James L. *German History, 1770-1866.* Oxford: Oxford University Press, 1994.

Sieglerschmidt, Jörn. "Social and Economic Landscapes," in Sheilagh Ogilvie and Bob Scribner, eds., *Germany: A New Social and Economic History*, Vol. II London: Arnold, 1996, 1-38.

Singman, Jeffrey L. *Daily Life in Medieval Europe*. Westport, CT: Greenwood Press, 1999.

Skopp, Douglas R. "The Elementary School Teachers in 'Revolt': Reform Proposals for Germany's Volksschulen in 1848 and 1849," *History of Education Quarterly* 22 (Fall 1982), 341-361.

Sreenivasan, Govind P. "The Social Origins of the Peasants' War of 1525 in Upper Swabia," *Past and Present* 171 (1), 30-65.

_____. *The Peasants of Ottobeuren, 1487-1726*. Cambridge: Cambridge University Press, 2004.

Soliday, Gerald L. Book Review, "Six Books on Central European Family History," *Journal of Family History* 14 (1): 79-90.

Spencer, Frank. "An Eighteenth-Century Account of German Emigration to the American Colonies," *Journal of Modern History* 28 (1956): 55-9.

Spierenburg, Pieter. "Social Control and History: An Introduction," in Clive Emsley, Eric Johnson, Pieter and Spierenburg, *Social Control in Europe*, Vol. 2, 1800-2000. Columbus: The Ohio State University Press, 2004: 1-21.

Stier, Bernhard and Wolfgang von Hippel. "War, Economy, and Society," in Sheilagh Ogilvie and Bob Scribner, eds., *Germany: A New Social and Economic History*, Vol. II. London: Arnold, 1996, 233-262.

Strauss, Gerald. *Law, Resistance, and the State: The Opposition to Roman Law in Reformation Germany*. Princeton: Princeton University Press, 1986.

Stuart, Kathy. *Defiled Trades and Social Outcasts: Honor and Ritual Pollution in Early Modern Germany*. Cambridge, UK: Cambridge University Press, 1999.

Theibault, John. "Community and *Herrschaft* in the Seventeenth-Century German Village," *Journal of Modern History* 64 (March 1992): 1-21.

Thompson, E.P. "Rough Music," in E.P. Thompson, *Customs in Common*. London: Merlin Press, 1991, 467-538.

Tille, Alexander. "German Christmas and the Christmas-Tree," *Folklore* 3 (Jun 1892): 166-182.

Tipton, Frank B. "The Regional Dimension: Economic Geography, Economic Development, and National Integration in the Nineteenth and Twentieth Centuries," in Sheilagh Ogilvie and Bob Scribner, eds., *Germany: A New Social and Economic History*, Vol. III. London: Arnold, 2003, 1-34.

Tishler, William H. "Fachwerk Construction in the German Settlements of Wisconsin," *Winterthur Portfolio* 21 (Winter 1986): 275-292.

Toch, Michael. "Aspects of Stratification of Early Modern German Jewry: Population History and Village Jews," in R. Po-Chia Hsia and Hartmut Lehman, eds., *In and Out of the Ghetto: Jewish-Gentile Relations in Late Medieval and Early Modern Germany*. Washington, D.C.: The German Historical Institute, 1995, 77-89.

Trevor-Roper, H.R. *The Crisis of the Seventeenth Century: Religion, the Reformation and Social Change*. New York: Harper & Row, 1968.

Ulbright, Otto. "Criminality and Punishment of the Jews in the early modern period," in R. Po-Chia Hsia and Hartmut Lehman, eds., *In and Out of the Ghetto: Jewish-Gentile Relations in Late Medieval and Early Modern Germany*. Washington, D.C.: The German Historical Institute, 1995, 49-70.

Vann, James Allen. *The Making of a State: Württemberg, 1593-1793*. Ithaca: Cornell University Press, 1984.

Vincent, John Martin. *Costume and Conduct in the Laws of Basel, Bern, and Zurich, 1370 1800*. Baltimore: The Johns Hopkins Press, 1935.

Walker, Mack. *Germany and the Emigration, 1816-1885*. Cambridge: Harvard University Press, 1964.

_____. *German Home Towns: Community, State, and General Estate, 1648-1871*. Ithaca: Cornell University Press, 1971.

Warde, Paul. *Ecology, Economy and State Formation in Early Modern Germany*. Cambridge: Cambridge University Press, 2006.

Wegert, Karl H. "Contention with Civility: The State and Social Control in the German Southwest, 1760-1850," *The Historical Journal* 34 (June 1991): 349-369.

_____. *Popular Culture, Crime, and Social Control in 18th-Century Württemberg*. Stuttgart: Steiner, 1994.

Wexler, Paul. "Languages in Contact: The Case of Rotwelsch and the Two 'Yiddishes,'" in R. Po-Chia Hsia and Hartmut Lehman, eds., *In and Out of the Ghetto: Jewish-Gentile Relations in Late Medieval and Early Modern Germany*. Washington, D.C.: The German Historical Institute, 1995, 109-124.

Wheatcroft, Andrew. *The Habsburgs: Embodying Empire*. London: Penguin Books, 1996.

Whitford, David M. "Luther's Political Encounters," in Donald K. McKim, ed., *The Cambridge Companion to Martin Luther*. Cambridge: Cambridge University Press, 2003, 179-191.

Wilke, Gerhard. "The Sins of the Fathers: Village Society and Social Control in the Weimar Republic," in *The German Peasantry: Conflict and Community in Rural Society from the Eighteenth to the Twentieth Centuries*, eds. Richard J. Evans and W.R. Lee. New York: St. Martin's Press, 1986, 174-203.

Willenbacher, Barbara. "Individualism and Traditionalism in Inheritance Law in Germany, France, England, and the United States," *Journal of Family History* 28 (2003): 208-225.

Wilson, Peter H. *War, State and Society in Württemberg, 1677-1793*. Cambridge: Cambridge University Press, 1995.

_____. *The Holy Roman Empire, 1495-1806*. New York: St. Martin's Press, Inc., 1999.

Wokeck, Marianne S. *Trade in Strangers: The Beginnings of Mass Migration to North America*. University Park, PA: The Pennsylvania State University Press, 1999.

Wunder, Heide. "'Old Law' and 'Divine Law' in the German Peasant War," in Janos Bak, ed., *The German Peasant War of 1525*. London: Frank Cass and Company Ltd., 1976, 54-62.

_____. "Serfdom in Later Medieval and Early Modern Germany," in T.H. Aston *et al.*, eds., *Social Relations and Ideas: Essays in Honour of R.H. Hilton*. Cambridge, 1983, 249-272.

_____. "Agriculture and Agrarian Society," in Sheilagh Ogilvie and Bob Scribner, eds., *Germany: A New Social and Economic History*. London: Arnold, 1996, 63-99.

_____. *He Is the Sun, She Is the Moon: Women in Early Modern Germany*. Cambridge: Harvard University Press, 1998.

Zinsser, Judith P. and Bonnie S. Anderson. *Women in Early Modern and Modern Europe*. Washington, D.C.: American Historical Association, 2001.

Index

About the Author

Teva Scheer earned a Ph.D. from the University of Colorado in 2000. *Our Daily Bread* is her second book of historical non-fiction. The first, *Governor Lady*, is the biography of the first woman elected a state governor. *Governor Lady* was nominated for best biography in 2001 by the Colorado Book Awards (Colorado Endowment for the Humanities).

Teva and her husband live outside Victoria, British Columbia, where she writes, teaches, and gardens.

Her website: http://www.tevajscheer.com.

Made in the USA
Lexington, KY
14 November 2017